Criminal Justice Research in an Era of Mass Mobility

We live in an era of mass mobility in which governments remain committed to closing borders, engaging with securitisation discourses and restrictive immigration policies, which in turn nurture xenophobia and racism. It is within this wider context of social and political unrest that the contributors of this collection reflect on their experiences of conducting criminological research. This collection focuses on the challenges of doing research on the intersections between criminal justice and immigration control, choosing and changing methodologies, while juggling the disciplinary and interdisciplinary requirements of the work's audience.

From research design to fieldwork to writing up, this book captures every part of the research process, drawing on a range of topics such as migration control, immigrant detention and border policing. It also reflects on more neglected areas such as the interpersonal and institutional contexts of research and the ontological and epistemological assumptions embedded within data analysis methods. It makes a significant contribution to our understanding of the major developments in current research in this field, how and why they occur and with what consequences.

This book seeks to shake off the phantom of undisturbed research settings by bringing to the fore the researchers' involvement in the research process and its products. An interdisciplinary collection, it can be used as a reference not just for those interested in the criminology of mobility but also as a learning tool for anyone conducting research on a highly charged topic in contemporary policy and politics.

Andriani Fili is a Research Associate at the Centre for Criminology, University of Oxford, and a doctoral researcher at Lancaster University, UK.

Synnøve Jahnsen is a Postdoctoral Research Fellow at the Uni Research Rokkan Centre, Norway.

Rebecca Powell is the Managing Director of the Border Crossing Observatory, Monash University, Australia.

Routledge Studies in Criminal Justice,
Borders and Citizenship

Globalizing forces have had a profound impact on the nature of contemporary criminal justice and law more generally. This is evident in the increasing salience of borders and mobility in the production of illegality and social exclusion. *Routledge Studies in Criminal Justice, Borders and Citizenship* showcases contemporary studies that connect criminological scholarship to migration studies and explore the intellectual resonances between the two. It provides an opportunity to reflect on the theoretical and methodological challenges posed by mass mobility and its control. By doing that, it charts an intellectual space and establishes a theoretical tradition within criminology to house scholars of immigration control, race, and citizenship including those who traditionally publish *either* in general criminological *or* in anthropological, sociological, refugee studies, human rights and other publications.

Edited by
Mary Bosworth, *University of Oxford*
Katja Franko, *University of Oslo*
Sharon Pickering, *Monash University*

**Gendered Harm and Structural Violence
in the British Asylum System**
Victoria Canning

Nordic Nationalism and Penal Order
Walling the Welfare State
Vanessa Barker

Criminal Justice Research in an Era of Mass Mobility
Edited by Andriani Fili, Synnøve Jahnsen and Rebecca Powell

For more information about this series, please visit: www.routledge.com/criminology/series/CJBC

Criminal Justice Research in an Era of Mass Mobility

Edited by Andriani Fili,
Synnøve Jahnsen and
Rebecca Powell

LONDON AND NEW YORK

First published 2018 by Routledge

2 Park Square, Milton Park, Abingdon, Oxon OX14 4RN
605 Third Avenue, New York, NY 10017

Routledge is an imprint of the Taylor & Francis Group, an informa business

First issued in paperback 2021

Copyright © 2018 selection and editorial matter, Andriani Fili, Synnøve Jahnsen and Rebecca Powell; individual chapters, the contributors

The right of Andriani Fili, Synnøve Jahnsen and Rebecca Powell to be identified as the authors of the editorial material, and of the authors for their individual chapters, has been asserted in accordance with sections 77 and 78 of the Copyright, Designs and Patents Act 1988.

All rights reserved. No part of this book may be reprinted or reproduced or utilised in any form or by any electronic, mechanical, or other means, now known or hereafter invented, including photocopying and recording, or in any information storage or retrieval system, without permission in writing from the publishers.

Notice:
Product or corporate names may be trademarks or registered trademarks, and are used only for identification and explanation without intent to infringe.

Publisher's Note

The publisher has gone to great lengths to ensure the quality of this reprint but points out that some imperfections in the original copies may be apparent.

British Library Cataloguing-in-Publication Data
A catalogue record for this book is available from the British Library

Library of Congress Cataloging-in-Publication Data
A catalog record for this book has been requested

ISBN: 978-1-138-28412-8 (hbk)
ISBN: 978-0-367-48257-2 (pbk)

Typeset in Bembo
by Apex CoVantage, LLC

Contents

Series editors' introduction viii
List of contributors x
Acknowledgements xiv
List of abbreviations xv

Criminal justice research in an era of mass mobility: a brief introduction 1
MARY BOSWORTH, KATJA FRANKO AND SHARON PICKERING

PART I
Producing and presenting knowledge in an era of mass mobility 13

1 Taking the border for a walk: a reflection on the agonies and ecstasies of exploratory research 15
   LEANNE WEBER

2 Manoeuvring in tricky waters: challenges in being a useful and critical migration scholar 28
   MAY-LEN SKILBREI

3 'Crimmigration' statistics: numbers as evidence and problem 41
   SYNNØVE JAHNSEN AND KRISTIN SLETTVÅG

4 Funnel politics: framing an 'irreal' space 55
   NICOLAY B. JOHANSEN

PART 2
Epistemological and methodological accounts in practice 67

5 Expectations and realities of fieldwork by a nascent qualitative researcher 69
BRANDY COCHRANE

6 Spotting foreigners inside the courtroom: race, crime and the construction of foreignness 85
ANA ALIVERTI

7 Migrant voices in the Global South: challenges of recruitment, participation and interpretation 100
BODEAN HEDWARDS AND SIRAKUL SUWINTHAWONG

8 Life and death in immigration detention 114
DOMINIC AITKEN

9 Making sense of the shifting 'field': ethical and practical considerations in researching life after immigration detention 130
SARAH TURNBULL

PART 3
The politics of positionality, ethics and emotions 145

10 Researching vulnerable women: sharing distress and the risk of secondary and vicarious trauma 147
ALICE GERLACH

11 In the absence of sympathy: serious criminal offenders and the impact of border control measures 160
REBECCA POWELL AND MARIE SEGRAVE

12 Reflexivity and theorizing: conceptualizing the police role in migration control 173
HELENE O. I. GUNDHUS

13 Race at the border 186
ALPA PARMAR

14 One of us or one of them? Researcher positionality, language, and belonging in an all-foreign prison 201
DORINA DAMSA AND THOMAS UGELVIK

15 Voices in immigration detention centres in Greece: different actors and possibilities for change 213
ANDRIANI FILI

Criminal justice research in an era of mass mobility: concluding remarks 226
SYNNØVE JAHNSEN, REBECCA POWELL AND ANDRIANI FILI

Index 235

Series Editors' Introduction

This book has its roots in an International Leverhulme Network Grant on External Border Control (IN-2013–041) that pulled together three research groups from Oxford, Oslo and Monash Universities. Over a three-year period, scholars from these three institutions participated in a variety of online and real-world activities. The chapters in this book offer a glimpse into the range and vitality of the work conducted in each institution.

In their focus on methodological strategies and research experiences, they illuminate the messiness of research and invite the reader to reflect on some of the complexities of researching borders and migration control within criminology and criminal justice. From the challenges of gaining and maintaining research access to heartfelt explorations of the emotional burdens of working in this field, the chapters draw in the reader with their honest and open style.

It is not common to admit to difficulties and challenges in research. Notwithstanding considerable debate by feminists and critical race scholars about positionality and reflexivity, the pressures of academic life continue to demand that ideas are presented as though they flow effortlessly; research findings stand alone – the process itself is glossed over. In such an approach to knowledge, not only is the labour of producing it diminished, but its political and ethical nature is denied.

This book, on the other hand, offers honest accounts of struggles and difficulties as well as ethical dilemmas encountered when doing border criminology. It could therefore be described as an attempt to articulate – to borrow Michael Polanyi's famous term – tacit knowledge within the field. It offers a reflection on experiences and skills that researchers have developed through practice and is full of insights that are usually not taught in university methodology courses. For example, how does one deal with "gatekeepers" which may control, and sometimes block, access to the research field? While the field of border control studies frequently addresses questions of foreignness, membership and race of those controlled by state power, the contributions in this volume reveal that also researchers themselves can, in their work and on a personal level, struggle with issues of race, suspicion and belonging.

As the world increasingly demands simple answers to complex problems, academics have an important role to play in pushing back. The essays gathered here start an important debate within this field of criminology, which is relevant to most, about our role in generating knowledge. In so doing, they acknowledge failures and set-backs, compromises and disappointments. These are all part of a complex world and should not be denied.

Mary Bosworth and Katja Franko, Oxford and Oslo

Contributors

Dominic Aitken is a DPhil student at the Centre for Criminology, University of Oxford. He is researching responses to deaths in custody, focusing on prisons and immigration removal centres.

Ana Aliverti is Associate Professor of Law at the School of Law, University of Warwick. Her research explores questions of national identity and belonging in criminal justice and of law, sovereignty and globalisation.'

Mary Bosworth is Professor of Criminology at the University of Oxford, where she is Director of the Centre for Criminology, Director of Border Criminologies and Fellow of St Cross College. She is, concurrently, Professor of Criminology at Monash University, Australia. Mary conducts research on immigration detention and has published widely on issues to do with incarceration, citizenship, race and gender.

Brandy Cochrane is a researcher and educator in criminology and sociology at Monash University. Her work focuses specifically on the impact of border securitisation on refugee and asylum-seeking mothers. Her research interests include gender, migration, security, methods, critical and queer studies.

Dorina Damsa is a doctoral research fellow at the University of Oslo. Her research focuses on migrant trajectories in an in/hospitable Scandinavian governance context, with a focus on embodiment and perspectives on equality, justice and rights. She is currently conducting research funded by the Scandinavian Research Council for Criminology on foreign nationals' perceptions and experiences of punishment in Scandinavia. She has published in *The British Journal of Criminology* and *The International Journal of Qualitative Methods*.

Andriani Fili is a Research Associate at the Centre for Criminology, University of Oxford, and a doctoral researcher at Lancaster University. Her previous research examined immigration detention, human rights and border control. She has published a number of articles and chapters on her topics of interest and is currently preparing her monograph on the issue of resistance against immigration detention in Greece.

Katja Franko is Professor of Criminology at the University of Oslo. She has published widely in migration, borders, security and surveillance of everyday life. She is, among others, author of *The Borders of Punishment: Migration, Citizenship, and Social Exclusion* (co-edited with M. Bosworth, OUP, 2013), *Cosmopolitan Justice and its Discontents* (co-edited with C. Baillet, Routledge, 2011), *Technologies of Insecurity* (co-edited with H.M. Lomell and H. O. Gundhus; Routledge-Cavendish, 2009) and *Globalization and Crime* (SAGE, 2007/2013).

Alice Gerlach received her BSc Arts (social ecology/psychology) at the University of Tasmania. She is working towards her collaboratively funded ESRC-HMIP DPhil at the Centre for Criminology, University of Oxford. Alice is a member of the Border Criminologies Group and has a background in the detention estate, including immigration removal centres, working as a researcher for HM Inspectorate of Prisons in the UK.

Helene O. I. Gundhus is Professor at the Department of Criminology and Sociology of Law at the University of Oslo and professor II at the Norwegian Police University College. She obtained her DrPolit in criminology at the University of Oslo in 2006. From 2015 to 2021 she is heading a project titled New Trends in Modern Policing, funded by the Norwegian Research Council. She has published widely on topics such as crime prevention, police professionalism, police use of technology and transnational policing.

Bodean Hedwards has recently submitted her PhD at Monash University, which examined the irregular migration of Tibetans on the Tibet–Nepal border. In addition to this, Bodean is a Research Associate with Monash University's Border Crossing Observatory and the University of Nottingham's Rights and Justice Priority Area, where she supports research on issues relating to irregular migration, human trafficking and slavery. Prior to this, Bodean worked with the Walk Free Foundation as a researcher specialising in government responses to slavery and at the Australian Institute of Criminology, where she conducted research on a range of topics, including human trafficking, indigenous justice and countering violent extremism.

Synnøve Jahnsen is a Postdoctoral Research Fellow at the Uni Research Rokkan Centre. Jahnsen's research interest lies at the intersections between social and criminal justice and includes studies on prostitution, human trafficking, forced labour, outlaw motorcycle gangs, policing of migration, police reforms, multi-agency cooperation and intelligence-led policing. Jahnsen's research includes ethnographic research on Norwegian and Australian police forces and speaks to problems of globalisation, security and crime.

Nicolay B. Johansen is Associate Professor at OsloMet–Oslo Metropolitan University, the Faculty of Social Sciences, in Norway. Johansen has published broadly on topics relating to social control: informal social control, politics regarding white-collar crime, drug use, immigration and crime control, as well as the theoretical underpinnings of social control as a sociological concept. He is currently doing research on social control in the welfare state.

Alpa Parmar is Senior Research Fellow at the Centre for Criminology, University of Oxford, and an Associate Director of Border Criminologies. Her research interests are in race and its intersections with criminalization particularly with regard to British Asian youth, race and border policing and minority ethnic group involvement in offending. Alpa is editor (with Mary Bosworth and Yolanda Vázquez) of a forthcoming book, *Race, Criminal Justice and Migration Control: Enforcing the Boundaries of belonging* (Oxford University Press, 2018).

Sharon Pickering is a Professor of Criminology at Monash University and Dean of Arts. She is also the Director and co-founder of the Border Crossing Observatory – an innovative virtual research centre that produces high-quality and independent research on border crossings. Professor Pickering researches irregular border crossing and has written in the areas of refugees and trafficking with a focus on gender and human rights.

Rebecca Powell is the Managing Director of the Border Crossing Observatory. She is a senior researcher on a number of irregular migration research projects hosted by the Border Crossing Observatory and has previous experience working as an international research consultant on trafficking in persons and smuggling of migrants. Rebecca is currently completing a PhD titled "I still call Australia home: The deportation of convicted non-citizens from Australia and the impact of policy and practice from a criminological perspective".

Marie Segrave is an Associate Professor in Criminology at Monash University and leads the Trafficking and Labour Exploitation research agenda of the Border Crossing Observatory. She is also an Australian Research Council DECRA Fellow researching unlawful migrant labour, exploitation and regulation (2014–2018).

May-Len Skilbrei is a Professor of Criminology at the University of Oslo, Norway. She currently heads the research project Transnationalism from Above and Below: Migration Management and How Migrants Manage (MIGMA) funded by the Research Council of Norway. Her previous research has been on various visa and return-migration schemes in Norway, migrants' experiences in transnational prostitution and human trafficking policies, and she has published on these topics in the form of reports and academic publications in e.g. *Ethnos, Women and Criminal Justice, Anti-Trafficking Review* and *British Journal of Criminology*.

Kristin Slettvåg holds a master's degree in criminology from the University of Oslo. Her research interests include criminalisation processes and migration management and control.

Sirakul Suwinthawong has a PhD in criminology from Monash University. She works as a lecturer at the College of Politics and Governance, Mahasarakham University, in north-eastern Thailand. Her research interests are on irregular migrant workers, cross-border challenges and human rights.

Sarah Turnbull is a Lecturer in Criminology at the School of Law, Birkbeck, University of London. Her current research examines immigration detention and deportation in the United Kingdom, with specific focus on the experiences of confinement and removal in relation to affective issues of home, belonging, and identity in contemporary Britain. She is the author of *Parole in Canada: Gender and Diversity in the Federal System* (UBC Press, 2016) and has published articles in *Punishment & Society, British Journal of Criminology, Time & Society* and *Canadian Journal of Law & Society*.

Thomas Ugelvik is Professor of Criminology at the University of Oslo. He is the co-editor of the Palgrave Studies in Prisons and Penology book series, and the head of the Penology and Criminal Law Research Group at the Faculty of Law in Oslo. His PhD thesis was published by Palgrave as *Power and Resistance in Prison: Doing Time, Doing Freedom*. His work has appeared in journals such as *The British Journal of Criminology, Crime, Media, Culture, Ethnography, The European Journal of Criminology, Punishment & Society* and *Qualitative Inquiry*. He is currently working on a project about post-release reintegration and desistance in Norway.

Leanne Weber is Associate Professor of Criminology and Australian Research Council Future Fellow in the School of Social Sciences at Monash University, Melbourne, Australia. She researches border control using criminological and human rights frameworks. Her books include *The Routledge International Handbook on Criminology and Human Rights* (with Fishwick and Marmo, Routledge, 2017), *Policing Non-Citizens* (Routledge, 2013) and *Globalization and Borders: Death at the Global Frontier* (with Pickering, Palgrave, 2011).

Acknowledgements

This book has benefited from assistance and support from a range of people. First of all, we owe a great many thanks to Mary Bosworth, Sharon Pickering and Katja Franko for trusting us with this endeavour. Their support in pushing us forward as editors for this collection has been an incredibly valuable and insightful experience as well as an opportunity for great professional development and growth.

We could not have completed this collection without the contributors to this volume, who spent a great deal of time and energy in writing, editing and discussing with us their chapters while they were kept busy with other writing projects, teaching and personal commitments.

Our thanks go to Aimilia Papadopoulou, who carefully conducted the language editing for this book. Her patience in waiting for our chapters and timely turnaround with her edits were very much appreciated.

We would like to acknowledge each other in coming together as an editing team, literally from across the world. Between the flurry of email exchanges, the book has greatly benefited from a meeting we had back in February 2017 in Athens and which was generously funded by the Leverhulme grant. The notes, discussions and chapter reviews that we shared over food and drinks provided intellectual inspiration and helped this project move forward in a period of great uncertainty.

We are fortunate and thankful to our colleagues who have offered support and advice along our editing journey.

And finally, we wish to thank our families and friends for their unwavering support and pride in the work that we do.

Abbreviations

AAT	Administrative Appeal Tribunal
ALLEA	All European Academies
ARC	Australian Research Council
CPT	Committee for the Prevention of Torture
CUREC	University of Oxford's Central University Research Ethics Committee
DCO(s)	detainee custody officers
EKKE	National Centre for Social Research (Greece)
EU	European Union
EUR	euros
FRONTEX	European Union Agency
HMCIP	Her Majesty's Chief Inspector of Prisons
IOOI	insiders outside/outsiders inside
IRC(s)	immigration removal centres
KRIPOS	Norwegian National Criminal Investigation Service
MI	motivational interviewing
MIDC	Maribyrnong Immigration Detention Centre
MSF	Médecins Sans Frontières
NGO(s)	non-governmental organisation(s)
NPIS	Norwegian National Police Immigration Service
NSD	Norwegian Social Science Data Services
POD	Norwegian Police Directorate
PPO	Prisons and Probation Ombudsman
PTSD	post-traumatic stress disorder
RCN	Research Council of Norway
UDI	Norwegian Directorate of Immigration
UK	United Kingdom
UNHCR	United Nations High Commissioner for Refugees
VAM	research programme Welfare, Working Life and Migration (Norway)

Criminal justice research in an era of mass mobility

A brief introduction

Mary Bosworth, Katja Franko and Sharon Pickering

Introduction

This edited collection has emerged from the Leverhulme Network on External Border Control, 2013–2017, that drew together three criminological research groups at Oxford, Oslo and Monash Universities working on the intersections between border control and criminal justice. Through the Network, a series of seminars was held at each of the Universities during 2015–2016 at which participants presented their research findings and process, the challenges they faced and how they overcame them (or sometimes failed to overcome them). As their papers made clear, researching border control requires a complex range of novel tools and concepts, as well as some more familiar ones. Many are gathered in this volume.

Criminal justice scholars interested in issues of border control and mass mobility face a number of challenges. As well as developing new tools, concepts and theoretical perspectives, they must find a home in a discipline that has traditionally shown scarce interest in migration or with the related matters of race, colonialism and globalisation. Despite the enduring presence of people born elsewhere and the impact of global networks of finance, mobility and governance, criminology, for the most part, persists in imagining a world implicitly bound by the nation-state, neatly divided by jurisdictions.

The points at which the criminal justice system and the immigration system coincide draw this vision of criminology into relief. They challenge assumptions about the role of the prison (Kaufman, 2015), the scale and scope of punishment (Bosworth, 2017a), the nature of policing (Bowling & Westernra, 2018) and the definition of crime (Aliverti, 2013). Elsewhere, foundational concepts and forms of governance like the welfare state are also recast (Barker, 2018).

In conducting research on such matters, scholars face a series of methodological and ethical challenges, many of which spring from the politically contentious nature of migration, borders and security and from the vulnerability of those subject to border controls. While criminologists are used to navigating hard-to-access places and populations, the polarised nature of the political debates over migration and the competing objectives of the different stakeholders make this field of study particularly demanding. Gaining trust from the increasingly watchful and restrictive state authorities while maintaining independent academic standards is particularly difficult. Producing work that has some meaningful impact on policy makers is more challenging still.

From the start, members of the Leverhulme Network on External Border Control sought to raise public awareness about issues of border control and to provide alternative voices to the often one-sided media coverage of migration issues. In addition to their independent work in this area, for instance in public presentations and engagement with local media, the Network engaged with new technologies to disseminate research findings in an accessible fashion. Two initiatives stand out. Firstly, through the Leverhulme funding, the group created the first open-access journal, on the SSRN platform. Hosted by the Border Criminologies website[1] at the Centre for Criminology at the University of Oxford, the *Criminal Justice, Borders & Citizenship Research Paper Series* made academic research produced by network members and other colleagues, freely available. At the time of writing, the series contains more than 220 papers, which have been downloaded nearly 37,000 times, indicating considerable appetite for this kind of research.

In addition to these article-length papers, the Network contributed to the creation and development of the Border Criminologies blog.[2] Now an established debate platform for migration scholars from across the globe and from a variety of disciplines, the blog attracts more than 10,000 unique visitors per month and is read by academics, students, policy makers, NGOs, lawyers and the general public. Showcasing research and policy work from contributors across the world, the blog captures the geographical and disciplinary richness of scholarship on borders and border control. Like the Border Crossing Observatory hosted at Monash University, which has an Asia Pacific focus and has worked to document border-related deaths in the region, Border Criminologies demonstrates the diverse, rapidly evolving and youthful nature of this area of study and its potential to destabilise existing scholarly hierarchies and imbalances (Aas, 2011).

A brief history of criminological studies of border control

By turning their gaze to migration and border control, criminologists and criminal justice scholars have, in the past decades, sought to test the ways criminological insights could be applied to widespread criminalisation and exclusion of foreign nationals (Pickering & Ham, 2015; Aas, 2007). In so doing, they found some theoretical approaches to be redundant, while others have been adapted and blended. This new field of scholarship, known variously as border criminology, the criminology of mobility and 'crimmigration law' (Stumpf, 2006), has identified new sites and subjects as well as the enduring nature of more familiar problems and practices (Pickering, Aas, & Bosworth, 2015; Bosworth, 2017a). Paying close attention to the intersections of inclusion, exclusion and coercive and administrative processes used to sort the desirable from the undesirable, scholars have highlighted the impact of national, racial and gendered borders (Bosworth, Parmar, & Vazquez, 2018).

Those who have sought to push criminology into a space where migration and border control intersect have invariably come up against the high-octane politics of the field. While engaging with the political front page of the press is not new for criminologists, the widespread nature of the populist anti-immigrant sentiment has generated specific methodological, ethical and conceptual challenges for scholars in this field. Those subject to border control are often particularly vulnerable. Such matters engender different kinds of challenges, from purely logistical ones that include locating participants who live without legal immigration status or have been deported to more affective matters. Border control can be hard to understand or endure. It wrenches families apart, and prevents individuals from living out their aspirations. Witnessing that and writing about it hurts. At the same time, not all of those subject to immigration controls generate sympathy. Maintaining emotional distance towards them can also be challenging.

More prosaically, governments the world over guard access to sites of border control jealously. Notwithstanding populist support for harsh policies, border practices remain controversial. Unlike the criminal justice institutions they often resemble, these forms of state power are relatively new; they are, therefore, often unfamiliar with and suspicious of academic research. As several contributions to this volume make clear, some countries lack reliable statistical data on border control, while others may present figures, but with insufficient record keeping and transparency.

Border criminologists have to negotiate research access and secondary data with care. They also need to employ new forms of practical, methodological and theoretical imagination. Marked by increasing complexity of social worlds and relations in a globalising society, the emerging bordered forms of penality often reveal the inadequacy of traditional scholarly vocabularies. As we have written elsewhere (Aas & Bosworth, 2013), we need to take a look at some of the central concepts that have defined the field of punishment and society and examine how they might be adjusted and rethought in the context of mass migration to capture the current transformation of penal power better. In a world in which deportation is increasingly used as a central element of penal power, there is a need to re-examine what is meant by the term 'punishment'. Also phenomena such as prisoner transfers abroad and all foreign prisons within national contexts blur traditional distinctions between the domestic and the foreign and demand a nuanced geographical penal imagination. They also make visible global dimensions of penal power and its colonial history and reiterations (Aas, 2013; Bosworth, 2017b; Bosworth, Parmar, & Vazquez, 2018).

As the numbers of people on the move worldwide continues, governments (and their allies in the private and third sector) remain committed to closing borders. Despite their inability to stem the flow of arrivals, and indeed, notwithstanding their financial dependence on a certain proportion of foreigners in the marketplace, states deploy with ever greater enthusiasm criminal justice–inspired policies against those born elsewhere. Such matters, as numerous scholars have noted (Stumpf, 2006; Aliverti, 2013; Aas & Bosworth, 2013), do not stay sequestered in the immigration system. Instead, just as criminal justice powers have been imported into the administrative system, so too have we witnessed in many jurisdictions a seeping of administrative practices into the criminal justice system. While traditional areas of criminal justice scholarship draw on relatively established and familiar standards of the rule of law and discourses about legitimacy, the emerging assemblages of bordered forms of penality present a challenge for these discourses (Bosworth, 2013, 2017a). Scholars may often find it challenging to anchor their claims in authoritative notions of rights and justice as new hybrid forms of control challenge and push the limits of traditional standards and categorisations.

Under these conditions, this collection of essays offers a timely account of the nature and purpose of academic research in this field of study. Together, the chapters focus on the challenges of doing research on the intersections between criminal justice and immigration control, explaining how scholars choose and change methodologies while juggling the disciplinary and interdisciplinary requirements of their work's audience. In their accounts, authors provide an intimate view of the experience of being a researcher in a highly politicised environment within an interdisciplinary field that is rapidly evolving.

This book incorporates research experiences and methods applied from criminology, law, sociology, police studies and psychology. It also spans a number of physical and geographical border sites and locations. Geographical borders include the Thai–Lao border, India–Nepal border, Greece as a European border frontier, Norway as a border site affected by the European migrant crisis and Australia as a destination country for people from South East Asia and the Middle East. Physical border locations include immigration detention centres in the UK, Greece, Norway, Australia and Jamaica as a country of return.

While the importance of *being* reflexive is acknowledged within social science research (Liebling, 2011), the difficulties, practicalities and methods of *doing* it are rarely addressed (although see Armstrong, Blaustein, & Henry, 2017; Bosworth & Kellezi, 2017a, 2017b). Indeed, while there is recognition that reflexivity is important in thinking about a research project, in practice few researchers give reflexive accounts or discuss how reflexivity can be operationalised. As a result, the implications of current theoretical and philosophical discussions about reflexivity, epistemology and the construction of knowledge for empirical sociological research practice remain underdeveloped. This book seeks to fill that gap by drawing together epistemological discussions and the nitty-gritty of research practice.

Essays examine a wide range of the hidden realities of conducting fieldwork at the border, from the impact of the researcher's race and nationality (Parmar and Aliverti) to the experience of secondary trauma (Gerlach). Many topics are emotionally charged. Marie Segrave and Rebecca Powell, for instance, depict how they grappled with a lack of sympathy for those whom they researched, while Jahnsen and Slettvåg, Turnbull, Cochrane and Weber all describe moments when their preconceived expectations of research were not met. Skilbrei and Gundhus focus on their contingent independence as researchers, while Hedwards and Suwinthawong, Damsa and Ugelvik lay out a variety of difficulties in gaining access to vulnerable migrant populations.

In drawing back the veil on the often-messy process of research, the essays in this collection demonstrate powerfully how the interpersonal and institutional contexts of research, as well as ontological and epistemological assumptions embedded within data analysis methods, can deeply influence research processes and outcomes. As the authors make clear, the 'choices' we make in our research are not solely motivated by intellectual concerns. The adoption of particular research methods also reflects our personal and academic biographies. The interpersonal, political and institutional contexts in which researchers are embedded play a key role in shaping these 'decisions'.

Chapter overview

All the chapters in this collection are structured around the following key questions:

1 What is the purpose of academic research in this field of study?
2 What are some methodological limitations of criminology in understanding border control?
3 What are some of the key ethical challenges in the field?

Authors use these questions to discuss all stages of the research project, from the initial design to the fieldwork and writing up. While some contributors focus on the political environment and its impact on their research, others reflect on the methodological limitations of traditional criminological strategies in understanding border control. Still others discuss key ethical challenges; for example, how does the level and kind of research access affect the production of knowledge? Some contributors probe more deeply the concern that academics are wedded to outmoded conceptions in order to understand and talk about detention and imprisonment of foreign national prisoners. They all consider the silences that arise in the writing-up process. As such, this is a book that seeks to shake off the phantom of undisturbed research settings by bringing to the fore the researchers' involvement in the research process and its products.

In the opening chapter, Leanne Weber 'Takes the Border for a Walk', Musing on research design and the agonies and ecstasies of exploratory research, she asks what is the field? Where is the border, where does it start and end, and what do researchers mean when we say we are going 'into the field'? In posing such questions the chapter scrutinises the epistemological and ontological perspective of border research methodology. Weber argues that 'scientific' inquiry relies on creative insights to a greater degree than is often acknowledged, while the apparent flouting of established methodological principles in exploratory research belies the deeper logic and discipline that are needed to keep this potentially wayward methodology on track.

May-Len Skilbrei, in Chapter 2, outlines the difficulties in producing useful and critical scholarship. Addressing the positionality of researchers in government-commissioned research in Norway, she discusses the challenges and expectations of 'seeing like the state' in producing research that is intended to be useful to the state. Is it possible to maintain independence, relevance and impact, she asks, in a project that accepts the state's problem as the state 'sees' it? In highlighting the uneasy relationship between the researcher and the state, this chapter calls for academics to engage directly with issues of power and independence in their work.

The chapter by Synnøve Jahnsen and Kristin Slettvåg draws on research on violations of immigration law in Norway. The chapter addresses the methodological challenges that critical scholars face when seeking numerical data and statistical knowledge in an emerging scholarly field. Laying out the difficulties they faced and how they overcame them, they offer tips as well as a warning to future researchers.

Chapter 4 by Nicolay Johansen considers what happens when research does not go according to plan and has to be reframed and reconstructed. This chapter centres on the 'failures' that Johansen experienced in conducting research with irregular migrants in the field in Norway. As Johansen makes clear, his research project was beset by a number of unexpected challenges. It was difficult to gain access to migrant populations, and data was unavailable. Entering the field with preconceived ideas, he initially found it difficult to adjust the relationship between his theoretical frame and the empirical data.

In Chapter 5, Brandy Cochrane concentrates on the diverging expectations and realities she encountered as an early career qualitative researcher from a quantitative background, she discusses some of the difficulties she faced in accessing and recruiting Afghan and Iranian refugee mothers for her doctoral studies. The chapter also covers the experience of interviewing these women and the daily realities of working with a translator. It sets out a series of methodological tools she deployed over three phases of her qualitative research project; providing detailed accounts of challenges and how they were overcome to guide nascent researchers in fieldwork with marginalised populations.

In Chapter 6, Ana Aliverti explores the methodological implications of the identification processes in research on criminal justice and border controls. In particular, she considers the challenges of conducting research as a foreign national researcher in criminal courts with high representation of foreign nationals' cases. She draws on a study of Birmingham criminal courts in which she explored the treatment of foreign national defendants to reflect on processes of identification inside the courtroom and their importance for shaping methodological choices and findings. Aliverti points out that legal scholars researching the significance of citizenship and migration status for criminalisation often rely on legal categories to identify research participants. In doing so, they neglect how ideas and assumptions about 'foreignness' by the researcher and research participants may influence findings. So too they overlook how these processes of identification may affect the research relationship and the legitimacy of the researcher.

Bodean Hedwards and Sirakul Suwinthawong explore migrant voices in the Global South, paying particular attention to recruitment, participation and interpretation. Drawing on two separate research projects, they compare their experiences of working at the Lao–Thai border and that of India–Nepal. Suwinthawong is a Thai national working in a local context, while Hedwards is an Australian, (non-native) researcher. Paying attention to positionality, together they explore the fluidity of power and the implications that this can have for fieldwork and research more broadly.

Dominic Aitken, in Chapter 8, describes some methodological challenges of researching everyday life in immigration removal centres (IRC) in the UK. He does so drawing on two research projects, one about staff in a UK immigration removal centre and another about responses to suicide in IRCs and prisons. Reflecting on the interviews he conducted, he seeks to understand the experiences of IRC staff and detainees within the centres and the experiences of IRC staff and others in responding to deaths in custody. He concludes that there is much to be gained from researching both the internal world of immigration detention and its broader social and political context.

In Chapter 9, Sarah Turnbull examines the challenges and opportunities of researching life after immigration detention. In a highly personal account, she describes her expectations and hardship conducting research in British immigration removal centres, the potential vulnerabilities of the 'female body' for the research, security issues doing research abroad in marginalised communities as well as trust and burnout. In a range of examples, she brings to life the 'messiness' of research and calls for ongoing dialogue and discussion of the process of doing this kind of work.

Alice Gerlach, in Chapter 10, offers a reflexive account of her experiences interviewing women who had spent time in immigration detention in the UK to illustrate similar issues. Though many colleagues in the field of border criminology have shared emotional responses to their work, very little is written to inform researchers how these emotions can sometimes hijack and limit projects. Thus in this chapter Gerlach delves into why border control research presents a risk to researchers, the consequences of secondary or vicarious trauma before offering suggestions for the management of symptoms.

Rebecca Powell and Marie Segrave, in Chapter 11, detail research on the use of border control measures in Australia on serious criminal offenders and what occurs when there is an absence of sympathy. In seeking to understand

and present the experience of this marginalised 'unsympathetic' group, the researchers struggled when participants revealed serious criminal offences during interviews about the deportation experience. Acknowledging their uneasy emotional response, Powell and Segrave reflect on the challenges of advocating for a fairer operation of criminal and migration law.

Helene O. I. Gundhus, in Chapter 12, reflects on her research about the police's role in migration control. Her chapter explores the process of gaining access to officers working in Frontex and the Norwegian Police. Building on matters of positionality set out in the previous chapter, Gundhus reflects on her role as an insider-outsider researcher engaged in observing border policing practices while working at the Police University College. In so doing, this chapter addresses the dilemmas and discomfort of institutional affiliation.

In Chapter 13, Alpa Palmar considers why explicit discussions about race have not advanced in much of the scholarship about the criminology of mobility. She outlines the consequences of this problematic 'blind spot' in the overall development of the field. In her study on the booking-in process at police custody suites, she observed how nationality, race and religion intersected in practice and how foreign-national offending (and fears about it) shaped the ways in which people suspected of a crime were treated by the police. Her analysis includes reflexive accounts of her own experiences as a British Asian woman of Hindu background researching the policing of migration in the UK.

Dorina Damsa and Thomas Ugelvik, in Chapter 14, explore researcher positionality, language and belonging in the only all-foreign prison in Norway based on the research they both conducted there. Their chapter discusses the challenges connected to the lack of a shared language between researchers and participants and the barriers this may create in the practice of research. Such matters, they point out, can also become important sources of data collection and analysis in their own right.

Finally, in Chapter 15, Andriani Fili examines the politics of representing voices from immigration detention centres in Greece. Drawing on examples from her research experience and her work in the non-profit sector, she explores the methodological, ethical and empirical challenges in attempting to 'speak for' immigrant detainees. In doing so, she considers how the third sector and academic research can help scholars understand and criticise detention, if at all. Rather than shying away from the civil society–academic gulf, her chapter seeks to connect these disparate institutions and explore ways to open detention sites in Greece to a global gaze.

Conclusion: engaging with and complicating the 'migration crisis'

In drawing together these diverse contributions, the editors of this collection offer more than a glimpse into the complex world of applied social science research. There has been in recent years a proliferation of edited collections

(Armstrong, Blaustein, & Henry, 2017), journal articles and special issues dedicated to issues of methodology and, more specifically, for example, to prison ethnography (Drake, Earle, & Sloan, 2015). However, although relevant, few of them address the specific challenges and risks that may be unique, or at least more present, in the field of studies of border control. The intense governmental and political investment in the field, the numerous preconceived ideas and expectations, the emotional difficulties of field work all make it pertinent to constantly question and challenge the existing frames of understanding and examine the conditions of academic knowledge production and debate. How did the knowledge come about, and who is it for?

Sadly, the dilemmas raised by this edited collection are increasingly hard, if not impossible, to resolve. "What is the proper role of research? Can we make a difference? Should we even try to do so?" These are questions that most migration scholars are struggling with on a daily basis as we face a world in which border control seems to be further entrenched by growing nationalism and xenophobia around the world and the role of expertise under attack.

In our own work, we have, with varying degrees of success, sought to reconcile attempts to contribute to public debates and policy work while preserving the academic standards and integrity of our own work as well as our research access (see, for example, Bosworth, 2016; Franko & Gundhus, 2016). Indeed, although a quick glance at current political debates on migration and border control may give an impression of being uninformed by academic research, we found this often not to be the case. Both journalists and policy makers have often shown eager interest in our work. Yet sometimes, their objectives and approaches have been difficult to reconcile with our own perceptions of objectivity, quality and nuance.

For example, when one of us was recently invited to hold a public talk on state responses to immigration, she was alarmed to see that the talk was advertised by the organiser as "Migration crisis for dummies". The event was extremely well attended and as such probably brought academic research closer to the general public. At the same time, it left a distinct impression that in order to make a difference to the public debate, academics need to adjust how they communicate their expertise. Most often this adjustment involves a considerable degree of simplification and an adjustment of time scale. Long-term studies, with years of careful accrual of evidence, fit with some difficulty into the 24-hour news cycle in which so much debate over migration is located.

Packaging expertise 'for dummies' or transmitting it in 280 characters through social media and reporting findings quickly raises a number of challenges and ethical dilemmas. The risks are manifold, most obviously in the push towards sensationalism, simplification and a reliance on simplistic binaries in a field whose practices are dominated by discourses and strategies of exclusion.[3] Academics may also lose control over how their knowledge and findings will be deployed. Such matters, in border control, take on a particular urgency due to the politicised arena in which we are operating. In Norway, for instance, as

May-Len Skilbrei describes how one sentence in her report on Nigerian sex workers became a standard phrase used by Norwegian immigration authorities in negative asylum decisions. So, too, at the Monash University Border Observatory,[4] the Australian Border Deaths Database[5] was widely cited by the government as evidence of the success of their harsh border control strategies, as the database showed a decline in the numbers of deaths at sea following the reintroduction of off-shore processing and boat turn arounds.

Such experiences are discouraging and may prevent some from participating in public debate all together. Others may simply argue that we anyway should exert caution in trying to produce "policy relevant research". As Oliver Bakewell (2008, p. 432) points out, striving for policy relevance encourages researchers to "take the categories, concepts and priorities of policy makers and practitioners as their initial frame of reference". Only by breaking away from policy relevance, Bakewell suggests, will it be possible to challenge the taken-for-granted assumptions that underpin much practice in the field and, eventually, bring much more significant changes to the lives of migrants. At the same time, however, as university funding increasingly hinges on proof of 'impact', academics are under ever more pressure to engage with policy makers, stakeholders and others outside the academy.

More than 20 years ago, Nils Christie (1997) pointed out that closeness to the state produces not only knowledge that reflects the state's perspectives on social problems but also that this kind of research is often marked by a high level of triviality. Perhaps it is particularly the latter which we should be concerned about. While production of social change may feel like a distant promise, migration knowledge which is trivial and predictable is all around us. Neither research close to policy makers nor that which is aligned to activism is immune from it. This book has bravely and honestly opened a conversation about these dilemmas, which are likely to continue for many years to come.

Notes

1 https://bordercriminologies.law.ox.ac.uk
2 www.law.ox.ac.uk/research-subject-groups/centre-criminology/centreborder-criminologies/blog
3 A culture that migration scholar Bridget Anderson (2013) captures with the distinction between 'us' and 'them'.
4 http://artsonline.monash.edu.au/thebordercrossingobservatory
5 http://artsonline.monash.edu.au/thebordercrossingobservatory/publications/australian-border-deaths-database/

References

Aas, K. F. (2011). "Crimmigrant" bodies and bona de travellers: Surveillance, citizenship and global governance. *Theoretical Criminology*, 15(3), 331–46.
Aas, K. F. (2007). Analysing a world in motion: Global flows meet 'criminology of the other'. *Theoretical Criminology*, 11(2), 283–303.

Aas, K. F., & Bosworth, M. (Eds.). (2013). *The borders of punishment: Citizenship, crime control, and social exclusion*. Oxford: Oxford University Press.

Aliverti, A. (2013). *Crimes of mobility: Criminal law and the regulation of immigration*. Abingdon: Routledge.

Anderson, B. (2013). *Us & them? The dangerous politics of immigration controls*. Oxford: Oxford University Press.

Armstrong, S., Blaustein, J., & Henry, A. (Eds.). (2017). *Reflexivity and criminal justice: Intersections of policy, practice and research*. London: Palgrave Macmillan.

Bakewell, O. (2008). Research beyond the categories: The importance of policy irrelevant research into forced migration. *Journal of Refugee Studies, 21*(4), 432–453.

Barker, V. (2018). *Nordic nationalism and penal order: Walling up the welfare state*. Abingdon: Routledge.

Bosworth, M. (2016). The impact of immigration detention on mental health: Literature review. In *Review into the welfare in detention of vulnerable persons: A report to the home office by Stephen Shaw*. London: HMSO, CM 9186.

Bosworth, M. (2017a). Border criminology and the changing nature of penal power. In A. Liebling, S. Maruna, & L. McAra (Eds.), *Oxford handbook of criminology* (6th ed., pp. 373–390). Oxford: Oxford University Press.

Bosworth, M. (2017b). 'Penal Humanitarianism? Punishment in an era of mass migration.' *New Criminal Law Review*. 20(1): 39 – 65.

Bosworth, M. (2013). Can immigration detention be legitimate? In K. F. Aas & M. Bosworth (Eds.), *Migration and punishment: Citizenship, crime control, and social exclusion* (pp. 149–164). Oxford: Oxford University Press.

Bosworth, M., & Kellezi, B. (2017a). Doing research in immigration removal centres: Ethics, emotions and impact. *Criminology & Criminal Justice, 17*(2), 121–137.

Bosworth, M., & Kellezi, B. (2017b). Getting in, getting out and getting back: Access ethics and emotions in immigration detention research. In S. Armstrong, J. Blaustein, & A. Henry (Eds.), *Reflexivity and criminal justice: Intersections of policy, practice and research* (pp. 237–262). London: Palgrave Macmillan.

Bosworth, M., Parmar, A., & Vazquez, Y. (Eds.). (2018). *Race, migration and criminal justice: Boundaries of belonging*. Oxford: Oxford University Press.

Christie, N. (1997). Four blocks against insight: Notes on the oversocialization of criminologists. *Theoretical Criminology, 1*(1), 13–23.

Drake, D., Earle, R., & Sloan, J. (Eds.). (2015). *The Palgrave handbook of prison ethnography*. London: Palgrave.

Franko, K., & Gundhus, H. O. I. (2016, November 30). Europamester I utvisning [European leader in deportation]. *Aftenposten*. Retrieved from www.aftenposten.no/meninger/debatt/i/K4Gm5/Europamester-i-utvisning

Kaufman, E. (2015). *Punish & expel: Border control, nationalism and the new purpose of the prison*. Oxford: Oxford University Press.

Liebling, A. (2011). Being a criminologist: Investigation as a lifestyle and living. In M. Bosworth & C. Hoyle (Eds.), *What is criminology?* (pp. 518–529). Oxford: Oxford University Press.

Pickering, S., Aas, K., & Bosworth, M. (2015). Criminology of mobility. In S. Pickering & J. Ham (Eds.), *Handbook of migration and crime*. Abingdon: Routledge.

Pickering, S., & Ham, J. (Eds.). (2015). *The Routledge handbook on crime and international migration*. Abingdon: Routledge.

Stumpf, J. (2006). The crimmigration crisis: Immigrants, crime, and sovereign power. *American University Law Review, 56*, 367.

Part I

Producing and presenting knowledge in an era of mass mobility

Chapter 1

Taking the border for a walk

A reflection on the agonies and ecstasies of exploratory research

Leanne Weber

Introduction

Artist Paul Klee famously described drawing as 'taking a line for a walk'. That phrase suggests spontaneity and exploration, an artistic technique not entirely devoid of judgement or restraint but sufficiently fluid to enable curiosity to lead the way towards the discovery of meaning. I see this concept as a metaphor for the type of exploratory social research I particularly value and to which I am intuitively attracted as a criminological researcher. Although devising explicit hypotheses based on existing theory or previous scholarship and testing them with empirical research is a time-honoured method in social science research, other strands of social inquiry adopt a more open ended and flexible approach.

In this chapter, I use an example of exploratory research in which I am currently engaged to illustrate the key characteristics of this easily misunderstood research genre. I trace the development of a multi-faceted research program 'Globalisation and the Policing of Internal Borders',[1] and report some of the challenges encountered in the early stages of implementation of that project. I begin by setting out some key ideas about exploratory research as an epistemological perspective[2] for social researchers and introduce 'border as method' as the particular example of that approach that informed my own research program. I then discuss the design (i.e. the theory and choice of data collection methods) for my study and recount some early fieldwork experiences, pointing out both the advantages and the pitfalls of starting out on an extensive research journey with a deliberately unfinished roadmap.

Epistemology: taking the border for a walk as an example of exploratory research

Stebbins (2001) has argued that exploratory approaches have a unique and valuable place in social research – not merely serving as a preliminary stage within a larger research project but instead offering a distinctive, stand-alone research rationale. He describes exploratory social research as a 'purposive and systematic undertaking' aimed at the production of 'inductively derived generalisations about the group, process, activity, or situation under study'.[3] This contrasts with deductive approaches that typically adopt a fixed and narrow theoretical framing from the outset, follow strict methodological rules and set out to test explicit hypotheses. Importantly, Stebbins insists that both exploratory (inductive) research, and predictive (deductive) research are forms of scientific inquiry. In fact, Stebbins notes, new knowledge can never be produced by deduction alone, and this applies to the hard sciences as much as to social science. While inductive research is particularly suitable for under-researched (or poorly researched) subject areas, deductive methods come into their own where an extensive empirical and theoretical literature already exists.

With its focus on the production of generalisations through reflexive processes of empirical observation and induction, exploratory social research is closely aligned with grounded theory (Glaser & Strauss, 1967). Exploratory approaches typically begin with a broad and open-minded examination of a topic, where the premature narrowing of the theoretical gaze is deliberately avoided. Since the primary goal is to develop an intimate understanding of a social process, it follows, according to Stebbins (2001), 'that the most efficacious approach is to search for this understanding wherever it may be found, using any ethical method that would appear to bear fruit'. Exploratory studies are therefore likely to adopt a mixed-methods approach to data collection, often combining both qualitative and quantitative data (Cresswell, 2011; Yin, 2009, 2012). While advocates of these approaches claim that considerable rigour can be built into mixed-methodology case study design, for example by developing systematic (albeit flexible) data collection protocols, Stebbins argues that exploratory research is driven more by the desire to produce original ideas than to demonstrate methodological perfection. Flaws in design tend to be corrected as they become apparent or in later studies that may arise from the work. While social researchers engaged in deductive empirical research typically emphasise methodology beyond all else, exploratory researchers, according to Stebbins, give equal regard to their role as methodologists, writers and theorists – if anything, with a slight emphasis on the production of theory.

Although I have always been attracted to the blue skies offered by exploratory work, my most recent opportunity to embark on a project of social exploration arose from circumstances beyond my control. Several years ago, I was struggling to develop a proposal for a major national award, the Future Fellowship, funded by the Australian Research Council (ARC). After years of research and writing on borders and border control, I was hoping to shift gear a little, to return perhaps to my pre-academic experience in applied policing research and combine it with a long-held desire to contribute to scholarship and activism on Aboriginal justice. The early feedback I received from faculty advisers at my university was not encouraging. The Future Fellowship, they said, placed far more emphasis on individual track record than did other funding schemes. Therefore, I would need to formulate a project that related directly to the topics on which I had already researched and published. Not only that, but moving into research on Indigenous issues was fraught with additional hazards, not the least of which would be establishing legitimacy in the eyes of possible participants and prospective research partners. There seemed to be no option but to beat a hasty retreat to the familiar territory of border research. However, the desire to do something new had taken hold, so I continued to ponder how I could balance these conflicting imperatives. The answer that came to me was to take the border for a walk.

Looking back over more than a decade of research and writing – as major funding applications always require – I realised that I had indeed been taking the border for a walk for quite a while. Once borders are understood not as physical locations but as governmental functions (Weber, 2006) that can be carried out using a variety of technologies (Weber, 2013a) in an expanding range of locations (Weber & Bowling, 2004; Weber, 2007), researching the border becomes an exercise in following the application of border control functions wherever they are performed. This perspective comes readily to critical criminologists who are concerned with relations of power. While some critical criminologists may choose ethnographic methods to challenge power by privileging otherwise silenced voices (see for example Gerard, 2014), others go straight to the heart of power in order to understand and critique it (e.g. Whyte, 2009).

Armed with the epistemological perspective of taking the border for a walk, I revisited an article I had published with Ben Bowling in order to find ideas that would help to structure a project on 'internal bordering practices'. In that article (Weber & Bowling, 2008), I wrote that borders served the important purpose, *inter alia*, of delineating boundaries of entitlement, belonging and citizenship. Such bordering practices might be constituted by governmental projects of expulsion from physical territory or might instead create borders through more nuanced processes of social exclusion.

Guided by these three themes, I formulated three case studies. The first one focuses on the 'structurally embedded border' that operates through law and divides populations on the basis of differential entitlement to essential services based on immigration status. These borders may be directed towards the production of 'voluntary' departures through the creation of unlivable lives but also serve the neo-liberal agenda of reducing public expenditure. The second case study, on the policing of public space, explores the idea that police encounters with the public can produce messages of belonging or non-belonging, depending on the reason for and quality of the encounter. These are borders created through practice, in which the exercise of authority inscribes the line between those who are included or excluded from the community of citizens deemed worthy of respect and protection. The final case study explores the idea of hierarchies of citizenship through an examination of compulsory income management, a policy that falls outside the usual domain of criminology. This policy operates by identifying certain welfare recipients as incapable of managing the responsibilities of neo-liberal citizenship, thereby necessitating state intervention in the management of their financial affairs. In the case of

Aboriginal people, who have been explicitly targeted, this appears to revitalise colonial assumptions and practices that pre-dated their formal recognition as citizens.

Surprisingly perhaps – given its unconventional framing – the project was funded. For tactical reasons, the proposal contained no mention of the process of 'taking the border for a walk' that had produced it. But writing in this context I am free to acknowledge that it was that exploratory and reflexive process that enabled me to cross both disciplinary and policy boundaries to develop a research programme that hangs together by what some would consider to be the barest of threads – the concept of 'internal bordering practices'. Taking this circuitous route towards research design allowed me to include some examination of policing practices and of policies that target Aboriginal people – which had been my original intention – while using the language of border control to link the study strongly to my academic history.

Later I discovered that what I had thought of as an audacious sleight of hand aligned remarkably closely with a well-articulated research philosophy within the field of border studies, namely 'border as method' (Mezzadra & Neilson, 2013). Sandro Mezzadra and Brett Neilson have coined this phrase to describe an epistemological approach that treats borders as epistemic viewpoints from which to analyse practices of inclusion and exclusion. Border as method entails:

> taking the border not only as research 'object' but also as an 'epistemic' angle ... [which] provides productive insights on the tensions and conflicts that blur the line between inclusion and exclusion, as well as on the profoundly changing code of social inclusion in the present.
> (Mezzadra & Neilson, 2013, p. viii)

In contrast with ethnography, which starts with lived experience, border as method requires the researcher to follow the logic of the border across 'diverse borderscapes' in order to transcend 'bounded space' and reach new conceptualisations of bordering practices. This emphasis on the pursuit of wholly new connections between ideas and bodies of knowledge aligns well with the account of exploratory research by Stebbins (2001) I have given already, as does the presentation of 'border as method' as an epistemological perspective rather than a fixed research methodology. The border can be conceived as a method because, in Mezzadra and Neilson's formulation, borders are relational, being concerned with struggles for domination and resistance to power. It is the relational nature of borders that leads analysis to cross both disciplinary and geographic divides to uncover 'new relations of connectivity across discrete spaces and organisations of data'.

This brings us to another key feature of border as method, that it values the integration and reinterpretation of existing knowledge as much as the collection of new empirical data. Mezzadra and Neilson advocate breadth in research design rather than the depth of inquiry that is favoured in much ethnographic research, for example, saying:

> We question the limiting perspective imposed by the view that the breadth of research compromises its depth and rigor. Rather, we proceed with the commitment that breadth can produce depth, or better, can produce a new kind of conceptual depth.
>
> (Mezzadra & Neilson, 2013, p. 10)

My discovery of Mezzadra and Neilson's work provided some legitimation for the broad and open-ended design I had intuitively been drawn to in my project 'Globalisation and the policing of internal borders'. Both border as method and my own approach of taking the border for a walk are intended to guide an exploratory inquiry aimed at uncovering linkages between what may appear on the surface to be unrelated bordering processes.

Methodology: uncovering the deep structures of internal borders

As set out in the previous section, taking the border for a walk gives rise to a particular orientation to border research that is inter-disciplinary, exploratory and focused on sites of struggle. I chose to collect data for the project through a series of mixed-method case studies, each showcasing a relevant policy area, since case studies are ideally suited for exploratory research because of their flexibility and responsiveness (Thomas, 2011; Thomas & Myers, 2015; Yin, 2009, 2012). Moreover, I elected to undertake not one but three apparently disparate case studies, each reflecting a different site of struggle within the domains of law, policy and practice. This approach could be criticised for pursuing breadth at the expense of depth, as discussed earlier. But in choosing this path I judged that opting for shallow and wide was exactly what was needed to uncover the 'deep structure' (Cohen, 2001) that connected the internal bordering practices under study.

The rationale for the research design is that Australia's internal borders are deeply embedded in everyday practices of service provision (mediated by immigration status), street policing (mediated by race, place and perceptions of belonging) and the administration of welfare (mediated by conceptions of individual desert and capability). Policing, here, is conceived broadly across these different domains to cover any authoritative intervention intended to selectively manage or 'police' populations (Neocleous, 2000). Because of this deep embedding, the research program has been conceptualized as an excavation aimed at exposing these submerged processes to critical scrutiny to enable the identification of contrasts and connections. Even in an extended research program, it is not possible to investigate every combination of citizenship status, enforcement modality and geographical context. Therefore, an 'ice-core sampling' method was employed to identify the case study topics. Dauvergne (2008, p. 3) explains this technique and its rationale as follows:

> To understand the layers, the scientist extracts a narrow sample that contains a trace of each element under examination. This is the antidote to breadth. Core sampling ... means drilling into each topic under consideration to extract a sample that in key ways reveals something about the whole.

Case study one examines how the internal border operates as a site of inclusion/exclusion through immigration checks at points of access to essential services. Although life necessities such as employment and housing are crucial for social integration, education and health care were chosen for this part of the study because of their institutional nature. This case study builds on previous research in which I coined the term 'structurally embedded border' to represent the deployment of information exchange between service-providing, regulatory and immigration control agencies (Weber, 2013b). Of the three case studies, this one aligns most closely with literal border control, although it takes place away from the physical border. To date, 26 semi-structured interviews have been completed with key informants from the education, health and legal sectors, and plans are now in train to conduct surveys with secondary schools and hospitals aimed at identifying the extent to which their institutions have become locations where the imperatives of border control are played out or resisted.

Case study two explores how perceptions of belonging or not belonging can be produced and reinforced through interactions between young people from visible minorities and people in positions of authority, such as police, transport officials and teachers. Data is being collected through focus groups with culturally and linguistically diverse youths. Participants express what belonging means to them then recount their encounters with authorities in a variety of public places that have reinforced or threatened their sense of belonging. From an initial starting point focused on the 'policing of public space', the scope of this case study has broadened somewhat beyond the state police to include interactions with a wider range of actors and authority figures than was originally intended. This has been led by the interests and concerns of the youth organisation that has been an active partner in the project. I plan to make further connections with agencies that support different cohorts of young people, such as community legal centres, in the hope that interactions with state police will come more prominently to the fore.

Case study three also looks at bordering practices that have the effect of creating hierarchies of citizenship – in this case separating responsible from irresponsible citizens through the imposition of compulsory income management on certain social security recipients. The policy on which this case study is based has undergone numerous transitions, trials and re-brandings since the case study was first conceived, rendering this topic a particularly elusive target for research.[4] When the income management policy was introduced in 2007 by a Conservative government into remote Aboriginal communities in the Northern Territory, the resemblance to openly discriminatory and paternalistic policies of the 'protectionist' era of colonial administration was immediately apparent. A subsequent Labor government kept many of the features of the policy but attempted to mitigate its discriminatory nature by extending its reach to more mixed, sometimes urban, communities in which Aboriginal people nevertheless featured strongly. A return to a Conservative government has redirected income management policies back onto communities in which Aboriginal people predominate. Since Aboriginal people are once again the direct target of these policies (which was not the case at the time the proposal was drafted), I am now exploring possibilities to partner with an indigenous researcher who may be well placed to conduct ethnographic fieldwork in affected communities.

Just as the data collection methods in an exploratory research design need to remain fluid and responsive to the unfolding realities of policies and study sites, exploratory research also demands a theoretical framework that guides the collection and interpretation of data but does not constrain it. While border as method provides the overall epistemological perspective for the study, leading to the adoption of an open-ended and exploratory research design as described, no over-arching grand theory about the nature of internal bordering practices underpins the collection of data. This is the case because exploratory studies tend to be theory building rather than theory testing. This means that existing theory is most likely to be deployed *post hoc* to aid interpretation rather than to provide a blueprint for a fixed, theoretically-derived research design. Even so, a well-prepared exploratory researcher will engage in some preliminary review of literature in order to guide the search for understanding and sensitise themselves to the themes that are likely to arise.

In my project, the case studies were carefully selected in the expectation that the theoretical continuities between them would be brought into view *post hoc* as the data collection and analysis unfolds. These continuities are likely to concern similarities in governmental objectives and technologies typical of neo-liberal modes of governance, continuities between immigration control and the management of other subaltern populations, and historical connections between exclusionary policies associated with colonisation and contemporary forms of boundary reinforcement in the face of rapid globalisation. The broad themes of race, place and citizenship are also threaded through the scenarios presented in the case studies. Clearly, each of these areas of knowledge has a huge literature from which to draw.

I have tried to create some order out of this theoretical complexity by situating the literatures that inform the study within a 'theory pyramid'. At the base of this conceptual pyramid are theories that explicate the structural factors that produce inequalities. Relevant literatures at this level include analyses of neo-liberal globalisation, historical imperialism and contemporary hierarchies of citizenship and social inclusion. In the second tier are literatures that shed light on the technologies that are employed to enact differential inclusion and exclusion. This includes theoretical insights concerning the relationship between policing and belonging and the manipulation of access to entitlements as a tool of governance. At the apex of the theory pyramid is published material that sheds light on the situation-specific determinants of internal border policing practices. This may include information about specific policies or practices that is not theoretical in nature but illuminates the particular processes being studied. Finally, when interpreting the research data, a conscientious exploratory researcher cannot avoid the need to consider the intersections of race, class and gender in response to emerging findings (see Walby, 2009, and other 'intersectionality' literature). However, unlike explicitly feminist research, for example, the open-mindedness with which the exploratory researcher approaches her research topic warns against embedding any of these perspectives too firmly within the initial research design.

Praxis: making connections or losing the thread?

So far I have explained how I arrived at a fluid yet systematic method that I believe is well suited to exploratory research aimed at uncovering the disparate faces of internal borders. I have also given a few indications of how the data collection process needed to adapt as the empirical work began. In this section, I identify some of the challenges that have arisen so far in translating the research plan into practice.

As it turns out, the very fluidity of design that was so appealing has also proven to be one of the project's most perplexing aspects. No matter how experienced the researcher, the early stages of any new project are often characterized by an overload of new information, confusion and a struggle to maintain or establish focus. The extreme flexibility of the design, while admirably fluid, has at times given rise to a feeling that I might drown in the plethora of possibilities that it opens up. While each of the case studies is structured around specific research questions, with the concept of 'internal bordering practices' providing a link between them, I soon found that the boundaries between the case studies were porous and easily blurred.

In the preliminary stages of the first two case studies, I could find myself on the way to a planning meeting or mulling over how to interpret information that had just been provided in an interview while struggling to recall which of the two case studies the research activity related to. At a similar stage in my previous research on migration policing networks (Weber, 2013b), I produced posters for myself using colourful marker pens that said 'Detection of Unlawful Non-Citizens', stuck them in strategic places around my office walls and had my small team of research assistants do the same. It was reassuring to return to this clear objective at the heart of that study whenever any of us felt overwhelmed by the effort to sort out what was relevant and what was not. While the motto

'Policing of Internal Borders' fulfils the same role within my current project, the disparate starting points, multi-layered theoretical framing and open-ended rationale of discovering contrasts and connections has at times undermined efforts to cut through the complexity. To some extent, exploratory research demands a belief that, with perseverance and a sound underlying design, order and understanding will emerge at later stages. Stebbins (2001) hints at something similar when he proposes that the exploratory researcher, unlike the tester of hypotheses whose focus is on implementing a strictly defined methodology, must give equal weight to the methodology, writing and theory-building phases of the research task.

Two straightforward examples illustrate how the case studies began to blur around the edges once fieldwork commenced. The first convergence was a thematic one. Preliminary discussions with an agency supporting young people that I hoped would help to recruit participants for the focus groups for case study two proved to be unexpectedly wide ranging. Guided by the real-world situations that confronted the young people from diverse backgrounds who used their service, the initial focus on policing and belonging soon expanded to include many immigration issues that were relevant to case study one. I found myself repeatedly explaining that I was planning to cover that issue in the other part of the study (necessitating more conversational detours to try to explain the big picture) and wondering if I had inadvertently slipped into conducting a de facto interview for the first case study that technically required a signed consent form. I left the meeting with a commitment from that agency to assist with the policing case study but also armed with copies of immigration-related documents that provided key insights relevant to case study one.

Secondly, I began to find that there were organisational overlaps between the first and second case studies. Youth workers had wide-ranging networks within the local community, many of which overlapped with the types of organisations I was hoping to include in my first case study on access to health and education services. For example, the youth support agency mentioned earlier had a close relationship with a nearby English language school that was the first educational experience for most newly arrived migrants, refugees and asylum seekers. Experienced youth workers also proved to have a wide range of individual experience that cut across case studies. One of them had previously worked on a government-funded contract to provide support to asylum seekers and had a wealth of firsthand knowledge about the difficulties faced by this group in negotiating access to essential services. She became a valued facilitator for case study two and a formal participant (complete with signed consent form) for case study one.

What seemed at first to be signs that I was losing the thread of what I was trying to achieve in each of the case studies gradually gave way to a sense of vindication of the multiple-case-study methodology. Although the precise nature of the links between these three different domains of policy and practice will not be fully elaborated until I move into the analysis, writing and theory-building phase, my apparently disparate case studies are showing signs of uncovering some deeper connections.

Another consequence of the complex research design has been the difficulty of communicating the research rationale to a diverse audience of potential partners and participants. As any researcher knows, recruitment depends on 'selling' the project to participants as something that is non-threatening, at the very least, and preferably of interest and value to them. In relation to the first case study, this has necessitated as many different descriptions as there are categories of participants. The stern and technical language contained in the Explanatory Statement format required by the university Human Research Ethics Committee can be alienating enough. I was also concerned that the unfamiliar language of border control would potentially add to the sense of threat amongst service providers who were not used to dealing with coercive practices.

For example, one secondary-school principal I approached after seeing media reports of her speaking out about immigration problems faced by some of her students initially declined to be interviewed, without offering an explanation. While she was of course entitled to take this position, it seemed to me that there might have been a miscommunication. A friendly follow-up reassured her that I was not looking for information about the visa status of any of her students or any specific information about individuals, as she had feared. The dynamics of my approaches to agencies offering legal support to asylum seekers and migrants have been completely different, as the professional remit and occupational culture of these research participants aligns more comfortably with the sometimes harsh realities of a law enforcement environment.

Another element of the first case study is a survey of secondary schools and public hospitals. For me, the survey is about the extent to which schools or hospitals are being drawn (unwittingly) into the immigration control apparatus. This is not an appealing way to describe the research to decision makers in these organisations who take the view that worthwhile research in their workplaces should be about improving educational or health outcomes. Describing the survey in neutral terms as being about the 'impact' of immigration control on the provision of services or the 'intersection' between immigration control and service delivery has proven to be more intelligible and less challenging, although the content of the survey still contains questions that will be confronting. This includes identifying occasions when immigration authorities have visited their school or hospital for immigration enforcement or information gathering purposes and instances when services have not been provided due to lack of legal entitlement. Indeed, at the time of writing, rejections are beginning to arrive in response to the numerous and protracted applications we have been required to submit to state health and education authorities.

On the other hand, after initially being reluctant to divulge too much detail about the overall project or use the theoretical jargon that appears in some of the project documentation, in the belief that this might make the project sound even more abstract and alien to the professionals I was approaching, I have learned not to underestimate their capacity to think beyond the usual parameters of their work. When I have ventured to explain the wider context and thinking behind the project, I have often been pleasantly surprised. Some participants have been intrigued rather than put off by the idea of the 'structurally embedded border'. Moreover, I have come to realize that providing this explanation, particularly in relation to the proposed surveys, may help to reassure potential respondents. The idea that certain requirements (e.g. to check immigration status, to recover costs where there are deliberate gaps in federal funding, to provide certain information when requested) are the product of national laws and policies and are therefore 'structurally embedded' has at times helped to allay concerns that the intention of the study is to criticize their individual institutions.

Conclusion: putting 'border as method' into practice

At first sight, it might be difficult to see what common thread links a survey on access to education and health care for non-citizens, focus groups on young people's interactions with authority figures and a yet-to-be commenced ethnographic study on the impact of income management policies on Indigenous welfare recipients. In this chapter, I have explained that they are all staging points along a circuitous journey set in train by taking the border for a walk, until the border becomes a metaphor for wider processes of social division. While this is a potentially productive approach, an open-ended and reflexive method coupled with an eclectic theoretical framework can at times confuse rather than clarify. This suggests that an exploratory research design might not be an ideal choice for a less experienced researcher or for those who prefer to apply and build on established theory. But, on the question of who should undertake exploratory research, Stebbins (2001) is clear on one thing – that exploration is not merely the preserve of creative artists and research elites:

> [E]xploration is not an obscure, mysterious process available only to a small coterie of insightful intellectual adventurers. On the contrary, anyone with the will to explore can do it, and I am convinced that social science theory would profit enormously were more of its researchers inclined to work in the field of discovery.

A while ago, I was speaking with a close friend who has made a major contribution to criminology through her experimental empirical research and predictive modelling, when the difference in our professional approaches came up as a point of conversation. Partly in jest, I suggested that this was because she approached her work like a scientist, whereas I approached it like a poet – although, ironically, I was the one who had undertaken scientific training before entering the field. Nevertheless, the more considered analysis that I have presented here about the nature of exploratory research argues against seeing these approaches in binary terms. Good science, as Stebbins (2001) contends, requires leaps of imagination in order to open up new fields of enquiry, just as good creative work demands an appreciation of underlying structure and logic.

While respecting both inductive and deductive traditions, I have acknowledged throughout this chapter my attraction to the 'poetry' of exploratory social research. I therefore cannot resist the temptation to conclude with a literary reference that supports the point just made. In a short story titled 'Too Much Happiness', Alice Munro (2009, p. 171) provides a fictional account of the real-life meeting of aspiring mathematician Sophia Kovalevskaya and her soon-to-be mentor Karl Weierstrass. This is how Munro describes the older man's first impressions of the young woman's abilities:

> All his life he had been waiting for such a student to come into his room. A student who would challenge him completely, who was not only capable of following the strivings of his own mind but perhaps of flying beyond them. He had to be careful about saying what he really believed – that there must be something like intuition in a first-rate mathematician's mind, some lightening flare to uncover what has been there all along. Rigorous, meticulous, one must be, but so must the great poet.

The message of this chapter is that combining the imagination and intuition of exploration with the structure and rigour more usually associated with scientific inquiry is not the sole preserve of the artistic and intellectual elite. Rather, it is an approach that can be widely applied and is especially suited to an emerging field of enquiry such as the criminology of the border. This chapter has been an attempt to demystify that process.

Notes

1 See http://artsonline.monash.edu.au/thebordercrossingobservatory/research-agenda/internal-border-control/globalisation-and-the-policing-of-internal-borders/ (funded by Australian Research Council Future Fellowship FT140101044).
2 Note that I distinguish epistemology from theory in this discussion: epistemology being the overarching philosophy of knowledge production that determines the general character of the research, while theory is the more specific set of ideas that is relevant to the topic under investigation.
3 Note that page numbers are not available for direct quotes since the material has been taken from online extracts from the book provided by the publisher at this URL http://dx.doi.org/10.4135/9781412984249.n1
4 A description of the policy at the time of writing can be found here www.humanservices.gov.au/customer/services/centrelink/income-management

References

Cohen, S. (2001). *States of Denial: Knowing about atrocities and suffering.* Cambridge: Polity Press.

Cresswell, J. W. (2011). *Designing and conducting mixed methods research* (2nd ed.). Thousand Oaks, CA: SAGE Publications.

Dauvergne, C. (2008). *Making people illegal: What globalization means for migration and law*. New York: Cambridge University Press.
Gerard, A. (2014). *The securitisation of migration and refugee women*. London: Routledge.
Glaser, B., & Strauss, A. (1967). *The discovery of grounded theory: Strategies for qualitative research*. New York: Aldine.
Mezzadra, S., & Neilson, B. (2013). *Border as method, or, the multiplication of labor*. Durham, NC and London: Duke University Press.
Munro, A. (2009). *Too much happiness*. New York: Vintage Books.
Neocleous, M. (2000). *The fabrication of social order: A critical theory of police power*. London: Pluto Press.
Stebbins, R. A. (2001). *Exploratory research in the social sciences*. Thousand Oaks, CA, London and New Delhi: SAGE Publications.
Thomas, G. (2011). *How to do your case study*. Los Angeles, CA, London, New Delhi, Singapore and Washington, DC: SAGE Publications.
Thomas, G., & Myers, K. (2015). *The anatomy of the case study*. New Delhi, Singapore and Washington, DC: SAGE Publications.
Walby, S. (2009). *Globalization and inequalities: Complexity and contested modernities*. London: SAGE Publications.
Weber, L. (2006). The shifting frontiers of migration control. In S. Pickering & L. Weber (Eds.), *Borders, mobility and technologies of control*. Amsterdam: Springer.
Weber, L. (2007). Policing the virtual border: Punitive preemption in Australian offshore migration controls. *Social Justice Special Issue on Transnational Criminology, 34*, 77–93.
Weber, L. (2013a). Visible and virtual borders: Saving lives by 'seeing' sovereignty. *Griffith Law Review, 22*, 666–682.
Weber, L. (2013b). *Policing non-citizens*. Abingdon: Routledge.
Weber, L., & Bowling, B. (2004). Policing migration: A framework for investigating the regulation of global mobility. *Policing and Society, 14*, 195–212.
Weber, L., & Bowling, B. (2008). Valiant beggars and global vagabonds: Select, eject, immobilise. *Theoretical Criminology, 12*, 355–375.
Whyte, D. (Ed.). (2009). *Crimes of the powerful: A reader*. Maidenhead: Open University Press.
Yin, R. (2009). *Case study research: Design and methods*. Thousand Oaks, CA: SAGE Publications.
Yin, R. (2012). *Applications of case study research*. Thousand Oaks, CA: SAGE Publications.

Chapter 2

Manoeuvring in tricky waters
Challenges in being a useful and critical migration scholar

May-Len Skilbrei

Introduction

In the last few years, the high number of arrivals of migrants to Europe has been depicted as a problem for the continent (Jurado, Brochmann, & Dølvik, 2013). This has been spoken of as a 'refugee crisis' or a 'migration crisis', not only in terms of how leaving one's country is difficult for migrants, but also how receiving and integrating migrants is a problem for European societies (see, e.g. BBC, 2016). In order to solve this perceived problem, policy makers and implementers at European and national levels turn to the evidence and knowledge generated by research. This entails an increase in the relevant funding so that such research may contribute more efficiently to the management of migration. An example of this is the 11 million EUR strengthening of the European Union funding on migration in 2017 entitled 'In response to the refugee crisis'.[1] Thus the heightened concerns for the potentially negative impact of migration on European societies and the belief that research can help European states to manage migration better mean that migration research has gained more funding, visibility and traction. But there are also some dilemmas created by this situation. One of them is that migration researchers become embedded, and thus implicated, in the European migration management efforts in ways that are both epistemologically and ethically challenging. The fact that policy makers and bureaucracies expect researchers to provide them with tools they need in order to develop and perform policies obliges researchers to contemplate on their role and impact. In this chapter, I present some examples from my own research that illustrate these dilemmas and discuss ways forward for a research agenda that is both relevant and critical.

For the last 20 years, I have been a project manager of or a research participant in various projects related to migration and its links with crime, such as prostitution, human trafficking, return migration of rejected asylum seekers, marriage migration and irregular migration. These topics are often objects of heated public discussions and exemplify areas in which policy makers and implementers have looked to research for solutions. My main research context is Norway, but I believe that the challenges migration researchers face there are also relevant for other contexts.

Researchers take part in producing the realities they seek to describe. The chapter brings up some points related to how contemporary ways of framing and regulating migration influence how and what we, as researchers, study and are able to see and say and how what we say is received. By investigating the context of our knowledge, I seek to perform what Wacquant (2011 in McBride, 2017) calls 'epistemic reflection'. To do this, I employ three examples of entanglements with state agendas from my own research practice to demonstrate how negotiations over the balancing of research integrity and relevance take place between commissioning bodies and researchers. The backdrop to my examples and discussions of them is not only the political debate climate but also the developments in research and research funding.

The problem of oversocialisation of researchers

In his influential paper 'For Public Sociology', Michael Burawoy (2005) looks more closely at different strands of engagement among scholarship and public and political demands. He particularly mentions the policy orientation of Norwegian sociology. In a Norwegian context the development of the welfare state and the disciplinary development of sociology are often represented to walk hand in hand. In an evaluation of Norwegian sociology that took place a few years ago, an important conclusion was that it was highly empirically oriented and problem focused. It was argued that this set Norwegian sociology apart (Research Council of Norway, 2010, p. 18): 'The view of the task of sociology as problem-oriented and grounded in social reality is the central legacy and characteristic of sociology in Norway'. The evaluation committee saw this as a consequence of how Norwegian state building had relied upon Norwegian social science for several decades and that this had ensured the continued generous funding of research but that state agendas had also framed social science and had an impact on what is researched. In criminology, Nils Christie has written about this as part of the problem of 'the oversocialization' (1997, p. 14): 'It is just not true that officials as a rule are negative to social research. On the contrary, they are encouraging of research, and they are eager consumers of the results. But what they ask for is answers to problems as seen by themselves, helpful answers for running the state'.

My own academic trajectory is typical of this dilemma since much of my own research on migration and crime has been funded by ministries and other governmental bodies. Also, migration scholarship offers a good example of the development and bonds which the report from the evaluation of Norwegian sociology (Research Council of Norway, 2010) and Burawoy's (2005) paper speak of. Much of migration research is funded by governmental bodies, the same bodies that are tasked with developing and implementing migration policies. This ensures that researchers engage with questions that are seen as relevant for policy makers and implementers, as these bodies often fund research based on what they identify as their challenges. The Norwegian government funds research directly and indirectly. Research is directly funded through the ministries and governmental bodies that are organised under the supervision of ministries. A relevant example is how the department that is tasked to govern migration – the Norwegian Directorate of Immigration (UDI) – is also a large funder of research. UDI is the body that receives and makes rulings on applications for asylum and evaluates and makes decisions on applications for work and tourist visas and family unification. It funds research that in different ways is intended to evaluate the various schemes and how UDI manages them. The needs for knowledge that UDI has are met by a combination of university-based researchers, staff at non-profit academically oriented research institutes and staff working in private consultancy companies.

Additionally, the Norwegian government funds research indirectly by allocating funding to the Research Council of Norway (RCN). RCN is the largest single funder of research in Norway and is also the contact point to the European Research Agenda. RCN establishes research programs designed to produce research that helps to solve societal problems. The largest single source of migration research in Norway is the RCN research programme Welfare, Working Life and Migration (VAM). The programme lists as its first aim to 'deal with questions of significance for politics, administration and other relevant stakeholders' (Research Council of Norway, 2013, p. 11). This is similar to how the European Commission research programme Horizon 2020 is described as dedicated to funding research that helps Europe tackle 'societal challenges'.[2]

While there may be particularly strong links between governmental bodies and social science research in Norway, the forms of entanglement that this chapter deals with are also relevant for other contexts, where other bodies and policies influence research agendas. The examples in this chapter are from my own research, which was funded directly by the Norwegian authorities and was also designed to meet knowledge needs of policy makers and implementers, but the dilemmas I describe are also relevant for research funded indirectly, through various government-funded research programmes. Thus, I argue that threats to the independence of research could affect anyone. This is particularly the case since the aim to achieve 'impact' in research has become increasingly central in the past few years. Les Back (2015) argues that while 'impact' can be interpreted as adding to research an 'emancipatory' potential or helping people critique their governments, it is often interpreted as 'relevant' and 'instrumental' to powerful institutions. Back has looked at the priorities of the UK academic evaluation scheme, the Research Excellence Framework, whereby academic institutions are ranked in terms of how well they perform based on, among other things, the capability to make an impact with their research. He argues that this influences how scholars think and prioritise and that the need for researchers to make an impact thus functions 'as a filter for our sociological attention'. Since impact is often thought of as agenda setting and policy changing, speaking to and meeting the needs of the powerful is what counts as impact. This is similar to the critique offered by the Norwegian anthropologist

Christine Jacobsen (2015) when she argues that researchers who are concerned about making an impact risk ending up being state centric (see also McAra, 2017). When researchers are expected to produce research that aids policy makers in their endeavours to reach their policy goals, not only when they perform commissioned research but also when engaging in fundamental research, this serves as a bias that narrows research and its ability to impact society in a broader sense.

What is researched at any given time, and thus what is known about migration and migrants, is political in the sense that it is directly or indirectly influenced by priorities among politicians, bureaucrats and NGOs, as much of contemporary European research on migration and beyond is expected to 'be relevant' for policy developments. There is, therefore, a danger that what is deemed interesting and necessary data about migration, and something governments are willing to fund, is closely linked to views about what migration is and what should be done about it. When the European Union increases its funding for research on migration as a response to increasing arrivals of migrants to Europe, as described earlier, it is not willing to fund migration research in general but only projects that are helpful according to a particular problem definition. The current definition of migration as a problem for Europe is thus something that has an impact on the priorities of funding bodies and the thinking of scholars.

In this chapter I describe my experience with performing research on migration and crime and discuss this in terms of its 'entanglements' with administrative-managerial agendas and what consequences this has for my independence as a scholar. However, I will first give a more detailed description of the relationship between research and the governance of migration.

Enlisting research in 'migration management'

It has been argued that migration and integration policies are now, more than before, thought and spoken of as 'migration management' (Geiger & Pécoud, 2010a). Borrowed from the corporate world, the term 'management' suggests control and efficiency and glosses over the multiple conflicts that are often involved within states, among states and between states and migrants. Due to the emphasis on this term, the implementation of migration policies becomes depoliticised and appears to be the work of public and private technocrats in national bureaucracies and national and supranational organisations. Speaking of 'migration management' may in this way contribute towards hiding power relations in society and instead highlight a 'post-control' spirit' (Geiger & Pécoud, 2010a, p. 15) that pretends 'to move beyond the narrow security-oriented policies of border control' (ibid, p. 15); as if migrants are steered rather than downright stopped, harmed and deported. Through this, policies that under other circumstances would have been critiqued are normalised. This is why it is important to investigate the role of research in this landscape. The phrase 'migration management' assigns a particular task to research; namely, that of evaluating and delivering evidence for the improvement of particular policies, such as particular visa schemes, ways of organising asylum reception centres or priorities in programmes for assisted return. In this way 'gathering facts' is integrated into the administration of migration policies. A result is a symbolic 'depoliticisation' of migration policies in the sense that it makes policies appear to be anti-political acts of necessity instead of the results of a political will (Bourdieu & Wacquant, 1999; Büscher, 2010). They become an act of 'management' and not 'control'.

Christina Boswell (2009, p. 3) contends that policy making in the field of migration now relies more on research than earlier. Policies are expected to be based on 'evidence' of what works, and their consequences are expected to be evaluated and adjusted based on research (see also McBride, 2017). But this does not mean that policies are developed, implemented and changed in line with research findings, since only some findings are taken on board while others are ignored. Furthermore, it may also occur that the same logic treats research-based knowledge as useful in this endeavour only to the extent it contributes to producing clear-cut answers to the perceived policy needs. Research is expected to document how migration management works as a machinery whose function can be improved if one tightens the right bolts. In this way, research becomes integrated in what is often presented as a 'policy circle' (Sutton & Levinson, 2001) in which it serves a purpose in improving but not fundamentally changing the system (Boswell, 2009). This function of research must therefore be expected to impact the relationship between governmental institutions that commission research and researchers, as the definitional power stays with the funder. When research is given the task of investigating specific policy instruments, more than serving as a tool to raise relevant questions, the capability of research to expand our thinking and increase our capacity to act is diminished.

Accordingly, when migration scholarship is enlisted in migration management, scholars are required to think critically about the role they play in the field (Armstrong, Blaustein, & Henry, 2017, p. 14). The need to be relevant and 'make an impact' easily becomes an act of complicity whereby the position of academic knowledge is used to legitimise harsh migration policies and silence their critique. Geiger and Pécoud encourage researchers to retain a critical perspective in a climate in which critique is often silenced by presenting migration policies as apolitical and administrative: 'A critical standpoint is necessary, to avoid remaining too close to its ["migration management's"] narratives and stated objectives, and to develop a counter-perspective to the proliferation of the so-called "policy-relevant" studies by "experts"' (2010b, p. xiii). Nikolas Rose (1996) describes a shift from governing without any attempts to steer and influence the participating experts to an 'advanced liberal mode' of rule in which experts, such as researchers, are subjected to evaluation, monitoring and management. Rose paints a bleak picture of loss of independence in knowledge production that engages with power. He describes the relationship between scholarship and policy making as instrumental and lacking in trust.

With an interest in understanding what kinds of dilemmas are created by the fact that contemporary migration management turns to research to improve its efficiency both in its inclusionary and exclusionary efforts, I will now present three different challenges for migration scholars who wish to make an impact on society in a broad sense while retaining at the same time the critical potential the research ideally has.

The problem of framing

As mentioned in the introduction, much Norwegian social science generally, and migration research in particular, is funded directly or indirectly by the Norwegian government based on its knowledge needs in terms of developing and implementing policies. The funding call itself usually formulates what a research project should be concerned with if it is to receive funding. In the text of the call, corresponding memos or contract meetings, funders communicate what their knowledge needs are. As described, both the European Commission and the RCN, as well as research councils in other European countries, aim to fund research that helps what at any given time and place is considered a problem and in need of research-based knowledge to be improved upon. Relevance is therefore a prerequisite for getting the research funded. This is also evident in calls from UDI and various ministries that fund much migration research directly, based on the need for research-based knowledge that their employees have reported to the research and development divisions. Calls from funding bodies communicate what researchers should prioritise in developing a research proposal but also communicate how the topic should be framed. In this, they often build on a particular problem definition and worldview. Herbert Blumer has pointed to the need to investigate the foundational ideas about what we study (1969, p. 24): 'The *entire act* of scientific study is oriented and shaped by the underlying picture of the empirical world that is used'. In the current flow of calls for funding research on migration, it is often expressed that migration *is a problem*.

For example, in 2015–2016, I headed an evaluation of the Norwegian efforts to offer assisted return to Nigerian citizens, funded by UDI. The call for proposals stated: 'The aim of the study is to establish knowledge on what effects cash benefits have for whether asylum seekers chose assisted return or not, and how the support contributes to reintegration in the country of origin'. The background of the various schemes for assisted return is an explicit aim to return overstayers, irregular migrants and rejected asylum seekers, and this was also the background to why they wanted to know whether their efforts worked according to their intentions. By responding to this call for proposals and signing a contract to do the research, I had, to some degree, accepted their problem definition. While we interviewed prospective returnees and people who had returned to Nigeria, the main aim was not to engage with the problem definition of the migrants but to look for their motivations and experiences in order to offer improvements of the policy. The report (Paasche, Plambech & Skilbrei, 2016) even included advice on how to improve the relevant return schemes, and we published an op-ed to communicate findings more broadly.

The challenge for us as researchers in such a project was that the premise for undertaking the research entailed that we accepted the starting assumption: that research on why more Nigerians do not return to their country of origin is needed, and that we were willing to contribute towards improving policies that we very well knew were not understood as 'voluntary' for many migrants (see e.g. Skilbrei & Tveit, 2011; Webber, 2011). The case shows how, by taking administrative divisions and corresponding policies as a starting point, researchers take part in fixing motivations and people, instead of broadening the discourse. Also, by taking on the task of evaluating a particular policy, researchers contribute towards dividing policies into small pieces of the puzzle without contributing to directing the attention towards the bigger picture of border control policies that impact the lives of migrants. Simply looking at what governments describe as 'voluntary return', without examining the relationship between this policy and the threat of deportation, hides the power states have and the lack of ability the migrants have in choosing whether to return to their country of origin.

Related to this is the issue of terminology in calls and communication with funders and other stakeholders. In several research projects I have been involved in, there have been discussions between the representatives of the funding body and researchers about what terms should be applied. A few years back, Norwegian governmental bodies spoke of 'voluntary return', which I and other researchers problematised in meetings with representatives of the government. Now, the term 'assisted return' is applied, and governmental representatives will no longer speak as if they believe that assisted return is not marked by its relationship with deportation. But the term 'deportation' sits uncomfortably with governmental representatives. They prefer the term 'enforced return' with the argument that this is the administrative term for it, and if we as researchers desire to get our points across to them, we need to use their terms.

The problem of embeddedness

Another example is a research project on credibility assessments in asylum procedures, which I headed in 2012–2014. One of the most important tasks an asylum case worker bears when deciding upon an asylum claim is to evaluate whether the story told by the claimant is credible. The project was commissioned and funded by UDI, the same body that is in charge of asylum procedures in Norway and operationalises 'credibility' in their instructions to staff members who are tasked with making decisions about applications for asylum. As researchers, we were eager to study how UDI case workers operationalised credibility in the decision-making process and in asylum interviews. There were several concerns regarding entanglements in this project. We were expected to work closely with UDI and were also very dependent on them to be able to perform a survey and qualitative interviews among case workers. At the same time we, throughout the duration of the project, took particular steps to keep a distance for both ethical and epistemological reasons. UDI initially wanted one of their representatives to take a leave of absence from her work during the project period in order to participate in the research group. We refused this request with the argument that it would be difficult to ensure the confidentiality of research subjects and protect them from any negative consequences if the interviewer was someone on a leave from UDI management who would return to management after the completion of the research. The research team did not experience this as an attempt to steer our research but instead as a sign that UDI did not share our understanding of the relationship between funders of research and researchers.

The project was closely followed up by a reference group consisting of members from UDI, the Immigration Appeals Board and the Ministry of Justice. We had regular meetings with this group and were expected to communicate and discuss findings with them. While this was a highly qualified, interested and interesting group to discuss with, this also kept us conceptually close to governmental agendas in the sense that when we described findings they were very active in offering their interpretations.

In the methodology chapter of the report, my co-authors and I wanted to present the dilemmas of working so closely with the funding body as we did in that particular project. We wrote (Bollingmo, Skilbrei & Wessel, 2014, p. 30, my translation),

> We reflected on whether this could reduce access to information that was not in line with the UDI's own understanding of issues linked to credibility. It was important to us that the research perspectives where not locked to the commissioning body's own understanding of the problem and possible solution.

We concluded in the report that, while UDI representatives had been very hands-on throughout the research process, this had first and foremost constituted a resource for the research. Later, I reflected more on what had happened in that particular project and on how the close contact between the researchers and UDI was intended to ensure that the research we conducted would impact the training for asylum case work. While as a researcher, I was also positive to contributing towards ensuring high-quality asylum procedures, it was very difficult for me to bring up issues which UDI had not beforehand defined as relevant. The contact with the reference group and the communication in relation to the writing up of the report made us stick to a more narrow understanding of context than we would under other circumstances. UDI had a very concrete need for research-based information in order to improve their internal training of case workers, and comments from the reference group were often in the form of questions about how this and that finding was relevant for the research question.

Also, the entanglement in this particular project was that of loyalty towards UDI representatives that we got to know quite well and who were sympathetic towards us. This is similar to how Bosworth and Kellezi (2017) describe their sense of obligation towards the institutions that had assisted them in planning and executing their study on immigration removal centres in Britain. This easily becomes a situation in which the researchers align with central aims of the institution, something that may hinder more critical and, therefore, more transformative thinking. The end result, in my opinion, is one in which the main contribution of the research was one strengthening UDI in their understanding of the problem and solutions more than offering analytical depth that enable them to transform how they were thinking about asylum decisions.

The problem of expected loyalty

When researchers are understood as taking part in attempts to improve how an institution approaches migration, this impacts the possibilities of critique and whether new perspectives are welcome. If researchers are understood as part of a team of 'migration managers', any indications that they are not in compliance may have consequences for the acceptance of their findings. The danger is that research findings will be perceived to be true when the sentiments of the researchers are in alignment with governmental goals and problem definitions and untrue if they are not. Accusations of research being biased thus typically arise when researchers align with the powerless and not with the powerful (Hammersley, 2000).

In the following example, I describe my own experience in which various stakeholder groups thought of me as a loyal or at least a friendly-minded outsider, but only up to a certain point.

I was presenting a report evaluating Norwegian efforts to provide protection to identified victims of trafficking at a public event organised by my employer, the Norwegian research institute Fafo. More than 100 people had turned up for the event, many of them representing ministries and different governmental bodies designated with the task of implementing Norwegian trafficking policies. The Norwegian state is bound in its effort by the UN Trafficking Protocol and the Council of Europe Convention on Action Against Trafficking in Human Beings, and both are clear in that governments should take care to return victims only if this does not infringe upon their safety and well-being. At the launch of the report, we conveyed central findings, and one of them was that victims felt uncertain about the future and the ability of the Norwegian state to protect them. In the report and at the event, we described that victims of trafficking are refused asylum and residency permits on humanitarian grounds and are instead returned to Nigeria, also against their will. My co-authors and I pointed to the inherent problems the Norwegian authorities encounter when offering the best assistance possible to victims while they are in Norway but at the same time not helping the victims with what they want the most and what would best protect them in the long run, namely residency in Norway. In a Q&A session about the results, I answered a question about how we could best help victims, and I said, half-jokingly: 'Of course, if it was up to me, they could all stay'.

After the event a contingency of representatives from the immigration police came up to me. They were very disappointed with me and wanted me to know that. One of them stated, 'We have followed your work with great interest and read everything you have written. But from now on, we can no longer trust anything you say'. I was perplexed at this, as I had a good working relationship with the police and did not understand why they had changed their perception of my research. They explained to me that now that they knew about my views on migration they would not trust my conclusions as objective.

The reason for bringing up this example is the fact that I was unprepared for the expectation of loyalty to governmental migration policies. I had good rapport with Norwegian stakeholders, including the police, and had not thought that a precondition for this was that I shared the views of the Norwegian government. I would for example not expect all police officers or social workers working with trafficking to be in agreement on what the right policy to apply was, so why did a lack of alignment with governmental goals conflict with trust in my research? Reading my work had not indicated a particular bias to them, but the short statement I had made in public made them question whether my conclusions were research based or political.

In later work, I have depended on the police for access and legitimacy. I have heard rumours about police questioning my neutrality, but my impression is that my access to the field was never hindered thereby. Whether this continued to impact negatively on the police's trust in me or other researchers or not is difficult to say. These particular police officers and others may have regained trust in me since then, but the said and later experiences made me reflect on what is taken for granted in relationships between researchers and various stakeholders.

Conclusion

What silences are produced by following up on just the themes that the funding bodies designate to be worthy of funding and frame questions in line with their priorities? And how are we disciplined by contact with stakeholders and expectations of loyalty? Research can serve as a starting point for transformation, but through the three examples described here, I argue that it may instead take part in reinforcing silences.

To return to Blumer's (1969) point, the examples from my research point to existing incentives not to problematise. This may lead to the 'oversocialisation' mentioned by Christie (1997), which is not an issue of censorship or self-censorship but rather an issue of how researchers' thinking is framed and thus limited by institutions and their perspectives. The examples in this chapter point to the power institutions have to (1) frame research topics in a particular way by how they formulate calls for proposals, (2) institutionalise the relationship between themselves and researchers in ways that may make researchers take on the bureaucratic gaze and (3) communicate expectations to align with state agendas. These are all powers that, one can argue, ensure that research is relevant and thus produces an impact, but they are also powers that may influence what researchers think, say and write. Taking on politicised understandings and administrative labels uncritically is something that limits our thinking and makes our contributions less radical than they could be.

The whole research field is structured by administrative and political categories and boundaries. Legally and administratively, the state makes a division between mobility and migration. Mobility is, in line with the EU lingo, a reference to intra-European human movement, while migration is a term for the mobility of third-country nationals into Europe through the various regulated entry-schemes (family reunification, student, expert labour, asylum) and irregular entry (Boswell & Geddes, 2011, p. 3). In one sense, the division is a very realistic and necessary delineation, as these are the terms and legal divisions that the people studied by researchers have to relate to. In another sense though, appropriating them uncritically redounds in normalising this as a legitimate and 'natural' division.

In a situation in which research is intended to provide evidence of how migration policies work and how they can be improved, research easily becomes a bolt in the machinery of migration management. This implicates us in the society's power relations and the injustices that they produce. Independence is a central scientific virtue encompassed in the concept of 'research integrity' that in recent years has become an important principle in European research ethics (ALLEA, 2017). Such independence is difficult to establish when research is framed, embedded and loyal in the ways I have described in this chapter, not as clear-cut attempts to steer conclusions but rather as part of the framework researchers operate within. 'Experts', such as researchers, are today part of and invested in state practices and policies with very dramatic and negative consequences on people's lives (Sharma & Gupta, 2006, p. 9). I would argue that this is not only done by how we ensure the design of governmentally fundable projects because we want to win research bids. The alignment of research with political priorities and administrative categories is also produced by ideals internal to research, such as an increasing demand to be relevant and produce impact.

Notes

1 www.h2020.md/en/commission-invest-%E2%82%AC85-billion-research-and-innovation-2017
2 https://ec.europa.eu/programmes/horizon2020/en/what-horizon-2020

References

All European Academies (ALLEA). (2017). *The European code of conduct for research integrity* (Rev. ed.). Berlin: ALLEA. Retrieved July 18, 2017, from http://ec.europa.eu/research/ participants/data/ref/ h2020/other/hi/h2020-ethics_code-of-conduct_en.pdf

Armstrong, S., Blaustein, J., & Henry, A. (2017). Impact and the reflexive imperative in criminal justice policy, practice and research. In S. Armstrong, J. Blaustein, & A. Henry (Eds.), *Reflexivity and criminal justice: Intersections of policy, Practice & research* (pp. 1–30). London: Palgrave.

Back, L. (2015, September 23). On the side of the powerful: The 'impact agenda' & sociology in public. *The Sociological Review* Blog. Retrieved July 16, 2017, from www.thesociologi calreview.com/blog/on-the-side-of-the-powerful-the-impact-agenda-sociology-in-pub lic.html

BBC. (2016, March 4). Migrant crisis: Migration to Europe explained in seven charts. Retrieved July 16, 2017, from www.bbc.com/news/world-europe-34131911

Blumer, H. (1969). *Symbolic interactionism*. Englewood Cliffs, NJ: Prentice-Hall.

Bollingmo, G. C., Skilbrei, M-L., & Wessel, E. (2014). *Troverdighetsvurderinger: Søkerens forklaring som bevis i saker om beskyttelse (asyl)*. Oslo: Fafo.

Boswell, C. (2009). *The political uses of expert knowledge: Immigration policy and social research*. Cambridge: Cambridge University Press.

Boswell, C., & Geddes, A. (2011). *Migration and mobility in the European Union*. New York: Palgrave Macmillan.

Bosworth, M., & Kellezi, B. (2017). Doing research in immigration removal centres: Ethics, emotions and impact. *Criminology & Criminal Justice*, 17(2), 121–137.

Bourdieu, P., & Wacquant, L. (1999). On the cunning of imperialist reason. *Theory, Culture and Society*, 16(1), 41–58.

Burawoy, M. (2005). For public sociology. *American Sociological Review*, 70(1), 4–28.

Büscher, B. (2010). Anti-politics as political strategy: Neoliberalism and transfrontier conservation in Southern Africa. *Development & Change*, 41(1), 29–51.

Christie, N. (1997). Four block against insight: Notes on the oversocialization of criminologists. *Theoretical Criminology*, 1(1), 13–23.

Geiger, M., & Pécoud, A. (2010a). The politics of international migration management. In M. Geiger & A. Pécoud (Eds.), *The politics of international migration management* (pp. 1–20). Houndmills: Palgrave.

Geiger, M., & Pécoud, A. (2010b). Preface to the paperback edition. In M. Geiger & A. Pécoud (Eds.), *The politics of international migration management* (pp. vii–xiii). Houndmills: Palgrave.

Hammersley, M. (2000). *Taking sides in social research: Essays on partisanship and bias*. London: Routledge.

Jacobsen, C. (2015). Communicating irregular migration. *American Behavioral Scientist*, 59(7), 886–897.

Jurado, E., Brochmann, G., & Dølvik, J. E. (2013). Introduction immigration, work and welfare: Towards an integrated approach. In E. Jurado & G. Brochmann (Eds.), *Europe's immigration challenge: Reconciling work, welfare and mobility* (pp. 1–148). London: I.B. Tauris.

McAra, L. (2017). Criminological knowledge and the politics of impact: Implications for researching juvenile justice. In S. Armstrong, J. Blaustein, & A. Henry (Eds.), *Reflexivity and criminal justice: Intersections of policy, practice & research* (pp. 149–168). London: Palgrave.

McBride, R-S. (2017). Towards hope, solidarity and re-humanisation. In S. Armstrong, J. Blaustein, & A. Henry (Eds.), *Reflexivity and criminal justice: Intersections of policy, practice & research* (pp. 81–100). London: Palgrave.

Paasche, E., Plambech, S., & Skilbrei, M-L. (2016). *Assistert retur til Nigeria*. Oslo: University of Oslo.

Research Council of Norway. (2010). *Sociological research in Norway: An evaluation*. Oslo: Research Council of Norway.

Research Council of Norway. (2013). *Programplan 2013–2018*. Program Velferd, arbeidsliv og migrasjon – VAM II.

Rose, N. (1996). Governing 'advanced' liberal democracies. In A. Barry, T. Osborne, & N. Rose (Eds.), *Foucault and political reason: Liberalism, neo-liberalism and rationalities of government* (pp. 37–64). Chicago: Chicago University Press.

Sharma, A., & Gupta, A. (2006). Introduction: Rethinking theories of the state in an age of globalization. In A. Sharma & A. Gupta (Eds.), *The anthropology of the state: A reader* (pp. 1–41). Malden: Blackwell Publishing.

Skilbrei, M-L., & Tveit, M. (2011). Mission impossible? Voluntarily and dignified repatriation of victims of trafficking to Nigeria. In T-D. Truong & D. Gasper (Eds.), *Transnational migration and human security* (pp. 135–146). Berlin and Heidelberg: Springer.

Sutton, M., & Levinson, B. (2001). Introduction: Policy as/in practice – a sociocultural approach to the study of educational policy. In M. Sutton & B. Levinson (Eds.), *Policy as practice – towards a comparative sociocultural analysis of educational policy* (pp. 1–22). Westport, CT: Ablex Publishing.

Wacquant, L. (2011). From 'public criminology' to the reflexive sociology of criminological production and consumption: A review of *Public criminology?* By Ian Loader and Richard Sparks. *British Journal of Criminology, 51*(2), 438–448.

Webber, F. (2011). How voluntary are voluntary returns? *Race & Class, 52*(4), 98–107.

Chapter 3

'Crimmigration' statistics
Numbers as evidence and problem

Synnøve Jahnsen and Kristin Slettvåg

Introduction

The purpose of this chapter is to consider some of the ethical and methodological challenges scholars face when seeking numerical data and statistical knowledge about criminal justice and migration. In it we focus on the value and challenges of quantitative research data and describe our own attempts to mend the shortcomings of existing secondary quantitative data. Drawing on empirical content from our own projects, we explore how researchers frame their work and collect and analyse data on criminal justice practices in an era of mass mobility.

The chapter is structured as follows: first we present our research background and mutual interest in numbers before we outline some of the most important challenges we encountered when seeking to combine our research interests on a joint project. In particular, we will explore the difficulties we encountered in identifying relevant sources of data. We warn against a false dichotomy between qualitative and quantitative research designs. Great attention is needed, we argue, to how categories are established within legal, organizational and political contexts. Examining the manner in which individual cases are classified at a practical level is a fundamental and necessary task for quantitatively and qualitatively oriented researchers alike.

Background

The two authors of this chapter come from a criminological and sociological background respectively, with an emphasis on critical gender and minority studies. Slettvåg's research interests include migration management and control, with a specific focus on illegal re-entry and migrants sentenced to prison for violations of entry bans into Norway (Slettvåg, 2016). The most recent development affecting her project has been the increased criminalization of expulsion followed by an entry ban lasting one, two, five or ten years or indefinitely. In 2014, the maximum prison sentence for violating the ban was raised from six months to two years, and her project explored the reasons behind the changes and the way they played out in court and in convicted migrants' stories. Importantly for the topic of this chapter, Slettvåg's study combined traditional qualitative methods with the use of quantitative data to describe the extent of and changes in state reactions to violations of the entry ban. The study also described how crime statistics are used to justify law reform with increasing penalties for certain groups of non-citizens allegedly responsible for larger volumes of crime.

Jahnsen's interest in criminal justice has grown out of a broader sociological interest in social inequality and feminist theories and a more specific interest in public discourses on commercial sex and organized crime. The recent history of this field is marked by the implementation of the United Nations Convention against trafficking in persons, especially women and children, which was introduced in 2000, and the following ratification by the Norwegian government in 2003. Therefore, her methodological interests have evolved from discourse analysis of debate forums for clients in prostitution (Jahnsen, 2008b), public debates and media representations of prostitution (Jahnsen, 2007, 2008a), towards ethnographic studies of coordination and policy implementation (2014 a, b, 2018b), intelligence-led policing (Jahnsen, 2018a) and the shifting and hybrid nature of crime and border control (see also Jahnsen & Skilbrei, 2015, 2017, 2018).

Though we have entered migration research from specific, and to some degree narrow, topical angles, we share interests in what can be described as a trend in which migration control and crime control are merging into novel forms of hybrid control regimes directed at non-citizens. Specifically, we share a keen interest in improving our understanding of the extent of the regulation of migration via punitive methods and techniques derived from the criminal justice system and the prevention of crime by targeting non-citizens through immigration control.

Limitations of available quantitative data have forced us to combine several sets of data, relying on both qualitative and quantitative sources. One of these was a shared data set provided to us by the Norwegian Police Directorate (POD) in 2015. The data set was aggregated and did not include detailed information about individual persons, but it covered offences registered per year for the years 2002–2014. It also included specified types of offences, as coded by the police at different stages, from the reporting of the offence until the issuance of the final decision by the police. For our respective projects, the data were used to get a better understanding of the statistical increase in registered migration-related crimes. This chapter is a result of our discussions about the challenges we faced in our research and what we learned from attempting to mend for the limitations of official records and data sets. In what follows, we will present some of our mutual major challenges, faced jointly or individually.

'Crimmigration' statistics

For criminologists and criminal justice researchers our research interests can be placed within the field of 'the criminology of mobility' (Aas & Bosworth,

2013), which has emerged as a critical site where scholars have made efforts to bridge traditional and novel forms of empirical and theoretical considerations. These efforts have resulted in analyses of how changes in policy and law introduced new forms of legal rationalities termed 'crimmigration law' (Stumpf, 2006) social control (Barker, 2017; Guia, van Woude, & van Leun, 2013) and punishment termed 'bordered penality' (Aas, 2014). Part of this research has pointed out the paradox that while governments have enthusiastically included criminal law provisions in immigration law in the name of crime prevention, national security and border control, they have shown less interest in securing our ability to measure and quantify this development (Aliverti, 2013). Put simply, official documentation of the new laws and their impact is rather less than the action in the field suggests (Aas, 2014). Even recent discussions on crime statistics (see, for example Maguire, 2012) have failed to include the drastic increase in immigration violations that has been presented, among others, by the Pew Research Center (Gramlich & Bialik, 2017).

In contrast to the efforts used to quantify criminal statistics, the scarce evidence on the development of border control reveals how the criminalization of migration has historically been a political 'non-issue', encompassing crimes unworthy of counting, and a form of crime control unnecessary for the government to account for. Other issues are also salient, including time, resources, and competence of researchers. Rigid ethical and legal regulations in this field might also explain why some social science researchers and analysts for pragmatic reasons leave out populations that are deemed to be too vulnerable, statistically marginal, difficult to reach or only partly or poorly represented in registered data. Unregistered populations, like irregular migrants, not only represent all the above but also automatically fall outside the scope of expectations towards mainstream quantitative research on social and crime-related problems (unless they are willingly included by design and seen as useful for political purposes).

Like Aliverti (2013), who has pointed out that some recent immigration statistics include a wider range of detailed information about people prosecuted and convicted for immigration-related offences, we find that there are considerable inconsistencies and potential under-recordings of 'crimmigration' offences and hybrid forms of control. This knowledge gap renders the reliability of available statistics questionable and raises a host of methodological and ethical questions. As we will discuss in what follows, we had to mend for gaps in quantitative data sets and unpack how counting practices took place in order to understand how the data could be useful for research purposes. We also had to take great care when disseminating and presenting our research. Together, we sought to understand what numbers mean, symbolically and politically, and how they are given meaning and produced within various governmental and organisational logic and counting practices.

(Ac)counting (for) 'crimmigration'

Social scientists, even those who are qualitatively oriented, tend to use numbers and statistics to show a 'bigger picture' or to respond to political and public demands for information of a quantitative nature. Statistics have the power to connect our life experiences with larger societal shifts and help us see beyond mundane, local and everyday realities. Scientists, as well as political advocates, use numbers to evoke a social imagination as they place their arguments within larger horizons of meaning and imagined futures. Numbers are used to question, problematize, provoke and console but also to legitimize or dispute political decisions and practices. In our projects, numbers served as a potent background and starting point for analytical work, as official statistics illustrated the rise (and to some extent fall) of "crimmigration" as a political issue. We have both used quantitative data to show how migration control is increasingly linked to crime control and constitute prominent concerns in public debate.

Quantitative data often appear as 'matters of fact', as undisputed premises for policy development, and not up for discussion. Whatever politicians might disagree about, some aspects of social reality seem to simply mirror a shared truth. This numerical truth is objective and translatable across languages and contexts. As such quantitative research seems both particularly valuable, but also prone to trivialization and manipulation. Numerical data and statistics may be sensationalized by media, as 'hard facts' (Düvell, Triandafyllidou, & Vollmer, 2010, p. 235) or as neutral descriptions that make a normative debate about an issue seem unnecessary (Dahl & Lomell, 2009, p. 85).

As the principles, techniques and rationale of financial accounting have become central to organizing all aspects of social life, from the governance of welfare services to the execution of war, researchers have also become increasingly influenced by what has been termed 'audit culture' (Power, 2003). Moreover, manipulation of numbers can cause severe harm, particularly in relation to sensitive political issues covered in criminal justice and migration research (Düvell, Triandafyllidou, & Vollmer, 2010, p. 235). This means that research should be performed with attention to measurement errors that may arise due to the established goals of an organization and the introduction of New Public Management. The way statistics are interpreted and correspond to the allocation of resources may very well be a crucial aspect of to the credibility of both migration- and crime management. It is important to recognize that holding governments accountable for the numbers they produce, or not produce, can both disadvantage and advantage a particular group or political standpoint. The same stands for data mirroring organizational practices, which may obstruct or enable certain prioritizations. Pointing out the lack of assistance schemes for male victims of trafficking, for example, when explaining why there are few registered cases of forced labour, can be more or equally useful information for groups seeking to improve the quality of assistance schemes, than knowing the exact number of victims of trafficking.

The problem of bureaucratic data and feedback effects

The obvious benefit of secondary quantitative data is that it enables researchers to apply already-established administrative categories and conceptualizations, thus simplifying our counting processes and facilitating the comparison between various registering systems. Such data, however, is also associated with a range of problems, one being that it might result in conceptual simplifications that hamper our understanding of the phenomena we aim to study. Since the bureaucratic collection of personal data serves different purposes than those of the researcher, we risk that 'the meaning of concepts is sometimes determined by the available data rather than vice versa' (Bartram, 2012, p. 51). In addition, available data are often limited by categorizations, such as 'criminal', 'refugee', 'economic migrant', 'asylum seeker', 'immigrant', 'illegal' and 'undocumented', that have been designated not only to meet the administrative needs of bureaucratic systems but also to serve certain ideological and political purposes.

While migration status is directly relevant to migration data, it usually has only secondary relevance to the study of crime (Marshall, 1997, p. 240). Regardless, our projects have shown how the notion of the 'criminal foreigner' is present in public debate and policy development (Jahnsen, 2007; Slettvåg, 2016), and numbers on actual correlations are in demand (Mohn et al., 2014). Such issues illuminate the biggest ethical risk associated with the use of administrative categorizations, namely that our critical research efforts, rather than improving the status quo, may trigger negative and aggravated feedback effects by cementing explanatory variables into the social world we seek to describe. One obvious example here is the over-representation of non-citizens in crime data. Not paying sufficient attention to the structural causes for the over-representation may strengthen the mechanisms that caused the over-representation in the first place. The discussion of whether non-citizens or groups of non-citizens, such as asylum seekers or undocumented migrants, commit more crime than the citizens and whether more immigration causes more crime illustrates this danger and fear (see for instance Adelman et al., 2017; Mohn et al., 2014; Marshall, 1997). In order to avoid further statistical over-representation it is important for researchers to be cautious formulating research questions, developing research designs and disseminating results (Pickering & Ham, 2014).

Should we count?

Related to the problem of bureaucratic feedback effects is the more fundamental question of researchers' autonomy and whether researchers should let their research questions be guided or influenced by political problem definitions (in this case in relation to migration). Put differently: should researchers always count, or is it better to leave certain aspects of human life and condition uncounted? Describing a group or population category by quantifiable means simply because they are seen to constitute a problem from a governmental perspective is not necessarily best practice for scientific conduct or the right path to scientific progress.

Such ethical considerations are particularly relevant in research conducted on individuals referred to as 'irregular', 'undocumented' or 'illegal migrants'. Residing and moving outside the reach of governmental control and available registers, such as census data, renders irregular migrant populations, their needs and representativeness of their experiences difficult to gain knowledge about. One might argue that describing their experiences and struggle to access basic societal goods should be prioritized as a central scientific task (Düvell, Triandafyllidou, & Vollmer, 2010), allowing us to move the discussion from whether to count towards a discussion about how we frame our questions and what we measure. In our perspective, it seems necessary to separate the question of whether and how we should gain more knowledge into the lived experiences of migrants from the question of whether and how we do research on crimes committed by non-citizens. In our view, aggregated statistical data and quantitative analysis can be fruitful when performed with proper caution throughout the development of research questions, execution and dissemination. However, a major obstacle for us has been to access data that accurately quantify the current criminalization processes of migration and the related transformation of criminal justice systems.

How should we count and what?

Today the transnational and national regulation of migration is increasingly entangled with domestic and local crime control regimes that target migrant populations through punitive techniques derived from the criminal justice systems (Aas, 2014; Aliverti, 2013). Migration influences the national criminal justice systems in novel ways, while crime control and national security measures migrate across jurisdictions and systems set up to manage and control migration (see for example Jahnsen 2018a). Seen from a methodological perspective, this means that our empirical starting point is the intersection of these two systems and their tendency to overlap. Put simply, we can approach these issues from at least two angles: the migration control perspective and the criminal justice perspective. In the overlapping of the two we find what we describe as 'hybrid crimmigration statistics', which contains data on the state's coercive and punitive repertoire (including its crime-preventive strategies as well as administrative measures) for the purpose of migration management and border control.

Once we overcome the theoretical or more conceptual problem, the next challenge is a practical one: how to manage the hybrid nature of the phenomenon by finding a way to constructively approach these hybrid sources of data. One way to start is to by seek information about civil immigration law enforcement, that is, migration regulation techniques that are not formally defined as criminal procedures or punishments but which can be punitive in nature and/or intent. With this approach, one is able to find information about the criminalization of migration as well as its regulation and control (see, for example, Bosworth, 2013), but also about how border control intersects with crime control and crime prevention strategies (Gundhus, this volume; Jahnsen & Skilbrei, 2017b; Jahnsen, 2018a). In more practical terms there are (at least) two ways to go about this. Such information can often be found in publicly available numbers on expulsions provided by national or state authorities. In some cases, one can also procure numbers of incarcerations of non-citizens and deportations directly from a police immigration unit.

As a second approach, one can acquire data on non-citizens registered in the criminal justice system as well as the numbers of registered immigration law offences. Usually, this type of data is the most readily available source for studying the use of the criminal justice system for the purpose of migration control. Migrants may figure in these data both as victims (Marshall, 1997, p. 228) and as perpetrators of crime (see, for instance, Adelman et al., 2017; Mohn et al., 2014; Marshall, 1997). In Norway, getting access to register data relates to the larger issue of gatekeeping and to the extent authorities regulate and facilitate access to personal data and statistical analysis of register data. In our case, we were able to acquire secondary de-identified statistical data on registered immigration offences, which allowed us to bypass an otherwise time-consuming process of applying for and negotiating access to data. This means that our data contained no personal information. Still, even though the purpose of our analysis was to study systems rather than populations, our ability to live up to ethical standards felt ambiguous, as our data essentially derived from institutions that had collected them for other purposes than research, either for administrative purposes or in order to initiate/bring about criminal proceedings. As such, the issue of consent is at best questionable, as with most data on crime.

In comparison a similar but more particular problem haunts the human trafficking research field, as data on victims are collected from a range of organizations, which usually report on information given by a person on the premise of receiving some form of help and assistance, and/or during criminal proceedings. On a very basic level this relates to the issue of informed consent. Usually victims of trafficking lack the option to reserve themselves from being included in national reporting systems nor holds the power to influence the interpretations of numerical facts and statistical representations, for political as well as research purposes. On the other hand, the right to personal data protection and various ethical considerations dictate that the data on trafficking in Norway have to be reported anonymized and aggregated. Consequently, public records at a national level are seriously flawed, as it is not possible to review registrations and confirm any errors. For example, the fact that some service receivers are in contact with multiple care providers over longer periods signifies a serious threat to the validity of such data, to the extent that it is questionable whether the data can be used for research purposes at all – beyond informing us about registering practices and how policies are being implemented. However, the problem with ignoring the data set completely is that, due to the public character of the annual reports, the numbers will still be used to inform public debates about trafficking, as if they mirrored the size of the problem.

The problem of researching 'a moving target'

As pointed out in the introduction, violations of the Immigration Act have traditionally been treated as offences against the state or as victimless crimes and hence they have by many, including Norwegian police officers, been disregarded as immaterial and not necessarily something to report on a systemic level. Furthermore, for a violation to appear in our data, a representative of the law, either an immigration officer or the police, has to make a decision to act, for example by identifying, intervening and questioning an offender, and finally an officer usually has to press charges for a given violation.

It is challenging to sort and interpret changes in a dataset, and one can describe this as the problem of researching a 'moving target'. Changes in registration practices can occur due to legislative changes and organizational practices connected to implementation of new policies but may also occur due to external pressures on the police, new strategies and prioritization. This has, for example, been the case with Norwegian anti-trafficking policies in which we can observe an increase in the registered cases of trafficking for labour exploitation in the last few years. To complicate this even further, these changes took place at the same time as police districts were pressured into reaching higher and new types of target numbers, set by the sitting right-wing coalition government as part of their anti-immigration and tough on crime policy profile. At the same time, as police and immigration officers are granted substantial discretionary powers, we find variations between police districts, police units and individual police officers. From the time Jahnsen started doing fieldwork in the police in 2010 until her latest interviews in 2017, she has observed a spreading and increased awareness of the administrative powers prescribed by the immigration legislation for members of operational police units. Administrative powers, as laid down in Norwegian immigration regulations, have for example been used to target migrant sex workers and protect certain areas from street prostitution (even though sex work is not illegal in Norway).

Parts of the statistical spike we found in violations of the Immigration Act, might be explained by the concurrent influx of migrants. However, as mentioned, a major problem for researchers is that organizational counting practices often change, for example over time or due to new forms of governing and policing strategies (see also Andreas & Greenhill, 2010; Pease et al., 1983; Coleman & Moynihan, 1996). This means that when data is gathered by someone other than the researcher, for example the police, it can be difficult to get a complete picture of the changes that might have taken place without testing for changes in the counting practices. These more traditional challenges associated with statistical data on crime are further complicated when dealing with 'crimmigration statistics' because of the overlapping between punitive and immigration control forms. In Norway for example, certain punishable migration-related crimes such as exploitation of migrant workers may be registered as either criminal or civil immigration violations or both, depending on the time a crime had occurred, where it occurred and who recorded it. Counting practices may also change due to political and legislative changes, as immigration violations are increasingly met with criminal punishment, as is the case of illegal re-entry (Slettvåg, 2016). At the same time Jahnsen has observed that varying counting practices may exist also within local police districts, as some omit to register certain crimes over certain periods, for example due to recourse shortages at the prosecutorial level. At the end of the day, it is only the cases that are acted upon and registered as crimes and violations in the system that will show up in researchers' data sets.

In summary, statistical changes can be explained from a top-down perspective by examining the increased political pressure on police organizations, their prioritizations and their strategies. Some policing and registration practices are, however, better understood from a bottom-up perspective that takes into account, on the one hand, the increasing number of police officers that have received training on how to implement immigration law regulations and, on the other hand, that many police officers see the exercise of administrative powers, such as entry bans, as part of crime prevention strategies and thus useful against repeat offenders and as a way to control certain areas or groups of migrants. One may say that the increase in registered offences against the Norwegian Immigration Act, rather than mirroring an increasing number of crimes, shines light on a shift in perception of migration as a crime problem, mirroring that the police no longer sees these crimes as harmless, and thus as actions that they can continue to overlook upon discretion.

For us, the aforementioned problems of finding our focus in the blur of a moving target felt much like opening Pandora's box. We were left with a continuous stream haunting questions and no treasure. As such our efforts to get an accurate picture of 'crimmigration' as a social and political problem by accessing statistical data demanded a focus on tracking how data are bound horizontally, for example within institutions and horizontally between policy domains, and different levels of governance.

The problem of nationally bound data

The usefulness of the publicly available statistical data on migration in Norway and the data we obtained from the Norwegian Police Directorate (POD) was limited. In fact, they only provided us with a small piece of a larger puzzle, in our mind only describing the end result of the administrative and institutional practices that produced the data rather than the phenomena we were trying to study. The issue is not exclusive to the field of crimmigration control. It is, however, particularly salient within this field. In addition, as we will describe in more detail in what follows, counting practices vary between nation-states, which makes it difficult to translate findings from national registry data and assess to what extent they constitute useful knowledge for international researchers.

In crossing the borders of nation-states, migrants move across bureaucracies with different counting practices and registers. Since most counting practices in the field of migration are meant to describe the activity of nation-states with regards to (external) border control or (internal) crime control, the categories are usually limited to the authoritative scope of the nation-state. This scope is for the most part geographically limited to a specific territory, which is also usually the geographical limit of the existence of a non-citizen in national registers. This discrepancy between nationally bound data and methodological approaches and transnational phenomena poses certain challenges for researchers, relating in our studies to the degree that immigration status was evident in registered crime internationally (see, for example Mohn et al., 2014), and whether it made sense to compare our data with research from neighbouring countries.

Sometimes researchers might find themselves arguing that having some (poor) data is better than having none, thus allowing their research to be flawed at best or misleading at worst. When Jahnsen tried to compare Norwegian data on exploitation of migrants with numbers from neighbouring countries, she found that any comparative approach would be deeply flawed, because the data available to her were insufficient to support any conclusions or analysis, as it was too challenging to navigate between diverging legal and political categorizations, labelling and reporting practises. Eventually, her findings led her away from even trying to compare cases of human trafficking across the Nordic region. Instead she used research reports from other countries as an inspiration for a more qualitatively oriented analysis focusing on how distinctions are drawn between legal and ethical liability in reference to definitions of human trafficking, forced labour and social dumping (Jahnsen, 2014b). In such cases, thinking 'smarter' when designing research projects is the same as thinking 'small'. We also recommend that researchers seek international partnerships and alliances. Jahnsen has though not given up on her initial idea and is now part of a Nordic research network on forced labour and human trafficking that provide a path to successfully answering her initial research question.

Making research(-ers) available for scrutiny

While people might disagree about social and political values, only on rare occasions are we exposed to the more fundamental questions of how to interpret, use and avoid misuse of statistical information. Often the misrepresentation of social phenomena in the media is not intended but rather derives from lack of information about studies' methodologies and sampling (Düvell, Triandafyllidou, & Vollmer, 2010). It is our opinion that social scientists' obligation to make their studies available to the public and research subjects also entails a responsibility to provide context and meaning to their findings. Quantitative studies with secondary data not only must make methodological decisions taken by a researcher or a research team available, they also must provide a level of understanding of the institutions that produce the data and as such the organizational logics behind them.

Using numbers and estimates in some areas may challenge a researcher's integrity, as dissemination has to be done with an understanding of what type of information is relevant and useful for different audiences, as well as for policy goals. While numbers are often seen as useful by those who wish to rally for political/or institutional prioritization and support, and as such feed a demand for quantitative research designs, it is our experiences that a separation between a purely quantitative and a purely qualitative research design is a false dichotomy on a practical and empirical level. In human trafficking research for example registered convictions in a police district is not representative – to any actual amount – of crimes. Rather numbers are more useful when trying studying if and why investigations are initiated and lead to successful verdicts but also to illustrate, where and how certain forms of human trafficking, such as prostitution, have been prioritized over other forms, and how this might vary between time intervals, police districts and nations. For example, if one tries to compare the impact of anti-trafficking policies in the Nordic region, one will quickly see that whereas Finland have almost exclusively prioritize exposing cases of forced labour in regulated parts of the labour market, Norwegian authorizes have prioritized identifying victims of sexual exploitation and prostitution.

Public discourse is part of the research process in which other professional standards will come into play. This is where journalists, politicians and other groups of users share responsibility in terms of how they interpret and make use of research. Researchers with competence and confidence to denounced false claims and offer alternative explanations should engage in these debates in order to avoid misuse of statistical data which might have negative consequences for criminal justice and migration control measures. Yet this task is one that researchers might avoid for various reasons, such as finding it hard to communicate a nuanced view in the media or seeing the concepts discussed in public debate as scientifically meaningless (Marshall, 1997). Essentially, this is about loss of control over interpretation. Insufficient experience of public and media discourse might make it particularly difficult to communicate research findings in appropriate and manageable ways without oneself becoming an object of politicized public debates. When Jahnsen, for example, published some of her findings from her master's thesis (Jahnsen, 2007) in local news outlets and pointed out the relationship between anti-migration sentiments and the sudden and rapid political support for the sex purchase law, she simultaneously found herself the target of labelling strategies by individuals and organizations heavily invested in supporting of the new prostitution policies. These actors were less open to the nuances and the complexities which Jahnsen wished to bring forward. Such experiences can be unpleasant, but we believe that public critique bears fruit when used constructively as a source of new insights into the logic of political systems and as a learning process which can make young scholars more eligible to handle polarized debates. Doing critical social and criminal justice research in the era of mass migration can thus potentially provide a fruitful ground for young researchers who are up for a challenge.

Final discussion

The combination of an increasing number of asylum seekers and refugees, their precarious life situations and the heightened political tensions surrounding irregular migration have increased the possibilities for political exploitation and breaches of established rules of conduct from the authorities as well individual researchers. As a consequence, there has been a growing concern over reports that indicate that some researchers are tempted to make ethical lapses, thinking that the ends justify the means in terms of getting access to migrants and refugees (Hugman, Pittaway, & Bartolomei, 2011). Because of the massive political interests invested in migration, justifications for research on migration are rarely explained (Düvell, Triandafyllidou, & Vollmer, 2010). Rather it seems, compared to other disciplines such as medicine, that social scientists are less keen to discuss and criticize others for unethical research practises or point out misconduct among colleagues. However, if we, as researchers, worry about criticizing colleagues, we miss out on important discussions that sharpen our abilities to make better decisions and improve our practises. The concern over ethics in migration research generally originates from projects conducted within a qualitative framework. The growing interest for research methodologies and ethics has not been translated into corresponding publications found in quantitative research on migration or regarding dangers associated with quantitative data. While qualitative projects tend to focus on challenges associated with representation and 'giving voice', research subjects in large-scale quantitative studies appear almost 'faceless', at the same time as the numerical nature of this human data is presented with scarce ethical discussions.

Because of the rapidly changing field and the international nature of our research we hope that our chapter may inspire continuous methodological discussions. the nature of secondary data on noncitizens, registered as part of state control.

Bibliography

Aas, K. F. (2014). Bordered penality: Precarious membership and abnormal justice. *Punishment & Society*, *16*(5).

Aas, K. F., & Bosworth, M. (Eds.). (2013). *The borders of punishment: Migration, citizenship, and social exclusion*. Oxford: Oxford University Press.

Adelman, R., Reid, L. W., Markle, G., Weiss, S., & Jaret, C. (2017). Urban crime rates and the changing face of immigration: Evidence across four decades. *Journal of Ethnicity in Criminal Justice*, *15*(1), 52–77.

Aliverti, A. (2013). *Crimes of mobility: Criminal law and the regulation of immigration.* London: Routledge.
Andreas, P., & Greenhill, K. M. (2010). *Sex, drugs, and body counts: The politics of numbers in global crime and conflict.* Ithaca, NY: Cornell University Press.
Barker, V. (2017). *Nordic nationalism and penal order: Walling the welfare state.* London: Routledge.
Bartram, D. (2012). Migration, methods and innovation: A reconsideration of variation and conceptualization in research in foreign workers. In C. Vargas-Silva (Ed.), *Handbook of research methods in migration.* Cheltenham, UK: Edward Elgar Publishing.
Bosworth, M. (2013). Can immigration detention centres be legitimate? Understanding confinement in a global world. In K. F. Aas & M. Bosworth (Eds.), *The borders of punishment: Migration, citizenship, and social exclusion.* Oxford: Oxford University Press.
Coleman, C., & Moynihan, J. (1996). *Understanding crime data: Haunted by the dark figure (crime and justice).* Buckingham: Open University Press.
Dahl, J. Y., & Lomell, H. M. (2009). Tallenes tale: Bruk av statistikk i den kriminalpolitiske offentligheten. *Sosiologi i dag, 39*(3).
Düvell, F., Triandafyllidou, A., & Vollmer, B. (2010). Ethical issues in irregular migration research in Europe. *Population, Space and Place, 16*(3), 227–239.
Gramlich, J., & Bialik, K. (2017, April 10). *Immigration offenses make up a growing share of federal arrests.* Retrieved September 24, 2017, from http://pewrsr.ch/2opgdT8
Guia, M. J., van der Woude, M., & van der Leun, J. (2013). *Social control and justice: Crimmigration in the age of fear.* The Hague, The Netherlands: Eleven International Publishing.
Hugman, R., Pittaway, E., & Bartolomei, L. (2011). When 'do no harm' is not enough: The ethics of research with refugees and other vulnerable groups. *British Journal of Social Work, 41*(7), 1271–1287.
Jahnsen, S. (2007). *Women who cross borders – black magic? A critical discourse analysis of Nigerian women in prostitution.* Master thesis, Institute of Sociology, University of Bergen.
Jahnsen, S. (2008a). 'Norge er ikke en øy': Mediedekningen av kriminaliseringsdebatten i Norge. In M. L. Skilbrei & C. Holmström (Eds.), *Prostitusjon i Norden.* København: Nordiska ministerrådet.
Jahnsen, S. (2008b). På nett med menn som kjøper sex: Analyse av diskusjonsforumet på www.sexhandel.no. In M. L. Skilbrei & C. Holmström (Eds.), *Prostitusjon i Norden.* København: Nordiska ministerrådet.
Jahnsen, S. (2014a). *Innestengt eller utestengt? Norsk prostitusjonspolitikk og kampen mot menneskehandel.* PhD thesis, Department of Sociology, University of Bergen, Bergen.
Jahnsen, S. (2014b). *Menneskehandel og tvangsarbeid. En forstudie om gråsoneproblematikk innenfortiltaksfeltet arbeidsmarkedskriminalitet.* Oslo: The Norwegian Police University College.
Jahnsen, S. (2018a). Banishing and banning outlaw motorcycle clubs. In K. Rønn, H. Gundhus, & N. Fyfe (Eds.), *Inteligenceled policing.* Milton Park, UK: Routledge.
Jahnsen, S. (2018b). Condoms as evidence, Condoms as a crowbar. In M. Laing & T. Sanders (Eds.), *Policing prostitution.* Milton Park, UK: Routledge.
Jahnsen, S., & Skilbrei, M. L. (2015, April). From Palermo to the streets of Oslo: Pros and cons of the trafficking framework. *Anti-Trafficking Review: Bangkok, 4,* 156–160.
Jahnsen, S., & Skilbrei, M. L. (2017). Leaving no stone unturned: The borders and orders of transnational prostitution. *The British Journal of Criminology,* azx028. https://doi.org/10.1093/bjc/azx028
Jahnsen, S., & Skilbrei, M-L. (2018). Norway. In S. Jahnsen & H. Wagenaar (Eds.), *Assessing prostitution policies in Europe.* Milton Park, UK: Routledge.

Maguire, M. (2012). Criminal statistics and the construction of crime. In R. Morgan, M. Maguire, & R. Reiner (Eds.), *The Oxford handbook of criminology*. Oxford: Oxford University Press.

Marshall, I. H. (1997). 10: Minorities and crime in Europe and the United States: More seminal than different! In I. H. Marshall (Ed.), *Minorities, migrants, and crime: Diversity and similarity across Europe and the United States*. London: SAGE Publications.

Mohn, S. B., Ellingsen, D., Solheim, Ø. B., & Torgersen, K. (2014). *Et marginalt problem? Asylsøkere, ulovlig opphold og kriminalitet*. Kristiansand: Oxford Research.

Pease, K., Bottomley, K., & Coleman, C. (1983). Understanding crime rates: Police and public roles in the production of official statistics. *The British Journal of Sociology, 34*(2), 269. doi:10.2307/590750

Pickering, S., & Ham, J. (Eds.). (2014). *The Routledge handbook on crime and international migration*. London: Routledge.

Power, M. (2003). Evaluating the audit explosion. *Law & Policy, 25*(3), 185–202.

Skilbrei, M., & Holmström, C. (2013). *Prostitution policy in the Nordic region: Ambiguous sympathies*. Farnham: Ashgate.

Slettvåg, K. K. (2016). *Å straffe ikke-borgere – en studie av brudd på innreiseforbud*. Master's thesis, University of Oslo, Oslo.

Stumpf, J. P. (2006). The crimmigration crisis: Immigrants, crime, and sovereign power. *American University Law Review, 56*.

Chapter 4

Funnel politics

Framing an 'irreal'[1] space

Nicolay B. Johansen

Introduction

Few things in life pan out exactly as planned. This chapter tells a story of a shipwrecked research project that was rebuilt at sea and highlights the significance of framing a research topic. Directing attention to the phase of discovery and implicit theorising, the concept of framing shows how results are created from the initial stages of research, including the choice of words to describe the topic. The project initially intended to analyse differences between socially marginalised groups with and without citizenship by looking at irregular migrants in reception centres and drug users in special housing facilities. However, soon after I began my research, the reception centres under examination were torched and completely ruined. The planned topos of the research was literally destroyed.

A phase of drifting followed, during which I attempted to find a new research design. The standard vision of research is that of verifying or rejecting a hypothesis. Emphasis can be put on inductive or deductive logic, but scientific endeavours are commonly visualised in Popper's famous terms as a dynamic of 'conjectures and refutations' (Popper, 1963). Data are in some way brought in to correct more or less reasonably founded assumptions. However, in this project, the most important data were available for the public, and their significant contribution did not derive from analysing them, but from reframing them. The necessary details were there for everybody to pick up. Therefore, through the process of reframing, my attention turned to the diffuse social spaces of which the research was "being a case of". In doing so, I ended up researching a social, or "irreal" space (Rose, 2000) in which irregular migrants are manipulated in order to conform to political goals. This was termed "funnel politics".

Funnels are practical devices used to lead things to a certain place. Through this metaphor, I seek to capture how contemporary policies construct situations that make attractive the choice to conform to political goals. Funnel politics differs from traditional crime control in that indirect measures are employed (Johansen, 2013, 2015). Whereas punishment used to be the preferred measure for policing unwanted behaviour, 'funnel politics' highlights how social control is increasingly conducted by forcing individuals into destitution (Johansen, 2014a). While the study focuses on Norway, it resonates with tendencies in other European countries (de Leun, 2003; Hynes, 2011).

To economise with space this chapter focuses on the part of my comparative study that was dedicated to the control of irregular migrants. The chapter will unfold as follows: firstly, I introduce the concept of 'framing'. Secondly, I describe how the research project's implementation failed, requiring a new approach. The third section outlines how the new frame was developed given the downfall of the original design. The final section presents the findings as a product of the new framework.

Framing as method

The methodological obstacles I encountered (for a full discussion see next section) during the research process, underlined the importance of framing. In this section, I outline the meaning of framing, a phenomenon that highlights some attributes at the cost of others. The politicised nature of immigration in contemporary European politics demands that researchers are particularly cautious with framing their research to avoid being interpreted as (secretly) providing arguments in favour of a certain political stance.

As a methodological tool, framing is based on Goffman's 'Frame Analysis' (1986 [1974]). It has been associated with media analysis but, as Becker reminds us, has a long history in sociology (2007). Goffman developed the concept of 'framing' as a mundane practice, a way of making and creating meaning in everyday interaction, but the activities he describes are also relevant for methodological issues (Agustin, 2012). To Goffman, the effort of making the 'umwelt' (Goffman, 1971) intelligible did not differ substantially in everyday settings and scientific endeavours.

Goffmans 'total institutions' famously puts prisons on par with monastries and concentration camps (1961). Hughes offers another useful example of framing with the term 'bastard institutions' (Hughes, 1984a). Hughes was famous for posing questions like 'what is the similarity between priests, psychiatrists and prostitutes?' By comparing morally unequal entities he provoked the reader (Becker, 1998: 107–108). Underneath this playfulness lies a serious sociological curiosity about how to frame a phenomenon. A 'bastard institution' resembles ordinary institutions in that they both 'distribute goods and services', though the goods and services offered there are not (openly) respected and often illegitimate. Under this label Hughes discussed several shady areas and their relations to the formally accepted society, such as gambling rackets, black markets and prostitution (see also Hughes, 1984b; 1984c). Putting it this way, Hughes framed the phenomena he wanted to study in a way that accentuated certain traits. And furthermore, he placed the phenomenon on a continuous scale (Becker, 1998, 2007). Hughes's 'trick' involves attention to words and denotations, as well as an element of imaginativeness.

Framing relates to the classic problem of language. It shifts attention to words, definitions and concepts. It allows the researcher to cut loose from the traps of conventional language for analytical purposes. As Becker notes, social scientists are never the first arriving on the scene when they study an institution or an organisation. There are always words used by the persons inhabiting the place of study, and words are not the objective signifiers of the situation that the researcher is expected to keep at analytical distance. They express the local users' experiences and perspectives. Adopting conventional words at the very start of the process commits researchers to one or more local understandings already present at the scene (Becker, 2007, p. 224). The choice of a certain word to describe something implies some associations that colour the understanding of this phenomenon. No language is free of associations and metaphors, as Lakoff and Johnson have made clear (2003).

In presentations of research designs, the decision-making process regarding words and frames is frequently omitted. Swedberg labels the initial phases of a research project as 'theorizing' (Swedberg, 2016). Most researchers become available to their audience through articles and books in the aftermath of the actual work. This is the 'context of justification', according to Swedberg. However, Swedberg (2014, 2016) suggests that more attention should be given to the context of discovery. The context of discovery does not fall into the neat categories and linear processes that usually appear in the final versions of the context of justification. Swedberg's goal is to bring attention to the processes within the context of discovery, to bring awareness and encourage nurturing competence in the formative part of research. While it is not possible to give a full account of the formative part of a research process, it is evident that imagination (Wright Mills, 1977) plays an important part.

In my research project, the term 'funnel' was eventually introduced as a tool to do a trick similar to that of Hughes mentioned above and Goffmans 'total institutions' (1961). It is a term that frames the policies according to the attributes they share. Hopefully, this will become clearer in the following part. Both fields of control, targeting drug users and irregular migrants (Guild, 2004) respectively, create a similar mechanism, enveloping the lives of the target groups and stripping them of resources for sustenance. The messy process leading to the introduction of the imagery of the 'funnel' is presented in what follows.

The tale of IOOI

This section tells the story of how the research project capsised and was rebuilt. The first part presents the design of the project as it was planned. Subsequently, phase two is introduced.

I embarked on the project entitled 'Insiders outside/outsiders inside' ('IOOI') in 2011. But as the story will show, the topos of research was already in ruins. The title was borrowed from an influential paper by Stumpf (2006) that described a conflation of immigration law and penal law in the US. Stumpf commented that penal law was being used for purposes that were traditionally considered as border control, regarding foreigners and aliens, and that immigration laws were used for penal purposes. IOOI sought to juxtapose the control of two marginal groups and compare how they were treated, politically and administratively, in Norway. The first group was formed of irregular migrants, namely, for mostly practical reasons, rejected asylum seekers. These are outsiders – non-members of the state, non-citizens. In the phrase of Norwegian officials and politicians, 'they have a duty to leave'. But their bodies are inside the territory of the state, hence the term 'outsiders inside'. The other group was formed of street-level drug addicts. Drug users are outsiders in terms of their relation to the main circuits of money and exchange in society. Yet they remain official members of society, identified as citizens. The phrase 'insiders outside' captured their position.

The project was to compare these two groups and see how they were 'controlled' in a broad sense. IOOI took a classical view of 'social control' by asking what processes produce order (Janowitz, 1975). Control, in this perspective, implies a broad view of all efforts used to promote a certain conformity. Controlling irregular migrants has the ultimate goal of making them leave the territory (Johansen, 2014a). Controlling drug users seeks to make the target group stop using drugs. The project was designed to scrutinise differences between the two marginal groups that differed in regard to their legal citizenship status. Limiting the scope to politics, the question was '*what is the importance of citizenship in the control of marginal groups in Norway?*'

Fieldwork was planned at a so-called 'waiting camp' for irregular migrants. Waiting camps would function as a diametrical opposite to a housing facility for drug users. For IOOI, waiting camps were expected to be 'microcosms' of control. Studying the smaller unit is intended to serve as a shortcut to the larger picture (Lincoln & Guba, 2000; Becker, 1998). The microcosms were intended to shed light on the broader phenomena, to "draw general hypotheses from single instances and the substantiating them by comparing them with hypotheses derived from other different instances" (phrase coined by Znanieckis, that condenses 'analytic induction', 1968, p. 262[2]).

The broader field of politics was conceptualised as 'governing spaces' (Rose, 2000). Governing spaces, or 'irreal spaces' as Rose also calls them, are socially defined and demarcated by distinctive forms of technologies and rationales. The governing spaces studied in IOOI were created by a set of institutional demarcations. Irregular migrants were cut off from welfare, work, health care, housing and the majority of the other organisations that would support them. Thus, the political field is defined by contributions from a number of dispersed institutions. It was unrealistic to study all these institutions.

According to Yin (2003) a case study must fulfil two requirements which also illuminate the story of IOOI. First, it investigates a contemporary phenomenon in its real-life contexts. Second, the boundaries between the phenomenon and context are not clearly evident (Yin, 2003, p. 13). These requirements are especially relevant when the cases are microcosms of political fields that are not properly defined or even acknowledged as distinct political areas. Governing spaces are social, not physical entities. As such, they are irreal in a methodological sense, but most importantly they are ontologically irreal in that their existence is disputed. Thus, the study did not scrutinise the targeted spaces in a 'real-life context'.

Eventually, the waiting camps did not illuminate the broader field of control policies. Firstly, they were not used by the people they were intended to assist. It was mostly the weak, disabled and sick among irregulars who used the facilities. Secondly, in the summer of 2010, both of the existing waiting camps were torched by some of the residents (Kjellberg & Rugeldal, 2011). In the aftermath, it was decided that they would not be re-established. The research was thus bereft of its empirical object.

With the research object in ruins, the entire framework of the project fell apart. This, in turn, led to a search of new ways to study the importance of citizenship for control policies. Attention had to be turned to the field of politics as such, without focusing on a specific institution, in order to tie the scattered elements together. The fragmented nature of the topic made it impossible to rely on the same kind of data gathering. Fieldwork is possible in defined and preferably sharply delimited settings. Researching control of irregular migrants and drug users would broadly require data gathering from welfare organisations, public health care, NGO health services, labour inspection, tax authorities, schools, workplaces, asylum reception centres, the police, immigration authorities and many more sites that contribute to the control landscape determining the lives of irregular migrants. I found it unrealistic to approach all of them, get familiar with them, find people to interview and perhaps participate in some of their activities.

The targets of control play a pivotal role in the perspective I chose. By focusing on how irregulars get by on an everyday basis, the importance of different organisations and institutions could have been tracked. The first plan was to interview a number of them. People without status are scattered and hard to find. They have few meeting points. As a general pattern, their situation leads to atomisation and individualised strategies for sustenance. However, this needed to be studied at close hand. The obvious strategy would be to interview them in depth and make them narrate their experiences with the institutions I found relevant and how they got along in everyday life. I was hindered in recruiting from the specialised health services, since there was a queue of researchers and the organisers were generally not happy with the presence of researchers in their facilities. I started inquiring in certain environments and asked some representatives of different ethnic groups to help me find respondents. I contacted activist organisations for asylum seekers, and I visited several asylum reception centres (where irregulars after some rounds of political haggling had been readmitted).

After a slow start these recruiting strategies paid some dividend. However, two factors made me end this line of inquiry. Firstly, it soon became clear that the depth of information that could be obtained by interviewing irregulars was limited. One experience illuminates this issue. I had found a man about 45 years old who had stayed in Norway as an irregular for more than 10 years. He had partly survived by working as a painter and had partly lived on the street as a drug addict. Now he was seriously ill, having suffered a stroke. He isolated himself in his room at a reception centre and spent most of the days watching television. From the start, it was difficult to get information on his background and the context of his situation more broadly, but then again this was not my main focus. I started to ask for his work relations, and after a brief description of his specific tasks, I turned to the question of how he had lost his position as a painter. 'Asshole' he replied (in Norwegian). I felt I needed something more to get a proper grip on the actual developments that led him to leave the work place. Probing more into the matter failed to produce anything else than the same response. After a few rounds I realised that it was unrealistic to expect information of the depth required.

Other interviews were more successful than the one mentioned, but it proved difficult to obtain information at a level of detail that could illuminate the complex matters I intended to study. I had to conclude that I could not underpin my project with my own data. The ambitions were perhaps too optimistic from the start. And as this insight dawned on me, I decided to end my pursuit of new informants. Besides, there were a number of other sources that could illuminate the life conditions of irregulars better than I could hope to achieve, including research reports of different kinds and even novels written by (former) irregular migrants describing their fates.

Instead I turned to secondary sources of different institutions and organisations, such as white papers, reports from authorities, reports from NGOs and the like. To some extent, these data drew on interviews with staff, personnel at NGOs, informal conversations and observations, newspaper articles and continuous dialogue with journalists covering parts of the field.

The second phase: on differences and similarities

From the outset, IOOI was designed to focus on differences between how drug users and irregular migrants are controlled. Drawing on the evidence I had collected, I found many examples of such differences. For a start, the ambitions of control differ: irregulars are expected to leave the country, whereas drug users are expected to end drug use. Irregular migrants can be deported. Drug users can be punished. The intention was to consider these differences in light of citizenship. However, my investigation and the challenges I experienced with the original research design turned out to illuminate the development of crime control in general and thus the similarities. The differences regarding citizenship receded into the background.

During a brief period of fieldwork at a reception centre, I became more sceptical of the differences. The first impression was that it was organised on similar principles with the housing facilities for drug users (Johansen & Myhre, 2005). Its architecture was similar, with distinctly defined areas for staff and inmates. The staff seemed to have been recruited from the same social strata and their daily tasks were the same as well. In addition, some of the routines were identical. The weekly inspections of the inmates' rooms took the same form as in housing for drug users, and the feeling about the occasional encounters between the parties was strikingly on par. The similarities were undeniable.

Most striking was the discovery of the emphasis put on the trademark technique 'motivational interviewing' (MI). MI is a technique that uses everyday conversations to manipulate the opposite party into adopting a desired behaviour. Six visits to other reception centres revealed that MI was used at all of them. It was also a requirement for obtaining a contract with the immigration authorities, that is, that staff was trained in MI.

Rather than using the cases as opposite poles contributing to the analysis of the importance of citizenship, a different problem came to the fore. What does the design of the institutions and the emphasis put on MI in both fields tell us about the control policies in these areas? The cases were planned to constitute contexts for each other, but after their reformulation the cases became two instances of a more general class of phenomena: control of marginal groups. The two cases could be seen as cases of one pattern in control policies. Similarities were brought to the fore.

In a way, the altered design was a step backwards. On the other hand, it gave an opportunity to reorganise the many 'data points' (in Yin's terms). The said situation called for overall redefinitions of the subject matter. The next section will present the core ideas in funnel politics, and the following section discusses the choice of words to frame it.

The reality of funnel politics according to IOOI

This section reports the findings of IOOI within the framework adopted in the second phase. The emerging picture was that of control strategies revealed by the deployment and maintenance of a certain mechanism. The mechanism is to create (and/or sustain) conditions that create a situation for the targeted group, which restricts their life chances to such an extent, that compliance (to the goals of control, in these instances: a drug-free life style and return to country of origin) becomes attractive. This way, the desired behaviour (exit and conformity) is made relatively more attractive than the present situation. The mechanism can be presented as an 'equation':

$$\text{Current conditions} < \text{alternative conditions}$$

The mechanism is to make the targeted people 'choose' the right side of the equation (the alternative conditions which are offered by the government) while the left side of the equation (the current conditions) is rendered as too harsh and unattractive. Politics focuses on manipulating the left side of the equation: the current conditions. If current conditions become more awful than the alternative conditions, every rational being will drift towards the alternative conditions.

The targets of control experienced strategies 'using freedom', in Rose's terms (2000). The said strategies consist of the implementation of policies by proxy, indirect measures, and government through choice. Thus irregular migrants and drug users were subject to similar policies (plural term intended) that were conceptualised under the term 'funnels'.

The focus shifted from a scrutiny of 'crimmigration law', as a new field of politics, to mapping uncharted ground. Immigration law and penal law are limited in scope. Funnels are made of any imaginable piece that adds 'pressure' (Zedner & Ashworth, 2013) on the target. This way, funnels become areas of politics. The different elements are aligned and coordinated, perhaps best described by Rose (2000). But they are not treated as distinct fields for policies or administration. On the contrary, there are few indications that the policies (deriving from the dispersed set of institutional efforts mentioned) are discussed as isolated phenomena. The combined result is rarely mentioned as a field of coordinated policies (this is why the plural term is used). Secrecy is a conspicuously large part of the studied fields of politics. The research, then, offers a perspective that counters the prevailing understanding of policy regarding the targeted groups. In this respect, to make the word accepted would imply that my competing understanding was acknowledged.

The cases revealed policies differing from traditional crime prevention in important ways. Most importantly, to regard control policies in this perspective implies that policies are directed at people defined by their status (drug addict or irregular migrant). Penal law, on the other hand, does from the classical period take pride in actively disregarding status, since everyone is, as a matter of principle, considered equal before the law, and punishment is meted out without consideration of the culprit's status ('Justice is blind'). Funnel politics target persons with regard to their status and create unfavourable conditions for them. Irregular migrants are denied access to work, social benefits, health and so forth because they are 'irregular migrants'. Drug users are treated as 'drug users' by police and authorities.

Maintenance of the control mechanism

After ensuring that the mechanism is in place, it is necessary to make sure it works. Regulations of aid and health care illustrate this part. In a new Immigration Act passed in the Norwegian Parliament in 2008 any form of health assistance to irregular migrants was prohibited. This decision was later lifted and replaced by a moderate version that merely prohibited contractual relations between citizens and irregulars (Søvig, 2013).[3] The effect of this regulation appears to have been insufficiently transparent at the time (the legislators didn't anticipate that every form of assistance would be criminalised), but the preparatory discussion for the law reveals that it was conceived with the conditions for irregular migrants in mind. The decision was more or less explicitly intended to underpin policies regarding this group. Analytically, the decision was a secondary effort to uphold a strategy already in place. It can be seen as a form of 'maintenance'.

Søvig (2013) claims that it is reasonable to consider assistance to people who actively violate a decision to leave the territory as a form of sabotage. This statement connects the aforementioned law with the broader political picture. If denial of welfare and residence were a means to pressure irregular migrants to leave, criminalising assistance to them was partly a way to uphold this pressure.

Another example fills out the same picture. In 2010, more than 100 irregular migrants from Ethiopia were disclosed as undeserving recipients of tax licenses. To hold a legitimate job in Norway, one needs a tax license, but irregular migrants are not permitted to join the labour market. These Ethiopians had, because of a flaw in the internal control regime within the tax authorities, been able to lead almost ordinary lives within the Norwegian society. The Ethiopians were deprived of tax licenses because the tax authorities were made aware of a loophole in their internal control. It was not a result of a change in politics. Neither was the decision made with their (un-)well-being in mind.

One must nevertheless differentiate between political decisions that actively manipulate conditions for irregular migrants (for the worse) and the kind of activity that upholds the political decisions in general. The decision taken by tax authorities was not made to limit the life chances of irregular migrants; it was a decision to maintain their ineligibility for work. Still, this decision added some pressure and contributed to life conditions that must be understood to ultimately lead them to consider leaving Norway voluntarily (Brekke & Søholt, 2005).

The main point is that these policies can be seen as connected to each other. It is evident from the mentioned developments that (1) irregular migrants to some extent experience concerted policies manipulating their conditions and (2) different measures to some extent are expected to reinforce each other.

But while this was rarely stated explicitly, these activities are bound to the policies on irregular migrants more broadly. They are woven into the same rationale of making life miserable for the targets of control.

Discussion: funnel politics as imagery

A funnel is a device used in kitchens and mechanics. It is a technical apparatus rarely referred to in sociology.[4] The practical uses of funnels illustrate the mechanism of the political fields in question by deploying fairly neutral imagery. If anything, it resonates with the industrial imagery associated with 'mechanism'. 'Mechanism' is a commonly used word in social sciences. Elster famously defined mechanism as a 'frequently occurring and easily recognisable causal pattern' (2007, pp. 36–37). But Elster uses the word to elaborate on the concept of causal explanation. A 'mechanism' as a metaphor brings associations to engineering and the industrial age. It is no coincidence that Elster supports his view with more words from the 'toolbox', literally speaking, of the industrial world: 'Nuts and bolts for the social sciences' (the subtitle of the referred and a former book). The industrial imagery works well for the present purposes too, but the intention is not to make an explanation.[5] The 'funnel' refers to a process whereby something is transformed, as in a factory. Intermediate goods enter the factory and a refined product comes out. A mechanism makes this transformation take place. The evoked imagery is muddled by Elster's former use of the same term, but the reference to industrial processes illustrates how humans and politicians (try to) control their environment with social engineering.

The term 'maintenance' refers to secondary efforts to uphold something that is already in place. In the words of Zedner, "the notion of order maintenance has the considerable virtue of capturing the minute and mundane activities of criminal justice agents in their everyday work" (2004, p. 6). The connotations of maintenance are coloured by the more dominant metaphor of 'mechanism'. There are important differences among those who build a machine, the people that ensure it works on a day-to-day basis, those who make sure the parts are not wrecked and that there is enough lubricant. But all parties contribute to the same result.

IOOI in its final form framed politics regarding irregular migrants and drug users by creating a mechanism, namely by isolating the targeted individuals in a social space of misery. The maintenance attempted to prevent the targeted group from escaping from this space.

The idea of creating favourable and less favourable conditions to manipulate people's choices is not new. On the contrary, this rationality ('less eligibility') was very much an intrinsic part of the liberal epoch which also saw the emergence of modern penal law (Sparks, 1996). The funnel metaphor puts current policies on par with traditional liberal doctrines. This way the cases are placed in a different context. Citizenship is undoubtedly an important aspect of control policies regarding marginalised groups. But the study concluded on a different level; an emerging pattern of funnel politics has replaced the traditional crime control. And there are indications that similar patterns can be found in other European countries too. Van der Leun (2003) identifies the emergence of a similar rationale in politics regarding irregular migrants with the so-called Linking Act, and Hynes (2011) argues that the dispersion of asylum seekers is part of the same way of thinking. But none of them goes as far as to identify a break with the established political rationality.

By putting these and other measures in the funnel frame, connotations on a higher political level become activated. They are made meaningful in a context of a political rationality on par with long historical trajectories regarding groups considered problematic. Funnel politics does the same trick as 'bastard institutions' by framing the phenomenon on a continuous scale that opens up for broader sociological comparisons.

This chapter is about the 'sphere of discovery'. By describing the misfortunes of the research project IOOI, focus was directed at the pragmatic search for data and eventually at a new design. This way theorising and framing the topic were brought to the fore. The vantage point was a broad understanding of social control, but the project moved from viewing two cases as antithetical to using them as instances of a broader phenomenon; order production regarding marginal groups became the context within the funnel metaphor.

Notes

1 The term 'irreal' spaces refers to how it is used by Rose (2000).
2 Quote made into a plural sentence.
3 In 2011 certain health centres was established, although not by the authorities.
4 It is sometimes used to describe the steps leading through the system of justice, from reported crimes to final conviction.
5 Becker notes that the idea of an explanation is also part of the sociological imagery (Becker, 1998, p. 63).

References

Agustin, L. R. (2012). Kvalitativ diskurs- og rammeanalyse. In M. H. Jacobsen & S. Q. Jensen (Eds.), *Kvalitative udfordringer*. Copenhagen: Hans Reitzel.
Becker, H. S. (1998). *Tricks of the trade*. Chicago: Chicago University Press.
Becker, H. S. (2007). *Telling about society*. Chicago: Chicago University Press.
Brekke, J-P., & Søholt, S. (2005). *I velferdsstatens grenseland*. Oslo: Institutt for samfunnsforskning.
Elster, J. (2007). *Explaining social behavior: More nuts and bolts for the social sciences*. Cambridge: Cambridge University Press.
Goffman, E. (1961). *Asylums*. New York: Anchor Books.
Goffman, E. (1971). *Relations in public*. New York: Basic Books.
Goffman, E. (1986). *Frame analysis*. Boston, MA: Northeastern University Press.
Guild, E. (2004). Who is an irregular migrant? In B. Bogusz, R. Cholewinski, A. Cygan, & E. Szyszcak (Eds.), *Irregular migration and human rights*. Leiden: Martinus Nijhoff.
Hughes, E. C. (1984a). Bastard institutions. In E. Hughes (Ed.), *The sociological eye*. New Brunswick, NJ: Transaction Books.
Hughes, E. C. (1984b). Dirty work and decent people. In E. Hughes (Ed.), *The sociological eye*. New Brunswick, NJ: Transaction Books.
Hughes, E. C. (1984c). On institutions. In E. Hughes (Ed.), *The sociological eye*. New Brunswick, NJ: Transaction Books.
Hynes, P. (2011). *The dispersal and social exclusion of asylum seekers: Between liminality and belonging*. Bristol: Polity Press.
Janowitz, M. (1975). Sociological theory and social control. *American Journal of Sociology*, *81*(1), 82–108.
Johansen, N. B. (2013). Elendighetstrakten. In N. B. Johansen, T. Ugelvik, & K. F. Aas (Eds.), *Krimmigrasjon?* Oslo: Universitetsforlaget.

Johansen, N. B. (2014a). Det strafferettslige kompleks. Strafferetten og biopolitikkens nye grenser anno 1902. In S. Flaatten & G. Heivoll (Eds.), *Straff, Liv, Historie*. Oslo: Akademisk Publishing.
Johansen, N. B. (2014b). Governing the funnel of expulsion. In M. Bosworth & K. F. Aas (Eds.), *The borders of punishment: Migration, citizenship, and social exclusion*. Oxford: Oxford University Press.
Johansen, N. B. (2015). Controlling Roma in Norway: Governing by an administration of distance. In A. Eriksson (Ed.), *Punishing the other*. London: Routledge.
Johansen, N. B., & Myhre, H. (2005). Skadereduksjon i praksis. *Rusmiddeletaten i Oslo*.
Kjellberg, J., & Rugeldal, C. (2011). *Illegal: papirløs i Norge*. Oslo: Spartacus.
Lakoff, G., & Johnson, M. (2003). *Metaphors we live by*. Chicago: University of Chicago Press.
Lincoln, Y., & Guba, E. (2000). The only generalization is there is no generalization. In R. Gomm, M. Hammersley, & P. Foster (Eds.), *Case study method*. London: SAGE Publications.
Popper, K. (1963). *Conjectures and refutation*. London: Routledge.
Rose, N. (2000). *The powers of freedom*. Cambridge: University of Cambridge Press.
Søvig, K. H. (2013). Straffansvar og straffeforfølgning av humanitære hjelpere ved ulovlig opphold. In N. B. Johansen, T. Ugelvik, & K. F. Aas (Eds.), *Krimmigrasjon?* Oslo: Universitetsforlaget.
Sparks, R. (1996). Penal 'austerity': The doctrine of less eligibility reborn? In R. Matthews & P. Francis (Eds.), *Prisons 2000*. London, UK: Palgrave Macmillan.
Stumpf, J. (2006). *The crimmigration crisis*. Bepress, Working Papers, no. 1635.
Swedberg, R. (2014). *The art of social theory*. New Jersey: Princeton University Press.
Swedberg, R. (2016). Before theory comes theorizing or how to make social science more interesting. *The British Journal of Sociology*, 67(1), 5–20.
Van der Leun, J. (2003). *Looking for loopholes: Processes of incorporation of illegal immigrants in the Netherlands*. Amsterdam: Amsterdam University Press.
Wright Mills, C. (1977). *The sociological imagination*. Middlesex: Penguin Books.
Yin, R. (2003). *Case study research: Design and methods (applied social research methods)*. Thousand Oaks: Sage.
Zedner, L. (2004). *Criminal justice*. Oxford: Oxford University Press, Clarendon Law Series.
Zedner, L., & Ashworth, A. (2013). *Preventive justice*. Oxford: Oxford University Press.
Znaniecki, F. (1968). *The method of sociology*. New York: Octagon Books.

Part 2

Epistemological and methodological accounts in practice

Chapter 5

Expectations and realities of fieldwork by a nascent qualitative researcher

Brandy Cochrane

Introduction

Coming from a quantitative background, my learning curve was steep in moving from numbers and statistics to recruitment and narrative interviewing with refugee and asylum-seeking mothers. Methods literature on qualitative research often attempts to universalise or minimise the challenges that arise in research (Edwards, 1998; Griffin, 2015; Smith, 2015), hence not providing an accurate view of the experience of being a researcher.

The advantage of utilising qualitative methodologies with marginalised populations has been well-documented (e.g. Dhamoon & Hankivsky, 2011; Knowles & Cole, 2008; Mccall, 2005; Simien, 2007). In research focused on the complexity of social difference, qualitative methodologies enable researchers to engage with ambiguity and fluidity as conceptual resources, advancing beyond rigid categorical knowledge and oversimplified numerical data. A qualitative approach creates space for experiential knowledge to emerge beyond simple categories and the individual to answer larger structural questions. As Dhamoon and Hankivsky (2011) argue in regards to their work on health inequities in Canada, mainstream qualitative research frameworks are ineffective in understanding the needs of marginalised populations as they attempt to neatly categorise vulnerabilities and social differences. Therefore, researchers must use qualitative methods in order to "investigate the interaction of numerous characteristics of vulnerable populations, not only at the individual level but also at structural levels" (Dhamoon & Hankivsky, 2011, p. 16).

Despite the importance of qualitative methods, there is a lack of knowledge in the procedure and the particulars of qualitative research with marginalised populations as experienced by the researcher. With the intention to reveal some of these challenges, I relate my experience as a novice researcher with marginalised populations and specifically with refugee and asylum-seeking mothers from Iran and Afghanistan.

States of the Global North are increasingly securitising their borders through physical and technological deterrent tactics aimed at the increasing migration of people from the Global South. For the vast majority of women from the

Global South there is no opportunity for legal migration to the Global North and therefore they must seek other means of transit already illegalised by states (Indra, 1999; Crawley, 2001; Palmary et al., 2010). The absence of legal transit has not suppressed women's desire to move across borders, as evidenced in the increase of women migrating, but instead forced them to pursue more dangerous modes of entry for access (Boehm, 2011; Fan, 2008; Jiménez, 2010; Pickering, 2011). Security and citizenship are precarious for these women, especially mothers, due to structural gender inequalities that are further complicated by migratory journeys (see Sixsmith, Boneham, & Goldring, 2003; Jones-Correa, 1998; Pessar, 2003; Sassen, 2003).

However, there is scant research on the experiences of refugee and asylum-seeking mothers who encounter border securitisation before, during, and after migratory journeys to Australia. The aim of the study was to illuminate the everyday security and citizenship fluctuations experienced by mothers in this era of mass mobility. Recruitment focused on women who were mothers and had come to Australia from two countries of origin, Iran and Afghanistan, as asylum seekers from these two countries of origin were the most likely to have been involved in irregular travel to Australia. I conducted interviews with 8 Iranian women and 11 Afghan women who ranged in ages from 24 to 50 and had from one to seven children. The majority of the women had arrived in Australia within the last 5 years (18), with one Afghan woman arriving in 2007. I chose the cut-off date of 2007 because of the substantial changes to asylum-seeker and refugee policies during this year. The Rudd government abolished the Pacific Solution, which resulted in the termination of offshore processing for asylum seekers and the closure of detention facilities on Manus Island and Nauru and ended the use of temporary protection visas. These changes, albeit briefly, marked a shift towards more humanitarian policies in Australia in regards to asylum seekers and refugees in line with the international protocol.

In order to illuminate my experiences as a novice qualitative researcher, I will provide a clear and concise set of methodological tools that I employed and their outcomes in regards to research with a recognised marginalised population. I have organised the chapter according to the methodological tools I engaged with within the three phases of my qualitative research project: Access and Recruitment, Participants and Interviews, and Interpreters. Pseudonyms are used throughout the chapter for participants and translators.

The chapter is structured to show the differences between the expectations and realities of fieldwork. I will also be incorporating a discussion of reflexivity throughout the chapter. Employing reflexivity within a project means that researchers critically reflect on chosen methods and the implementation of methods throughout the interview process (Ambert et al., 1995; Mackenzie, McDowell & Pittaway, 2007; Marshall & Rossman, 2011). In doing so, reflexive methods replace the so-called objectivity of positivism with epistemological subjectivity that focuses on power imbalances and the positionality of the researcher.

Just the 'basics': recruitment and access

Expectations

In the initial stages of the project, and drawing on methodological qualitative literature (Cohen & Arieli, 2011; Jacobsen & Landau, 2003; Noy, 2008; Sommers, 2001), I reasoned that a strategy of recruitment for participants that included flyers, website posts, and verbal communication, distributed with the assistance of refugee and migrant support organisations, would be sufficient for attracting a significant number of refugee and asylum-seeking mothers. My strategy, also, included building rapport with informal contacts during the interviewing process and they, along with the research participants, would inform other potential participants. This type of recruitment, known as snowball sampling, has been criticised for its lack of representative sample and selection bias based on already-established relationship bonds (Sommers, 2001; Jacobsen & Landau, 2003). There is also the risk of sensitive information being transmitted within groups (Sommers, 2001; Jacobsen & Landau, 2003).

However, snowball sampling is likely the most widely used sampling method in qualitative research for a number of reasons. Firstly, this method allows the sample to emanate from the participants' group rather than from the top down (van Meter, 2000; Jacobsen & Landau, 2003; Noy, 2008). Secondly, this approach creates space for the choice to participate being bounded by the participant (Jacobsen & Landau, 2003; Noy, 2008; van Meter, 2000). Lastly, snowball sampling is also particularly helpful in regards to recruiting marginalised, difficult-to-reach, or so-called hidden populations, such as members of gangs, drug users, and sex workers (Noy, 2008). Indeed, the foundations of snowball sampling reflect the traditional feminist research methods that bring the participant and their agency to the centre.

As Cohen and Arieli (2011) discuss in their work with displaced people in conflict zones, snowball sampling has three benefits: locating, accessing, and involving research participants. This method, then, aids in mediating interactions with gatekeepers who may take a protective stance due to the population's possible exploitation (Groger, Mayberry, & Straker, 1999). Recruiting Afghan and Kurdish refugee populations within New Zealand, Sulaiman-Hill and Thompson (2011) found it necessary to employ snowball sampling to locate and identify participants, build trust, and circumvent barriers of remoteness and gatekeeping. Additionally, they employed it with a number of different agencies in order to decrease selection bias that has been a previous critique of the method.

Based on this, I determined that the method well suited my research with asylum-seeker and refugee mothers. I also decided to attempt multiple initiation points via various refugee and asylum-seeker support organisations in order to obtain a more diversified sample.

Realities: languishing at the gate

In this section, I provide more details about my recruitment strategy within Melbourne. As Jacobsen and Landau (2003) report in their review of methodologies regarding research with refugees and displaced people, there is a lack of details on issues and barriers in regards to recruiting. Despite the solid basis on which I founded my recruitment methods, as discussed, the realities in this realm differed greatly from my expectations. In what follows, I first identify the challenges of building contacts in Australia after moving from the United States for my PhD and, second, the organisational attitudes I encountered. Thirdly, I discuss how I overcame these barriers.

The difficulties surrounding recruitment reveal the amount of power that gatekeepers hold. My overly simplistic idea of hanging posters and waiting for the calls to come in was based on literature that did not describe the challenges and power dynamics that exist within groups and organisations. Therefore, in the midst of recruitment, I needed to change my methodological approach to build trust with gatekeepers first and gain a better understanding of the inner workings of the services offered by each organisation. The product of this reflection was to conduct 10 informal interviews with individuals from refugee and asylum-seeker organisations across the Melbourne metropolitan area from a variety of areas, including health, policy, and housing.

Conducting research in a new country means establishing relationships from the ground up, an experience that is relevant for many academic researchers. Having worked with refugee and immigrant populations in the United States within small community legal clinics and with organisations that relied on my services for support, I did not fully understand how difficult it would be to make contacts within Australia, specifically within the metropolitan area of Melbourne. My previous work had allowed me an easy access point to migrant populations in a professional capacity, and I hadn't realised that contacts would be difficult to build from scratch without the organisation inroads that my job had provided me.

The difficulty of recruitment, beyond my lack of established contacts in Australia, was further exacerbated by the attitudes of some refugee and asylum-seeker organisations. As refugee and asylum-seeking populations are considered vulnerable and over-researched populations by many organisations, there was hesitancy to allow recruitment for my interviews. Non-governmental organisations play an important role in both advocating and interloping among refugees and asylum seekers and researchers. Their main aim is to provide a buffer so that their beneficiaries are not exploited during research.

However, there were times during my research when an organisational stance interfered with the agency of clients to participate. For example, many organisations would not meet with me to discuss my research, were not interested in allowing me to volunteer, nor would they distribute or hang posters about the study in their offices, thus blocking access to marginalised populations. This is, of course, not to undermine the important role that the organisations play in assisting asylum seekers and refugees. In fact, these organisations were often mentioned by mothers who participated in my study as being essential in helping them.

Yet I hereby explain the several-month-long process that I went through to engage with multiple entry points in the community and to build trust with gatekeepers and agencies in order for other researchers to appreciate the challenges inherent in accessing this population. I began my recruitment for participants, as mentioned, by contacting agencies by email and telephone with my proposal for research. I wrote a blog post and used various email lists and social media outlets in my attempts to recruit participants. After resistance from gatekeepers and a general lack of response, I decided I needed to employ a more personalised approach in regards to recruitment. So I approached targeted people within the organisations via email requesting an informal interview about the organisation. This method allowed me to understand better the refugee and asylum-seeker organisations in Melbourne and their roles within the community, as well as to build in-person rapport. After the informal interviews with employees and/or volunteers, I wrote blog posts about the organisation, with their permission, for the Border Crossing Observatory[1] website.

In my inquiry for the interview, I stated that I was a student but also a researcher who could offer social media exposure and share with other researchers what the organisations were undertaking. During the interviews, I was also able to speak with volunteers and employees from organisations about my research project. All of the individuals who met with me were receptive and supportive of my research. Some were unable to help with recruitment due to their roles or organisational policies, but several others offered to pass along my name to other gatekeepers who worked more closely with refugee and asylum-seeking mothers.

From those interviews, I was able to gain access to three gatekeepers who allowed me to recruit participants from within their English language courses and mothers' groups. After I received access to these spaces, I was able to follow in the ethnographic process of 'being there' and engaging with possible participants to encourage their participation in the research (Sixsmith, Boneham, & Goldring, 2003). Gaining access to women's everyday lives can be difficult, and the slow building of trust in the weekly mothers' group or near the snack table at the English-language group was sometimes frustrating, but the process highlighted the patience required for qualitative research with marginalised populations. In some cases, participants signed up to participate in the research right away, and in other cases such as the mothers' group, the process of recruitment gained momentum over time.

The difficulties surrounding recruitment revealed the amount of power that gatekeepers held. The protective stance of organisations may unknowingly contribute to the silencing of refugee voices within the community and research. Endowing and attributing agency to refugees and asylum seekers, as they wish to do, means that their beneficiaries should be able to choose whether to participate. Organisations can, indeed, play an important role in helping refugees and asylum seekers to understand what the opportunity to participate in research means and the issues that might come with it (Bloch, 1999). By facilitating individuals to have a voice within research, organisations may also receive information and feedback on how better to support refugees and asylum seekers.

It is easy in hindsight to minimise the frustration that I felt during the recruitment process or to judge whether I could have been more efficient throughout those initial stages. However, by uncovering my own experiences and failures, as well as the tools I used to gain access through gatekeepers, I aim to add to the necessary discussion of qualitative methods with marginalised populations and inform nascent researchers of these challenges before entering the field.

Navigating narratives: participants and interviewing

Expectations

The process of qualitative interviewing is a basic mode of inquiry engaging participants in order to understand their lived experiences. This section examines my interviewing methods by drawing on the literature on narrative interviewing, a method driven by participants' voices on which I based the research project. As I sought to let the participants create the parameters of the interview rather than me determining the course, I chose the life-story narrative method (Adriansen, 2012; Bamberg, 2010; Bauer & Gaskell, 2000; Messerschmidt, 1999; Smith, 2015), which centres on lived experiences and personal views, meanings, and practices while allowing subjective conception to be linked with social and historical contexts (Messerschmidt, 1999; Adriansen, 2012). In employing this method, I hoped women would guide me through their experiences of motherhood before, during, and after their irregular migrant journeys.

This technique is especially appropriate in research dealing with sensitive personal experiences. It is a type of qualitative, in-depth interview that moves beyond question and response and uses everyday conversation, especially storytelling and listening (Bauer & Gaskell, 2000). A narrative has the power to convey what matters in an individual life (Mason, 2004) and can be understood as a way of constructing identity (Bamberg, 2010). As Bauer and Gaskell (2000) suggest, the narrative interview is particularly well suited to the exploration of social problems that may be embarrassing, of a highly personal nature, or carry negative social implications. The telling of stories also plays an important role in day-to-day interactions, and some authors argue that the sharing of stories has therapeutic meanings in the realm of creating order and making sense of difficult life experiences (Orbuch, 1997; Holloway & Jefferson, 2000; Plummer, 2001; Wengraf, 2001).

The importance of narratives within qualitative methodologies with refugee and asylum-seeking women has also been highlighted by multiple authors (Katz, 2004; Luibhéid, 2013; Smith, 2015). The method is supported by Smith (2015), who conducted narrative interviews with asylum-seeking women within the UK. She argues that the experiential knowledge that emerges from the narratives of these women rarely enters public and political discourse (Smith, 2015). Instead of allowing women's voices to take centre stage, the focus is on their victimhood and bodies. The methodological choice that I made in regards to narrative interviewing allowed for the mothers' voices to be at the centre of the research project rather than marginalised. I chose to use semi-structured narratives to allow interviews to be placed within mothers' comfort zones and give them space to explore themes of their choice.

Realities: stumbling over the obstacles

Reflecting upon my interviewing methods, I realised that the life-story narrative approach was neither straightforward nor universal in its results and was instead dependent on the participants. For example, the majority of the Iranian women with whom I spoke had no problems guiding the interviews based on their experiences. Often the stories were chronological and detailed and emphasised points of crisis. Traumas in home countries, distressing stories of boat journeys, and harrowing time in detention centres both on and offshore Australia, were presented in a format that fits the idea of a life-story narrative and its goals. This is not to say that these stories were told without emotion or struggle on the part of the women. However, as opposed to women who had not had to endure the asylum process, these women had to communicate their stories in an organised and coherent narrative to asylum authorities. As Kleinman and Kleinman (1996, p. 10) argue, the stories of these women are a part of the spectacle of suffering for the Global North, as they have 'become the currency' for those seeking refugee status.

On the other hand, the majority of Afghan women with whom I spoke preferred a question-and-answer format for the interview. The difference in format may be due to multiple factors, but perhaps most obvious was that the majority of them did not have to tell their stories during an asylum process, as they came to Australia on partners' visas. I had to alter the interview format to accommodate the women, many of whom had come to Australia via plane on refugee visas and had not told their narratives outside of private spaces. At first, this was difficult to navigate, as I just had basic prompts prepared. Additionally, my lack of confidence in my interviewing skills meant that on-the-spot adjustment was difficult for me. The answers proved to be short and simple, even with additional prompts to discuss experiences, as reflected in this exchange with Mina, mother of four.

ME: I guess, sort of just telling her story starting from when she was thinking about leaving.
INTERPRETER: She wants to just answer the questions.
ME: Okay. How did you – when you decided to leave where you were originally from, how did you decide to do that? Did you come with your children or? Sorry. A little nervous. I guess we could start with sort of a basic one then.

I was uncertain during these interviews, as evidenced in the excerpt. I was also constantly considering power and positionality within the research. Smith (2015) explains that in her focus on her position as the one with power, she found the process led to being careful around sensitive questions, often to the detriment of the research. She goes on to state that 'achieving the right balance of caution and forwardness in interviews' was challenging throughout the cross-cultural interview conducted by herself as a white British woman interviewing black Botswanan women about sensitive topics.

I struggled with this situation within the narrative interviewing process, too. The data collection of irregular migratory journeys, as one might expect, is often wrought with difficult topics of times of war, frightening journeys, and months within crowded detention centres. Despite understanding that sensitive issues would emerge, I didn't have the tools to navigate some of the issues without visible discomfort. Specifically, on the subjects of hinted sexual violence or the death of a child, I found I would sometimes deflect in order to alleviate perceived stress of the participant and actual stress for me. My fear of abuse of my powerful position to gain details that mothers were not comfortable giving, paired with using my interview structure to move past difficult topics for the participants and myself, was a double-edged sword, which had an impact on my interviews.

In some cases, this dynamic interfered with the trust-building work and comfortable interview dynamic that had earlier been established. My own discomfort, upon self-reflection, hindered mothers from giving their full narratives, as it made some of them uncomfortable or suspicious of my motives. Therefore, the data collected was likely limited and less rich than if I had allowed mothers the agency to direct the interviews without my interruption. One such example would be this discussion through an interpreter with Kashmala, an Afghan mother whose daughter had died:

ME: Did she say her daughter in Pakistan passed away?
INTERPRETER: She said, 'I have no clue what happened because baby was in my home and there was a big explosion. The bomb exploded, and after two days the child died.'

ME: Okay. And so was she having mental issues in Pakistan? Did she go to the hospital for them at that time?
INTERPRETER: From the day that that bomb exploded in front of the house, killed the baby, she got a problem. She is taking depression pills even now and at that time. Now, she is taking three different sorts of pills because she cannot forget that moment and her daughter.
ME: And so then she flew to Australia with her children?
INTERPRETER: Yes. But not her daughter who had died.
ME: Could you ask her to talk a little bit about how that was and whether she was excited or nervous or what?

When reflecting on the narrative, it becomes clear that Kashmala wanted to talk about the death of her daughter. Twice, I attempted to turn the conversation away from what I deemed a sensitive topic, and yet she brought the discussion back. In this example, I could have given her room to discuss her child's death by asking additional questions around it.

Space during the interviews was also an issue. Since the majority of my interviews with Afghan women was through mothers' groups, often the interviews would also take place in this setting. The rooms were at a school, where the children played on one side and the women sat in semi-circles on children's chairs while a volunteer used children's books to teach the women the days of the week and how to count to 10. Several sewing machines were in the rooms, where the women or the volunteers were sewing a variety of materials. There was a small room attached to the playroom off to the side that was used for storage where many of my interviews took place. A typical experience was me sitting on one of the children's chairs in the storage room or directly in the playroom, depending on what made the mother more comfortable for the interview. Hot, strong tea and biscuits were always on offer, and the noise level never lingered at a lull. My recorder was usually perched precariously on one of those tall art stools, and I was trying to ask questions and take notes while sometimes holding a squirming child.

Due to the inherent nature of motherhood, in that the responsibility towards children is wrapped up with all activities, these dynamics also affected interviews conducted in mother's homes or at mothers' group centres. Children came in and out of the room looking for their mums or staring at me to figure out why I was there. The youngest children were held in mothers' arms or were sometimes passed to me so that another child could be comforted. At times children became disruptive, in very direct vocal and physical ways, to garner attention from me, their mothers, and the interpreter. Whether it was one or two children in an interview in a home setting or the more than 30 children who were present at the mothers' group, their influence was felt during the interviewing process. Although they were not directly participating in the study, their voices were often a part of the narrative both directly and indirectly in a way which I had not fully comprehended before entering the field.

They sometimes made comments, answered questions, or performed informal translating for their mothers.

After attempting to canvass the literature in regards to the presence of children, I found little that even mentioned children being present when they weren't specifically being interviewed (Schensul, Schensul, & LeCompte, 1999; Holloway & Jefferson, 2000). As I progressed through the interview process, I learned to bring colouring books, felt pens, and stickers to help keep the children busy. Most importantly, though, I learned to just let the interview ebb and flow based on the needs of mothers and their children.

Attempting to maintain a controlled research environment only made the situation frustrating for me. My own inexperience and insecurity in my interviewing skills meant that I hadn't realised that the shifting environment was something that was quite normal in qualitative research. I couldn't have been prepared for these obstacles per se, but the importance of flexibility when encountering the unknown is essential in qualitative research (Ambert et al., 1995; Mackenzie, McDowell, & Pittaway, 2007).

Lost and found in translation: interpreters

Expectations

The addition of an interpreter is often necessary in cross-cultural research. There has been a multitude of literature that discusses the use of interpreters within academic research. Focusing on reflexivity, Edwards (1998) argues, it is important to consider the interpreter as a key informant in the research. The interpreter is not merely a verbatim translator but an interpreter of interactions. According to Greenhalgh, Robb, and Scambler (2006), there are three dynamics at play when utilising an interpreter: participant/interpreter, interpreter/interviewer, and participant/interviewer. To ignore the place and role of the interpreter before, during, and after the interview would signify misunderstanding the importance of reflexivity within qualitative research. As Smith (2015) details in her chapter about being a cross-cultural researcher, interpreters can be cultural mediators and assist in interviewing hidden populations. However, there are of course difficulties with interpreters, such as levels of language, threat to the accuracy of the data, purposeful misinterpretation, relationships between interpreter and participant, cultural biases, and controversy around taboo topics (Griffin, 2015; Smith, 2015).

Bounded in the feminist methodology and the ideas of fostering trust and understanding, a cultural interpreter, apart from being just a verbatim interpreter, would assist in the interviewing process. A truly verbatim interpretation from one language to another would lose cultural norms, specific terms and slangs, values of the language, assumptions of meanings, and emotions behind certain word choices (Griffin, 2015).

I explored two options for interpreters for my project: first, a translation service and second, attempting to find someone within the community of the women to translate for me. After canvassing the options, budgetary concerns, and flexibility around interview times and spaces, it became clear that a professional interpreter was not a viable option (Griffin, 2015), so I decided to rely on my contacts within the organizations who worked with women for referrals of trusted interpreters. I also relied on women whom I was interviewing to translate for others in some cases. The interpreter who was also a participant was not revealed as such to other interviewees unless she self-identified.

Realities: deciphering the messages

In this section, I will discuss some challenges I faced with the interpreters that were involved in the study and the benefits thereof. All three were volunteers who gave their time in support of my project and were either refugees or asylum seekers themselves. In what follows, I focus specifically on issues of modified interpretation, complex relationships, and the benefits of cultural guidance.

One of the challenges I faced with all the interpreters at different points was that at times I could tell that the participants' stories were being changed by the interpreter. In other cases, I would receive one or two sentences after long-winded soliloquys. When I tried to follow up, I was often told that it didn't translate well. There could be several reasons, including limited language skills or fatigue of interpreters, especially during multiple interviews. In one case, on a day that I had three interviews, by the third, that interpreter became briefer in interpreting what the participant was saying and in translating my questions.

A particular viewpoint could also change the translation. In this example, I discuss an interview in my fieldnotes:

> I'm recognising that it might be a bit problematic having [name] translate for me, for a number of reasons; one of them being that she definitely puts her own views in there and definitely isn't doing a great translation of what people are saying. I think, as far as I can tell she is omitting some things, as well as trying to put a positive spin on people's stories, like really moving away from the fact that [participant] was very ostracised in her country because – well, she was divorced twice, because she smoked, and because she drank.
>
> (28 June 2014)

Although it could be remarked that perhaps the interviewee refrained from saying anything due to the disapproval by the interpreter (Jacobsen & Landau, 2003), I didn't find it to be true. Due to the interviewee's English skills, it was obvious in her narrative that she was proud of having left the oppressiveness of 'the scarf' behind and was not ashamed about her divorce from an abusive husband.

Issues can arise around complex relationships or sensitive information being made known by interpreters who are part of a cultural community (Jacobsen & Landau, 2003). I encountered issues around this on a small scale throughout interviews, but the most striking time was when I was working with Cas, a young asylum seeker translating for me. During my last interview with him, about five minutes in, I realised that the participant was his mother. At this juncture, I confirmed that both Cas and the participant wanted to continue with the interview. As the interview further unfolded, it became clear that this was a very emotional interview for Cas and his mother, and it thus became difficult for me as well. I suggested several times that maybe we should stop the interview, as it felt like I was interviewing both of them, but there was consensus in continuing.

After the interview, the three of us had a debrief. Cas's mother mentioned how although they talked at home about the trouble in Iran, the boat journey, detention, and settlement, that it 'just sounded different in English.' Cas's mother said that she felt it was important that I knew her family's story, so she wanted to finish. Despite the debrief and the declarations, after the emotional interview, I received no more return phone calls from Cas to interpret, which blocked access to the group.

Reflecting on the tense nature of the situation, I arguably should have stopped the interview despite Cas's and his mother's assurances of well-being. There is a point in the interview where the obvious discomfort of participants may outweigh continued data collection. While giving a space for them to tell their story was important, the cost for Cas was possibly too high. I can only conjecture that as he and I did not speak again, but I assume the stress of the interview caused him to discontinue following up with me for further translations. During the process with Cas, from building trust and engaging him as my interpreter to apparently losing that trust and receiving no further contact, I understood the complications of working with interpreters among the group of participants.

However, it is essential to emphasise the benefits I received from engaging interpreters of similar backgrounds. The importance of the cultural mediation that occurred in the interviews around religion, practices, and issues in home countries was immense. The interpreters unveiled how my own actions also affected the participants' reactions to the interview process (Griffin, 2015; Smith, 2015).

When considering these benefits, I immediately think of the vast assistance provided to me by Tasleem, the volunteer for the mothers' group where I spoke to many of the Afghan participants. The first interview in through which Tasleem acted as an interpreter took place in a public library two blocks from the mothers' group location. As described above, there was a definite shift in the interview style with Afghan mothers, distinct from discussions with Iranian women whom I had talked to previously. We only had one interview that day, as only one of the four women showed up. After the interview, which had obviously been stressful for me and had gone quite awkwardly, Tasleem took the opportunity to clarify for me a number of issues, as well as to tell me her own story of travelling over by boat with her parents.

Being a nascent researcher, I was not confident in my skills as an interviewer and was also quite concerned with abusing my power as a researcher of marginalised migrant mothers. Immediately after the interview, while shaking her head at me, Tasleem told me to stop fidgeting and being nervous because no one would talk to me otherwise. She proceeded to explain how it was important to act differently with Afghan mothers than perhaps with the Iranian mothers I had spoken to before. She said that many of the Afghan mothers were of low education level and were very sceptical of universities and governments. She further told me that the woman I had interviewed suggested I was so nervous because I allegedly worked for the government and wanted to disprove her story. The woman also mentioned to her right before the interview that the other mothers had not shown up because they figured I worked for the government, because I wanted to talk to them separately from the other women at the mothers' group. At this juncture, I was embarrassed but also beginning to understand that I needed to have more flexibility.

Tasleem also gave insights after the interviews about the things that I might have missed or how what she had translated actually implied something else, such as domestic violence or sexual abuse. Although it would be easy to dismiss these as personal opinions of Tasleem, it became clear that she valued the importance of the research, the quality of what I wrote about the mothers, and my understandings of her culture reflected by her sharing with me her passion for attending graduate school and university in the future. She felt it was her duty as an interpreter and impromptu cultural guide to improve my research, which benefitted the work greatly.

Conclusion

This chapter addresses the awkward moments and feelings of inadequacy by describing some of the challenges that I encountered as a nascent qualitative researcher. Drawing on my experiences, I argue that researchers, instead of expecting circumstances to conform to ideals of tidy research methods, must be flexible in dealing with complex circumstances and shifting situations. Nascent researchers are, usually, thrown into the deep end of the pool to fend for themselves. Like my experience, this will likely mean making mistakes, feeling frustrated and distressed at certain points, emotions and experiences, which the literature on methods does not necessarily prepare researchers for. However, researchers must also be prepared to navigate the unknowable.

For this, I wrote an open and honest account of my struggles in hopes that it will support other qualitative researchers who may experience similar research challenges. The information provided here can assist in understanding the challenges that may arise when navigating work with marginalised populations, specifically in the realms of recruitment and access, narrative interviewing, and interpreters. These challenges and the experiences of conducting research in an era of mass mobility are essential in expanding our methodological understanding of enquiry with women on the move and more specifically with refugee and asylum-seeking women.

Note

1 The Border Crossing Observatory is a research centre based at Monash University that 'connects Australian and international stakeholders to high quality, independent and cutting-edge research on border crossings' (website, n.d.).

References

Adriansen, H. K. (2012). Timeline interviews: A tool for conducting life history research. *Qualitative Studies*, *3*(1), 40–55.

Ambert, A.-M., Adler, P. A., Adler, P., & Detzner, D. F. (1995). Understanding and evaluating qualitative research. *Journal of Marriage and the Family*, *57*(4), 879–893. Retrieved March 27, 2017, from www.ssc.wisc.edu/irpweb/initiatives/trainedu/igrfp/readings05/Ambertetal1995.pdf

Bamberg, M. (2010). Who am I? Narration and its contribution to self and identity. *Article Theory & Psychology*, *21*(1), 1–22. doi:10.1177/0959354309355852.

Bauer, M. W., & Gaskell, G. (2000). *Qualitative researching with text, image and sound: A practical handbook*. London, UK: SAGE Publications.

Bloch, A. (1999). Carrying out a survey of refugees: Some methodological considerations and guidelines. *Journal of Refugee Studies*, *12*. Retrieved October 17, 2016, from http://heinonline.org/HOL/Page?handle=hein.journals/jrefst12&id=377&div=30&collection=journals

Boehm, D. A. (2011). US-Mexico mixed migration in an age of deportation: An inquiry into the transnational circulation of violence. *Refugee Survey Quarterly*, 30(1), 1–21.

Cohen, N., & Arieli, T. (2011). Field research in conflict environments: Methodological challenges and snowball sampling. *Source Journal of Peace Research Journal of Peace Research*, *48*(484), 423–435.

Crawley, H. (2001). *Refugees and gender: Law and process*. Bristol: Jordans Publication.

Dhamoon, R. K., & Hankivsky, O. (2011). Why the theory and practice of intersectionality matter to health research and policy. In *Health inequities in Canada: Intersectional frameworks and practices* (pp. 16–50). Vancouver: UBC Press.

Edwards, R. (1998). A critical examination of the use of interpreters in the qualitative research process. *Journal of Ethnic and Migration Studies*, Taylor & Francis Group, *24*(1), 197–208. doi:10.1080/1369183X.1998.9976626

Fan, M. D. (2008). When deterrence and death mitigation fall short: Fantasy and fetishes as gap fillers in border regulation. *Law & Society Review*, *42*(4), 701–734.

Greenhalgh, T., Robb, N., & Scambler, G. (2006). Communicative and strategic action in interpreted consultations in primary health care: A Habermasian perspective. *Social Science & Medicine*, *63*(5), 1170–1187. doi:10.1016/j.socscimed.2006.03.033.

Griffin, G. (2015). *Cross-cultural interviewing: Feminist experiences and reflections.* Abingdon and New York: Routledge.

Groger, L., Mayberry, P. S., & Straker, J. K. (1999). What we didn't learn because of who would not talk to us. *Qualitative Health Research, 9*(6), 829–835.

Holloway, W., & Jefferson, T. (2000). *Doing qualitative research differently: Free association, narrative and the interview method.* Thousand Oaks, CA: SAGE Publications.

Indra, D. (1999). *Engendering forced migration: Theory and practice.* New York: Berghahn Books.

Jacobsen, K., & Landau, L. B. (2003). The dual imperative in refugee research: Some methodological and ethical considerations in social science research on forced migration. *Disasters, 27*(3), 105–206.

Jiménez, T. R. (2010). *Replenished ethnicity: Mexican Americans, immigration, and identity.* Berkeley, CA: University of California Press.

Jones-Correa, M. (1998). *Between two nations: The political predicament of Latinos in New York City.* Ithaca, NY: Cornell University Press.

Katz, C. (2004). *Growing up global: Economic restructuring and children's everyday lives.* Minneapolis, MN: University of Minnesota Press.

Kleinman, A., & Kleinman, J. (1996). The appeal of experience; the dismay of images: Cultural appropriations of suffering in our times. *Daedalus*, 1–23.

Knowles, J. G., & Cole, A. L. (2008). *Handbook of the arts in qualitative research: Perspectives, methodologies, examples, and issues.* Los Angeles, CA: SAGE Publications.

Luibhéid, E. (2013). *Pregnant on arrival: Making the illegal immigrant.* Minneapolis, MN: University of Minnesota Press.

Mackenzie, C., McDowell, C., & Pittaway, E. (2007). Beyond do no harm: The challenge of constructing ethical relationships in refugee research. *Journal of Refugee Studies, 20.* Retrieved March 27, 2017, from http://heinonline.org/HOL/Page?handle=hein.journals/jrefst20&id=303&div=23&collection=journals

Marshall, C., & Rossman, G. B. (2011). *Designing qualitative research.* Newbury Park, CA: SAGE Publications. Retrieved March 27, 2017, from https://books.google.com.au/books?hl=en&lr=&id=RbqXGjKHALoC&oi=fnd&pg=PR1&dq=reflexivity+refugee+qualitative+research&ots=BMmBvm_e5V&sig=53mHcmhHgsjA-VNI4_hQoLnt4_k#v=onepage&q=reflexivity refugee qualitative research&f=false

Mason, J. (2004). Personal narratives, relational selves: Residential histories in the living and telling. *The Sociological Review*, Blackwell Publishing Ltd, *52*(2), 162–179. doi: 10.1111/j.1467-954X.2004.00463.x.

Mccall, L. (2005). The complexity of Intersectionality. *Signs, 30*(3), 1771–1800.

Messerschmidt, J. W. (1999). From the SAGE social science collections. *Theoretical Criminology, 3*(2), 197–220.

Noy, C. (2008). Sampling knowledge: The hermeneutics of snowball sampling in qualitative research. *International Journal of Social Research Methodology, 11*(4), 327–344. Retrieved October 17, 2016, from http://nbn-resolving.de/urn:nbn:de:0168-ssoar-53861

Orbuch, T. L. (1997). People's accounts count: The sociology of accounts. *Annual Review of Sociology, 23*(1), 455–478. doi:10.1146/annurev.soc.23.1.455.

Palmary, I., Burman, E., Chantler, K., & Kiguwa, P. (2010). *Gender and migration: Feminist interventions.* London: Zed Books.

Pessar, P. (2003). Engendering migration studies. In *Gender and US immigration: Contemporary trends* (pp. 22–42). Berkeley, CA: University of California Press.

Pickering, S. (2011). *Women, borders, and violence: Gender, unauthorised migration and the feminisation of survival.* New York: Springer.

Plummer, K. (2001). The call of life stories in ethnographic research. In *Handbook of ethnography* (pp. 395–406) in Atkinson, P., Coffey, A., Delamont, S., Lofland, J. & Lofland, L. (eds.) Sage Publications.

Sassen, S. (2003). Globalization or denationalization? *Review of International Political Economy*, *10*(1), 1–22.

Schensul, S. L., Schensul, J. J., & LeCompte, M. D. (1999). *Essential ethnographic methods: Observations, interviews, and questionnaires* (Vol. 2). Walnut Creek, CA: Rowman Altamira.

Simien, E. M. (2007). Doing intersectionality research: From conceptual issues to practical examples. *Politics & Gender*, Cambridge University Press, *3*(2), 264–271. doi:10.1017/S1743923X07000086.

Sixsmith, J., Boneham, M., & Goldring, J. E. (2003). Accessing the community: Gaining insider perspectives from the outside. *Qualitative Health Research*, SAGE Publications, *13*(4), 578–589. doi:10.1177/1049732302250759.

Smith, K. (2015). Stories told by, for, and about women refugees : Engendering resistance. *ACME: An International E-Journal for Critical Geographies*, *14*(2), 462–469.

Sommers, M. (2001). *Fear in Bongoland: Burundi refugees in urban Tanzania*. New York and Oxford: Berghahn Books.

Sulaiman-Hill, C. M., & Thompson, S. C. (2011). Sampling challenges in a study examining refugee resettlement. *BMC International Health and Human Rights*, *11*(1), 2. doi:10.1186/1472-698X-11-2.

van Meter, K. M. (2000). Sensitive topics – sensitive questions: Overview of the sociological research literature. *Bulletin de Méthodologie Sociologique*, SAGE Publications, *68*(1), 59–78. doi:10.1177/075910630006800126.

Wengraf, T. (2001). *Qualitative research interviewing: Biographic narrative and semi-structured methods*. Thousand Oaks, CA: SAGE Publications.

Chapter 6

Spotting foreigners inside the courtroom

Race, crime and the construction of foreignness

Ana Aliverti

> "The West Indian does not by being born in England, become an Englishman".
> Enoch Powell, speech at Eastbourne on 16 November, 1968
> —(quoted in Gilroy, 2002, p. 47)

Introduction

In this chapter, I draw on a study of Birmingham criminal courts in which I explored the treatment of foreign national defendants to reflect on processes of identification inside the courtroom and their importance in shaping methodological choices and findings. Legal scholars researching the significance of citizenship and migration status for criminalisation often rely on legal categories to identify research participants. In doing so, they neglect how ideas and assumptions about the 'foreignness' of the researcher and research participants may influence findings. So too, they overlook how these processes of identification may affect the research relationship and the legitimacy of the researcher. In this chapter I explore the methodological implications of the identification processes in research on criminal justice and border controls. I argue that by being more reflexive on how social hierarchies and norms shape our research we can uncover the mechanisms leading to social injustice and inequality rather than help reproduce them.

As I will show, issues of citizenship and migration status are articulated through the language of national belonging and race by court operators. In identifying foreign nationals, court operators use racial cues and images and resort to longstanding stereotypes about particular national groups and associations among nationality, crime and race. In short, identification involves racialisation through the ascription of racial identities to specific groups which are, in turn, contraposed to the vernacular population.

The criminal courts are atypical spaces to research these more banal forms of commonsense racism. These spaces are more often imagined as unblemished by illiberal forces from the outside social world, where racism is to be combated and neutralised. Despite certain sporadic episodes tainting this image, the criminal courts have consistently commanded high levels of public trust, holding on to their place as Britain's most treasured institutions, the embodiment of the rule of law and founding blocks of democracy. Yet it is precisely this place in the public and civic imagination that makes these institutions a fruitful site to investigate the crafting of ideas about the nation and national belonging. As I have argued elsewhere (Aliverti, 2016), criminal courts are civic forums where a particular self-image of the British nation as strong, sovereign and governed by the rule of law is communicated through its grand architecture, formal language and rituals and the myriad of symbols that decorate them. In them, court participants are appraised against civic expectations and values and assert their belonging to the nation by aligning themselves with those civic parameters.

The analysis is focused on the criminal courts of Birmingham and draws from observations and reflections arising from conducting a research project which aimed at investigating the relevance of migration status and citizenship to criminal justice adjudication. Observations were conducted between March and August 2015[1] in the magistrates' court. When possible, the cases of interest – those involving foreign national defendants – were followed up until completion. At a subsequent stage, I requested and analysed the court files in cases of interest. I selected cases according to a number of indicators – including whether the defendant required assistance by an interpreter. In total, I followed up and analysed 88 cases. The project also relied on formal and informal interviews with various actors: judges, magistrates, defence lawyers, prosecutors, interpreters and probation officers.

The chapter proceeds as follows: in the first section, I describe the context in which the project took place, noting how the multicultural environment outside the courtroom shapes its inner life while intensifying stratifications and highlighting contradictions in the operation of the law. In this microenvironment of the criminal courts, exploring the relevance of citizenship and migration status for decision making is particularly challenging. It exposes the methodological pitfalls of using formal, state-sanctioned categories, which I explore in the next section. By taking these categories for granted, I argue, we risk failing to appreciate how processes of identification are shot through with ideas and images of the 'citizen' and continuously challenged by the uncertain, complex and fluid nature of identity in the context of mass human movement.

Doing research in the Birmingham courts

Doing research in the Birmingham courts was irreducibly shaped by the diversity of the city. Second only to London, Birmingham is home to a population more likely to have been born outside the UK and less likely to be white British than the national average (Birmingham City Council, 2013). In 2011, 22.2 per cent of Birmingham's residents were born abroad, compared to the national average of 13.8 per cent; nearly half of them arrived in the UK between 2001 and 2011. Pakistan, India, Ireland, Jamaica and Bangladesh were the most-reported countries of birth outside the UK among Birmingham residents. The last census reported Birmingham as the local authority that allocated the highest amount of national insurance numbers to foreign nationals outside London. The highest number of national insurance registrations to foreign workers between 2002 and 2012 were allocated to Pakistani, Polish and Indian citizens (Birmingham City Council, 2014).

Before the 1960s, Birmingham's migrant population was mostly made of people born in Ireland, Jamaica and India. In the following decades, migration from Ireland and Jamaica receded, while new arrivals hailed from India, Pakistan and Bangladesh. Since the 2000s, nationals from Eastern European countries – particularly Poland and Romania – outnumbered other national groups. The successive waves of international migrations have shaped the contemporary urban distribution of the city, which is still highly segregated by the ethnicity and nationality of its residents (Lambert, 1970). The recent rebranding of Birmingham as 'open for business' has taken stock of its rich social and cultural life, portraying it as the vibrant face of multicultural Britain. The city has also been infamous for staging Enoch Powell in his inflammatory 'Rivers of Blood' speech and for providing a local platform for the rise of the far right in the 1960s.[2] More recently, its vote to leave the EU in the national referendum laid bare deep social fragmentations and resentment towards the vernacular version of 'unruly multiculture' (Gilroy, 2012, p. 384).

Inside the criminal courts that serve this city, these tensions are revealed in the cases that arrive daily before them and in the accounts of court actors. As such, they frame research in this site and need further explanation. They not only shape interactions among those under analysis but, I found, had an effect on how people viewed me as well. Legal scholars seldom reflect on the bearing of their identity, or their positionality, on research methodology and findings. Yet as some social scientists have shown, the social location of the researcher and her identification by research participants and audience can significantly shape key aspects of research design, findings and impact, such as access, cooperation, trust and legitimacy (Vanner, 2015; Ryan Kofman & Aaron, 2011; Sanghera & Thapar-Björkert, 2008). In the context of a highly politicised and racialised debate on migration, the identification of the researcher as 'foreigner' may cast doubts and suspicion on her academic credentials and findings.

Questions of national belonging surfaced constantly in discussions about immigration and the foreign national clientele of the court. As I will discuss in more detail in what follows, they also sprang up in discussions about me. In both cases, court officers exhibited a certain level of suspicion about or even disdain for those born elsewhere. One of the solicitors who was local to the court described his hometown as a patchwork of different communities – Romanians, Polish, Kurdish, new arrivals and more established communities. In his version of the 'unruly multiculture', he connected crime, nationality and class to make sense of the diversity in the court's clientele and distance himself as a child of immigrants from the 'wetbacks', the newcomers: 'EU people get in trouble because they have different standards of child-rearing and are short-sighted. They don't care about sending kids to school'. Alluding to the 'cultural issues' underpinning 'their' incivility, he continued: 'in my community there is another perception of adults' responsibility'. Immediately after, he speculated that his parents would have probably acted in the same way when they arrived in the UK. In the messiness of this multicultural space, this lawyer deployed class and length of residence to align himself with whiteness and deflect racialisation while staging competing claims for national belonging and inclusion (Delgado, 2016).

Diversity intensifies the already stratified space of the courtroom and casts doubts on the alleged universality of the language of the law. Court actors make recurrent appeals to the 'common sense' of jurors and judges, exhorting them to use their everyday knowledge to guide their assessment of the evidence in the case and determine the plausibility of the party's version of events. Common sense, Rock (1993, p. 77) asserts, can be conceived as an 'objectification of the practical knowledge that motivates, explains, and organizes mundane experiences'. The importance of common sense in criminal proceedings takes for granted the existence of a single, uniform and homogeneous frame of reference under which defendants, practitioners, judges and juries operate. Such an assumption is, however, denied over and over again through abundant signs of normative fragmentation. Moreover, references to 'common sense', as Sara Ahmed explained, 'not only defines what we should take for granted (that is, what is normalized and already known as the given), but it also involves the normalization of ways of sensing the difference between common and uncommon' (Ahmed, 2000, p. 29). She argues that appeals to commonsense referents are techniques of knowledge: 'information is not given about how to tell the difference between normal and suspicious, because that difference is already "sensed".'

In the courtroom, appeals to common sense give legal credence to mundane, collective signifiers. In one of the cases before the magistrates' court I observed, the prosecution appealed to this technique when implicitly casting doubts on the 'normality' of a street encounter of the defendant with two young men. The case involved a middle-aged, non-white man who worked as a taxi driver and was accused and found guilty of 'plying for hire' for offering his services without prior booking and in an area where he was unlicensed to operate. In her presentation of the evidence, the prosecutor relied on CCTV footage which showed that the defendant picked up two young white men on the streets of Birmingham. The defendant argued that these were his friends and denied any commercial transaction involved in the ride: 'If any of my friends need help, I help', he explained to the court. His defence did not hold sway. Implicit in the construction of the prosecution case was the oddness of the scenario depicted by the defence. Race was crucial for persuading the bench about its implausibility.

Looking at court practices and discourse through the lens of citizenship brings to the fore the tensions and resistance to diversity and the challenges and complexities of conducting research in this field. Yet how do we fit such issues into our analysis? The world of the law and its practice is racially and gender coded at the same time that it is putatively racially and gender neutral. Unlike other institutions, the legal profession remains overwhelmingly white, British and male, particularly at the most senior levels. This holds true for describing the demographic composition of the criminal courts in Birmingham despite their relative heterogeneity if compared to other courthouses. In this hyperdiverse and stratified milieu, court staff – clerks, ushers, lawyers – are well versed in the classification of the 'sea of undifferentiated strangers' going through the court (Rock, 1993). They spot cues and assign individuals into their judicial typology of salient groups. My outsider status was rapidly spotted by 'insiders' (clerks, ushers, counsel and judges), who often mistook me for a journalist or an interpreter. My stubborn presence throughout the day in the otherwise empty public gallery disrupted the intimacy and familiarity of the court's circle. On one occasion, a woman magistrate addressed me directly: 'Are you observing us today?'

Above all, my name and accent rendered me different and thus visible. In interviews with court staff I was often asked about where I was from, and the interviewees speculated about my 'origin'. In such moments, I was being subject to identification too. As Koobak and Thapar-Björket (2012, p. 126) explained, our markers of identity are contingent and relational, they change 'dramatically once we crossed geographical and national boundaries'. Being visible because of my 'foreignness' may have raised suspicions and affected trust and willingness to participate.[3] In my case, language worked to highlight both my foreignness and my class status. On the one hand, my accent reminded interviewees of my foreignness and might have raised doubts among some about my 'impartiality' in pursuing a research project on foreign nationals before courts. On the other hand, mastering English, along with my university affiliation, might have worked to highlight my privileged class status and credentials as a 'respectable' migrant. Rendering the link among language, class and racialisation explicit, a magistrate – interviewed for the project – speculated that a defendant who requested a Chinese interpreter during a hearing did not actually need assistance, so adding: 'I'm positive that he actually spoke English – he was too well dressed'. English proficiency is an important aspect of migration policies in the UK with their neoliberal emphasis on picking the 'best and brightest' (Aliverti & Seoighe, 2017). It is connected to expectations about the 'good' migrant – high skilled, educated, cosmopolitan – and to stereotypical assumptions about some migrant groups as uneducated, insular and unwilling to mix up.

As I argue in the remaining part of the chapter, conducting empirical research on citizenship in these courts highlights the complicated nature of identification and the need to pay attention to the socially constructed nature of citizenship in research on 'crimmigration'. Such matters are not separate from methodological concerns, but rather they are intimately connected. Reflecting on court operators' strategies to spot foreigners exposes pitfalls in utilising legal categories uncritically within the legal research on border controls. It is to the analysis of this body of work that I now turn.

Searching for foreigners in the courtroom: citizenship and its elusiveness

For some time, legal and socio-legal scholars have documented the increased alignment between immigration and criminal justice policies and law enforcement and have theorised about the legal, symbolic and material implications of these developments (Stumpf, 2007). The new political and policy imperative to control migration in the Western world, these academics argue, is altering the architecture of the criminal justice system, criminal justice standards and the very purpose of punishment (Chacón, 2009; Eagly, 2013; Aliverti, 2012; Aas & Bosworth, 2013). As they showed, citizenship and migration status matter for understanding the contemporary contours of punishment (Bosworth, 2016). Lack of citizenship, others found, makes punishment more onerous in form and intensity (Aas, 2014; Light, Massoglia, & King, 2014).

Some of this literature, however, takes for granted the notion of 'citizenship' and fails to scrutinise its socially constructed nature as both gendered and racialised (Friedman, 2005; Sanchez & Romero, 2010). This failure to question state-sanctioned categories, critics suggest, obscures the unequal impact of immigration and penal laws on racialised groups (Armenta, 2017; Romero, 2008). It also disguises its effects on the research process and its impact or effects.

Taking formal status at face value and as a self-contained category overlooks how different aspects of people's positions in the world intersect and the complexities involved in defining (and documenting) civic attachments (Parmar, 2016a; Griffith, 2012; Aliverti, 2016). So too, the classification of people into citizens and non-citizens can be dehumanising and perpetuate subordination. As Tuhiwai Smith (1999, p. 8) explains, research can realise imperialism and colonialism 'in the myriad of representations and ideological constitutions of the Other in scholarly and "popular" works, and in the principles which help to select and recontextualize those constructions'. These pitfalls are most apparent in attempts to measure the effect of citizenship in levels of punishment (e.g. Light, 2017; Wu & D'Angelo, 2014). Not only do these studies assume that criminal justice decision makers operate with full information about the offenders' status and that establishing this is straightforward; they also neglect how ideas and images of the 'citizen' aid this classificatory exercise, belying assumptions about neat and discrete categories such as gender, age, ethnicity and class.

Highlighting the limitations of adopting a purely formal approach to citizenship to account for social stratification, some scholars insisted on the importance of paying attention to alternative forms of membership. Through the lens of national belonging, we can better grasp how and where the boundaries of inclusion and exclusion lie and appreciate the porosity and contested nature of these divisions. As Powell's quote makes clear, Britishness or Englishness is not squarely aligned with British citizenship. Race is key for understanding this mismatch.

In her extensive study on Britain's detention regime, Mary Bosworth (2014) documents the multi-layered dimension of detainees' identities, which defies the simple binary that justifies their confinement by border control bureaucrats and vanquishes attempts by detention staff to make sense of their jobs. Despite efforts to turn those confined persons into strangers, their familiarity and shared humanity makes their exclusion both onerous and painful for detainees and their custodians. Similarly, Emma Kaufman (2015) in her ethnographic research on prisons reflects on how the process of identifying foreign nationals for deportation is far more complicated and political than prison policies show. Rather than being a question of administrative expediency, she describes how the segregation of foreign national prisoners in specific prisons in the UK – under the 'Hubs and spokes' programme – is intimately implicated in the politics of race and the configuration of the borders of national belonging. These observations have methodological implications for researchers working on borders and penality. Empirical research is better fit to capture these richer, more textured and complex dimensions of subjectivities. As my research on the courts vividly illustrates, the endeavour of 'finding foreigners' (Kaufman, 2012) brings to the fore the complications involved in fixing bodies to cartographic spaces.

In the UK, the policy drive to remove foreign national offenders has placed the police and the prison service under increased pressure to identify and track down foreigners through the criminal justice system to ensure they do not fall through the cracks and they are expelled as soon as possible. Under the remit of a nationwide initiative branded 'Operation Nexus', immigration officers are embedded in police stations to conduct identity checks on arrestees, identify individuals 'of interest' and route them out of the country. At the receiving end of the criminal justice pipeline, the prison estate has been appended to this institutional chain to facilitate removal. Despite the insistence of court operators on the contrary, border controls have percolated the courtroom, opening up new vectors of stratification while casting new lights on familiar ones (Carlen, 1976; Hudson & Bramhall, 2005; Eaton, 1986). As one of my interviewees discovered, immigration enforcement is ubiquitous but shadowy. The Home Office singles people out and, he felt, emasculated his judicial authority: 'sometimes they say the person in custody, even if you bail them, isn't going to get released because they are going to be taken away by the immigration people who have already got them, so whatever you do on this offence, the immigration people will still hold them'.

Unlike other countries, English criminal courts do not collect information on individuals' migration or civic status, and their employees vehemently deny its relevance to the treatment of defendants. In asserting fairness, equality and the centrality of the rule of law, these court operators connive in reproducing what Doreen McBarnet (1981) called the 'dominant ideology of democratic rights', which simultaneously preserves the rhetoric of justice and due process while serving the pragmatic function of controlling crime by obscuring how the legal system is tipped in favour of conviction. This rhetoric is also a reminder of the centrality of legality in British self-identity as a colonial power (Comaroff, 2001; Armitage, 2000). Court staff often have a superior view of Britain's commitment to due process. This view was conveyed in comparisons they drew with other jurisdictions. Commenting on the difficulties involved in sentencing people with criminal records elsewhere, this crown court judge expressed concern at the differential standards of justice away from the British Isle: 'As you know there's been a case fairly recently where a defendant's bad character was put in and I think he had been tried in his absence in Bulgaria, where the process of, the administration of justice was not what we would expect in this country'.

Few of my interviewees thought that defendant's status might be relevant to their decision on the case. One of the crown court judges I asked about the bearing of these issues on the case was visibly irritated:

> I don't think they present a legal challenge at all. The only consequence of them being a foreign national is that they cannot speak English. Then obviously we need to use an interpreter. And the only effect that has – it makes the proceedings a little longer because what is said needs to be interpreted.

In his view, the only reason nationality was salient was logistical. Eliding language proficiency and nationality, this man had a particular image of the 'foreign national' (Aliverti & Seoighe, 2017). As it transpired, he ascribed features to the 'foreignness' of court participants which bear no apparent relationship to their citizenship status. Questioned about what proportion of his clients were 'foreign nationals' a local solicitor quickly gauged it at 70 to 80 per cent. On reflection, he requested clarification and amended his estimate:

> Define to me what you mean by foreign nationals? Not English? . . . If they are foreign nationals, I would say probably 10–15 per cent. I represent a lot of people who are second generation, Muslims that are British. But foreign nationals, probably 10 per cent, if that, and maybe less than that.

The ostensibly simple question about identification I put to a woman who sits as lay magistrate prompted a similar, disconcerted answer:

> if you're looking just at the name, the surname, and of course you can't always guess from that that they are a foreign national – I've got a foreign

surname and I'm British – but if you look at it on face value, you could say 70 per cent of that list are foreign nationals from some sort of background.

Despite the apparent difficulty she encountered, she confidently continued, 'I have noticed that increasingly, the names are becoming more and more apparent, complex in terms of the Polish names, Romanian names, all of those surnames are coming through in line with the general news that you hear that there's an increase in European migration . . .'.

These operators' characterisation of the court clientele defies neat distinctions based on formal status and lays bare assumptions about the identity of the 'foreigner' which links to discourses of race and national belonging. I explore in more details the content of these accounts in the next section.

Shaping foreignness: race and crime in the multicultural city

As my research unfolded, I became aware of how thorny the task of finding foreigners was. In Birmingham, this was particularly hard. The elusiveness of citizenship status raises doubts about the purpose of criminal justice policies around 'foreign national offenders' and the academic focus on measuring its impact on punishment. My enquiry then turned to unveiling court operators' – judges, magistrates, defence counsel, probation officers, prosecutors – assumptions about national belonging and how they were articulated through the language of race. They were explicitly invited to reflect about the presence of 'foreign nationals' in the courtroom and the challenges they pose to the everyday work of the courts. Some of the interviewees characterised them as timid, subdued and reticent, others as blatantly uncooperative and manipulative. As a Probation Service employee observed with frustration: 'they are generally very apprehensive and my experience is that they will often give you very little. So the [pre-sentence] reports are even more threadbare than they usually are'. In one of the hearings I observed, the defence counsel of a man who pleaded guilty to involvement in the cultivation of cannabis tried to argue that his client was a minor and had a marginal role in the larger operation. Incredulously, the crown judge moaned: 'I never dealt with Vietnamese nationals, save for cultivation. It is a common trend that they say that they are younger than they appear to be'.

In the judicial crime typologies, the label of 'criminal foreigner' was often pinned on specific national groups. The 'Romanians' featured prominently in narratives with the foreign national clientele of the court. Their presence sometimes met disgust and annoyance. A solicitor conveyed this feeling thus:

> I think – this is just a sensation I have – there is a general feeling of dislike for the type of offence they commit, for the fact that they are so identifiable – there is the national dress, the way they behave in court is so

stereotypical and I think people see a Romanian name and there is a general rolling of eyes and an "Oh, what have they done now?".

Familiar intersections of class, race and gender appeared in others' characterisations of the innate criminality of this group. For another solicitor their alterity and abjection was connected to their values and their 'way of life':

> I have had people say to me in the past 'we have to survive and we have to do what we can to survive, including stealing' which is obviously not the rule here. It seems to be ingrained into some people, the way they think. . . . It seems to be almost a way of life for them, which some of them have imported from Romania to here and they carried on here. If I'm generalising, I'm sure that there are some very legitimate hard-working people there. . . .

Reviving Lombrosian terminology, he explained their offending in cultural terms as a quasi-biological feature, something they carry with them. While offending by foreigners was generally explained through appeals to culture (Aliverti, 2018), offending among the vernacular population was more likely to be depicted as instrumental – for instance, to fund their drug or alcohol addiction.

On these accounts, the perception that an increased share of 'Romanians' are passing through the courts contributed to their visibility and racialisation. Many of my interviewees remarked the apparent surge in this group, connecting it to policy decisions and the attractiveness of the UK. Conveying the UK's perceived desirability as rich, tolerant and naïve, this magistrate subtly hints at the predatory nature of foreigners' criminality and the victimhood of the national (Ahmed, 2014, p. 3):

> I think a lot of magistrates would take probably the view that in coming to this country, there are certain expectations that you will appreciate a certain standard of living. If one says to somebody 'why do you want to come to the UK?' 'Better life' is often the phrase I heard before. And yet in coming to this country, by whatever means, this better life that they want for themselves and their family, involves them committing crimes . . . maybe they think there's a right to claim certain things or to get certain things and if they can't claim it because they know they're not legal or have got documentation to prove that, so that the only way they can get things is through theft, which is often the way . . . and I think there's a perception that perhaps in the UK that we are not quite as harsh in our justice system [as in their own country] so they think that they can get away with it more.

The representation of Romanians as irredeemable, predatory petty thieves in court connects with broader social stereotypes about this group. As Fox and colleagues (2012) observed, whiteness and the privileges attached to it come in shades. Romanians have been denuded of their whiteness through policies and media representations that highlight their otherness by dint of their uncivilised behaviour in the form of begging, theft and benefit fraud. The narratives about Romanians inside the courtroom reveal the shifting and contingent boundaries of race. These can be traced down to the aftermath of the EU enlargement and the changes to class relations it brought home and shows the racialising effects of some migration and labour policies.

Foreignness brings to the fore connotations that legal categories hide. In singling out certain national groups as 'foreigners' and ascribing to them familiar stereotypes, my research shows that identification processes inside the court both rely upon and contribute to the racialisation of these groups in line with the public mood about immigration outside the courthouse. Given the heightened public sensitivity of debates around migration in the UK and elsewhere, researchers working on borders and criminal justice need to be reflexive on the assumptions, ideas and even images that underpin their research and on how their social position may shape their research by facilitating or thwarting it. Identification processes involve power dynamics, and we need to pay more attention to how 'foreignness' unsettles or reinforces traditional power relationships between the researcher and the researched (Mikecz, 2012).

Conclusion

In his seminal book *There Ain't No Black in the Union Jack* (2002), Paul Gilroy alerted us to the peculiar interweaving of race and nation in contemporary British history. Racism and nationalism, he observed, are mutually entangled, yet the intimate connection and the centrality of race for delineating the borders of the nation are persistently disavowed by conservatives and liberals alike. The symptomatic reluctance to acknowledge the embeddedness of colonialism with its attendant racial hierarchies in British patriotism and the relegation of racism to the extreme and the exceptional lie at the heart of Britain's chronic problem in dealing with 'race', Gilroy diagnosed. According to him, discussions about 'race' are often consigned to the abhorrent acts of extremists, which can be safely remedied through the law and its enforcement. On this account, the ubiquitous presence of race and the more elusive and subtle forms of everyday racisms are conveniently disguised while the role of the law and its institutions for perpetuating racial hierarchies remains unearthed.

The endurance and pliability of the language of race under the guise of culture, religion and nationality, and the persistence of flagrant social inequalities affecting racialised minorities in the UK point to the importance of understanding how racial difference is constructed and legitimised in everyday life (Parmar, 2016b; Phillips, 2008; Bosworth, Bowling, & Lee, 2008). Discourses around migration and crime have been historically a privileged site for the currency of ideas and imageries about the nation and its boundaries. Race and racial representations have provided the raw material for delineating the borders of national belonging (Ahmed, 2000; Gilroy, 1990). Three decades of public obsession with 'immigration' have forged a sturdy and rich receptacle of what Gilroy calls the 'folk grammar of common sense racism' (Gilroy, 2002, p. 87), which was unleashed during the electoral campaign to pull Britain out of the European Union.

While sociologists of race have documented the connections between race, nation and crime, criminologists and criminal justice scholars have been far less interested in exploring these questions (Bosworth, Parmar, & Vazquez, 2018). As I have shown in this chapter this oversight has diminished our understanding of the practical aspects of conducting research on migration. As a foreigner studying the treatment of foreigners in criminal courts, I found myself subject to the same kinds of processes and language of identification as the defendants. Reflecting the intersectional nature of identity, I did not inhabit quite the same status. My gender, and above all my education and university credentials, affected how I was perceived. Yet I remained labelled as different and perceived as such.

Looking at legal practices and discourses through the lens of citizenship brings to the fore the limitations of formal categories to understand social stratification and the importance of empirical work for teasing out the nuanced, labile and subtle ways in which subordination is produced and rationalised (Phillips & Webster, 2013; Bulmer & Solomos, 2004). In particular, it sheds light on how the language of citizenship is carefully articulated to avoid race while revealing resistance and tensions to 'multicultural conviviality' (Phillips, 2012).

The increased focus on foreign national offenders in criminal justice policies and the recurrent efforts to make them recognisable and visible encounter ethical, practical, legal and political difficulties. In the courtroom, these are met with ambivalence and some level of resistance. Yet these policies rely on a receptacle of images and cues about 'foreignness'. The 'foreign national' is already recognised as someone who does not belong. Searching foreigners in the courtroom has a reinforcing effect: it relies on markers of difference which are the product of prior processes of racialisation. In turn, difference and non-belonging legitimise immigration controls. Court staff's accounts on foreign nationals reveal how processes of identification in demarcating the boundaries of belonging warrant those controls.

Notes

I am grateful to Rachel Seoighe for her research assistance, and to Mary Bosworth and the editors of this collections for constructive feedback and encouragement.
1 An additional period of observations was done between November and December 2016 at the magistrates' court.
2 Powell pronounced his speech at the Conservative Conference in Birmingham in April 1968, where he advocated for the halting of immigration and mass repatriation of citizens from former British colonies. Four years earlier, in the outskirts of

Birmingham, in the industrial town of Smethwick, Conservative Peter Griffith had won his seat in Parliament after what was branded the 'most racist' election in British history: Buettner 2014.

3 To give an example of the difficulties in recruiting participants and the low response rate, only two lay magistrates agreed to participate in formal interviews for the project at Europe's largest and busiest court, which houses 22 courts and employs around 400 magistrates and district judges: Birmingham Post, 'Birmingham's Hidden Spaces: Victoria Law Courts became jewel in "terracotta city"' available at: www.birminghampost.co.uk/business/birminghams-hidden-spaces-victoria-law-8304428.

References

Aas, K. F. (2014). Bordered penality: Abnormal justice and the precarious membership. *Punishment & Society, 16*, 520–541.

Aas, K. F., & Bosworth, M. (Eds.). (2013). *The borders of punishment: Criminal justice, citizenship and social exclusion*. Oxford: Oxford University Press.

Ahmed, S. (2000). *Strange encounters: Embodied others in post-coloniality*. Abingdon: Routledge.

Ahmed, S. (2014). *The cultural politics of emotion*. Edinburgh: Edinburgh University Press.

Aliverti, A. (2012). Making people criminal: The role of the criminal law in immigration enforcement. *Theoretical Criminology, 16*, 417–434.

Aliverti, A. (2016). Researching the global criminal court. In M. Bosworth, C. Hoyle, & L. Zedner (Eds.), *Changing contours of criminal justice: Research, politics and policy*. Oxford: Oxford University Press.

Aliverti, A. (2018). Strangers in our midst: The construction of difference through cultural appeals in criminal justice litigation. In M. Bosworth, A. Parmar, & Y. Vazquez (Eds.), *Race, and migration control criminal justice*. Oxford: Oxford University Press.

Aliverti, A., & Seoighe, R. (2017). Lost in translation? Examining the role of court interpreters in cases involving foreign national defendants in England and Wales. *New Criminal Law Review, 20*.

Armenta, A. (2017). Racializing crimmigration: Structural racism, colorblindness, and the institutional production of immigrant criminality. *Sociology of Race and Ethnicity, 3*, 82–95.

Armitage, D. (2000). *The ideological origins of the British empire*. Cambridge: Cambridge University Press.

Birmingham City Council. (2013). *Population and migration topic report, 2011 census in Birmingham*. Birmingham: Birmingham City Council.

Birmingham City Council. (2014). *2012 to 2013 international migration*. Retrieved from www.birmingham.gov.uk/downloads/file/4615/2012_to_2013_international_migrationpdf

Bosworth, M. (2014). *Inside immigration detention*. Oxford: Oxford University Press.

Bosworth, M. (2016). Border criminologies: How migration is changing criminal justice. In M. Bosworth, C. Hoyle, & L. Zedner (Eds.), *Changing contours of criminal justice*. Oxford: Oxford University Press.

Bosworth, M., Bowling, B., & Lee, M. (2008). Globalization, ethnicity and racism: An introduction. *Theoretical Criminology, 12*, 263–273.

Bosworth, M., Parmar, A. & Vázquez, Y. (Eds.) (2018). *Race, criminal justice and migration control*. Oxford: Oxford University Press.

Buettner, E. (2014), '"This is Staffordshire not Alabama": Racial Geographies of Commonwealth Immigration in Early 1960s Britain', *Journal of Imperial and Commonwealth History*, 42:4, 710–740.

Bulmer, M., & Solomos, J. (2004). Introduction: Researching race and racism. In M. Bulmer & J. Solomos (Eds.), *Researching race and racism* (pp. 1–15). London: Routledge.
Carlen, P. (1976). *Magistrates' justice*. London: Wiley-Blackwell.
Chacón, J. (2009). Managing migration through crime. *Columbia Law Review Sidebar, 109*, 135–148.
Comaroff, J. (2001). Colonialism, culture, and the law: A foreword. *Law & Social Inquiry*, 305–314.
Delgado, D. (2016). And you need me to be the token Mexican?: Examining racial hierarchies and the complexities of racial identities for middle class Mexican Americans. *Critical Sociology, 42*, 679–698.
Eagly, I. (2013). Criminal justice for noncitizens: An analysis of variation in local enforcement. *New York University Law Review, 88*, 101–191.
Eaton, M. (1986). *Justice for women?* Milton Keynes: Open University Press.
Fox, J., Moroşanu, L., & Szilassy, E. (2012). The racialization of the new European migration to the UK. *Sociology, 46*, 680–695.
Friedman, M. (Ed.). (2005). *Women and citizenship*. New York: Oxford University Press.
Gilroy, P. (1990). The end of anti-racism. *Journal of Ethnic and Migration Studies, 17*, 71–83.
Gilroy, P. (2002). *There ain't no Black in the Union Jack*. Abingdon: Routledge.
Gilroy, P. (2012). 'My Britain is fuck all' zombie multiculturalism and the race politics of citizenship. *Identities, 19*, 380–397.
Griffith, M. (2012). Anonymous aliens? Questions of identification in the detention and deportation of failed asylum seekers. *Population, Space and Place, 18*.
Hudson, B., & Bramhall, G. (2005). Assessing the 'other': Constructions of 'Asianness' in risk assessments by probation officers. *British Journal of Criminology, 45*, 721–740.
Kaufman, E. (2012). Finding foreigners: Race and the politics of memory in British prisons. *Population, Space and Place, 18*, 701–714.
Kaufman, E. (2015). *Punish and expel: Border control, nationalism, and the new purpose of the prison*. Oxford: Oxford University Press.
Koobak, R., & Thapar-Björket, S. (2012). Becoming non-Swedish: Locating the paradoxes of in/visible identities. *Feminist Review, 102*, 125–134.
Lambert, J. (1970). *Crime police & race relations: A study in Birmingham*. London: Oxford University Press.
Light, M. T. (2017). Punishing the 'Others': Citizenship and state social control in the United States and Germany. *European Journal of Sociology, 58*, 33–71.
Light, M. T., Massoglia, M., & King, R. D. (2014). Citizenship and punishment: The salience of national membership in U.S. Criminal Courts. *American Sociological Review, 79*, 825–847.
McBarnet, D. (1981). *Conviction: Law, the state and the construction of justice*. London: Macmillan Press.
Mikecz, R. (2012). Interviewing elites. *Qualitative Inquiry, 18*, 482–493.
Parmar, A. (2016a). Intersectionality, British criminology and race: Are we there yet? *Theoretical Criminology, 21*, 35–45.
Parmar, A. (2016b). Race, ethnicity, and criminal justice: Refocusing the criminological gaze. In M. Bosworth, C. Hoyle, & L. Zedner (Eds.), *Changing contours of criminal justice* (pp. 55–69). Oxford: Oxford University Press.
Phillips, C. (2008). Negotiating identities: Ethnicity and social relations in a young offenders' institution. *Theoretical Criminology, 12*, 313–331.
Phillips, C. (2012). *The multicultural prison: Ethnicity, masculinity, and social relations among prisoners*. Oxford: Oxford University Press.

Phillips, C., & Webster, C. (2013). Introduction: Bending the paradigm: new directions and new generations. In C. Phillips & C. Webster (Eds.), *New directions in race, ethnicity and crime* (pp. 1–17). Abingdon: Routledge.

Rock, P. (1993). *The social world of an English crown court: Witnesses and professionals in the crown court centre at Wood Green*. Oxford: Oxford University Press.

Romero, M. (2008). Crossing the immigration and race border: A critical race theory approach to immigration studies. *Contemporary Justice Review, 11*, 23–37.

Ryan, L., Kofman, E., & Aaron, P. (2011). Insiders and outsiders: Working with peer researchers in researching Muslim communities. *International Journal of Social Research Methodology, 14*, 49–60.

Sanchez, G., & Romero, M. (2010). Critical race theory in the US sociology of immigration. *Sociology Compass, 4*, 779–788.

Sanghera, G. S., & Thapar-Björkert, S. (2008). Methodological dilemmas: Gatekeepers and positionality in Bradford. *Ethnic & Racial Studies, 31*, 543–562.

Stumpf, J. (2007). The crimmigration crisis: Immigrants, crime, and sovereign state. *Lewis & Clark Law School Legal Research Paper Series, 2007–2*, 1–44.

Tuhiwai Smith, L. (1999). *Decolonizing methodologies: Research and indigenous Peoples*, London: Zed Books.

Vanner, C. (2015). Positionality at the center. *International Journal of Qualitative Methods, 14*, 1609406915618094.

Wu, J., & D'Angelo, J. M. (2014). Unwarranted disparity in federal sentencing: Noncitizen crime as a social/group threat. *Criminal Justice Review, 39*, 58–80.

Chapter 7

Migrant voices in the Global South

Challenges of recruitment, participation and interpretation

Bodean Hedwards and Sirakul Suwinthawong

Introduction

The criminalisation of migration, as well documented, produces vulnerabilities for migrants, largely because it does not prevent migration but instead pushes those who cannot access regularised migration avenues to irregular border crossing pathways (see Khosravi, 2009; Bosworth & Guild, 2008; Hudson, 2007; Weber, 2007; Pickering & Weber, 2006). As such, irregular and criminalised migration practices remain hidden and largely inaccessible to researchers. This chapter examines a unique and contextually specific view on some of the shared methodological challenges in conducting research on irregular migration. It draws on two projects, undertaken in two very different border settings, that focus on common forms of irregular migration[1] in the Global South; Suwinthawong researched irregular labour migration from Laos to Thailand and Hedwards researched asylum seeking from Tibet to India via Nepal. Both studies were designed with an emphasis on understanding the experiences of irregular migrants during border crossing and afterwards, in the country of destination.

The chapter follows the fieldwork processes and stages, starting, first, from the recruitment of the participants, moving to their participation and then ending with the interpretation of interviews. In doing so, this chapter seeks to advance the way we understand the inherent complexities of the processes involved in qualitative fieldwork. While the experiences of the participants are not the focus of this chapter, by examining the fieldwork experiences of researchers across these two specific projects and the nature of the participants' narratives, this chapter explores the fluidity of power and positionality and the implications that this can have for fieldwork and research more broadly. These practical implications are explored through the preconceptions and expectations of the researchers and university ethics committees as a way to demonstrate how local realities shift and shape the research at different stages, in different ways and for different stakeholders.

Background: the two research projects

The two projects examined in this chapter were finite, doctoral research projects. They were undertaken in close time proximity (the Thai research was conducted in 2015 and the research in India was undertaken in 2013), and while they had a different research focus, there are methodological convergences between them, as well as significant points of contrast. The research with Tibetan refugees in India was undertaken in a highly politicised context. In the decades that followed the Chinese occupation of Tibet in the 1950s, the situation in Tibet has been shaped by the ongoing social and religious oppression, intense surveillance practices and forced displacement; all largely in the name of 'development' (Human Rights Watch, 2016a, 2016b, 2013). Inside Tibet, there are severe restrictions on movement, particularly for ex-political prisoners, who are required to have permission to move beyond their own township, meaning that those who try to flee end up doing so illegally, and thus they are often unable to return legally. This impacted the research because participants were highly vigilant and attuned to the possibility that anything they said could lead to their deprivation of a legal return to Tibet.

Conversely, the research undertaken in Thailand was largely accepted within – albeit irregular – labour migration flows. The long, and relatively poor border enforcement between the Northern Thai province of Mukdahan and the Southern Lao province of Savannaket makes Thailand a viable and accessible option for Lao migrant workers who seek better employment opportunities. In addition to the lack of job opportunities and lower wages in Laos, the high demand for low-skilled, cheap labour in Thailand has sustained a relatively unregulated labour migration flow across the Thai–Lao border (Luanglatbandith & Leuangkhamsing, 2016; Phouxay, 2010; World Bank, 2006). So while also irregular, as per participants in Tibet, the gravity of being identified as irregular and/or the vigilance in the articulation of the irregular border crossing was quite different at this border crossing and, in contrast, more relaxed.

Both projects sought to map the impact of the 'border' and the ways in which bordering practices emerged via the lived experiences of migrants. However, the main points of convergence were found in the methodologies used. The research design included semi-structured interviews informed by various feminist research frameworks, specifically, by the methods that seek to privilege the perspectives, experiences and voices of participants (Ackerly & True, 2010, 2008). Beyond this, given the positioning of both researchers as middle-class, young females (and, in the case of Hedwards, also as a foreigner), the research design and methodologies required a significant level of reflexivity so as to understand the impact that their positioning could have on the fieldwork and the research outcomes more broadly (Hett & Hett, 2013; Bonnin, 2010; Aléx & Hammarström, 2008).

Recruiting participants at the research site – from ethics applications to negotiating participants' status and the role of the gatekeepers

While there was a range of anticipated challenges in conducting the research (see Miller, 2004), both Hedwards and Suwinthawong faced the same main challenge: accessing participants. The challenges were informed by the influence of the participants' migration status and the contextually specific, often fluid role of authorities or gatekeepers. Given the different contexts, both researchers took different approaches in order to navigate the implications of the said two factors.

The research in Thailand involved semi-structured interviews and observations with two key groups: Lao female migrant workers and Thai stakeholders, including local authorities, NGOs and local community groups that work with irregular migrant workers. A total of 33 interviews were conducted; 21 with Lao women who were working as domestic workers, pig farmers, shop helpers, restaurants workers and construction site workers, and 12 interviews with Thai stakeholder groups, including marine police officers, border patrol police officers, employers and NGO staff members. A snow-ball methodology was used to recruit migrant workers, starting with NGOs that worked with Lao migrant women, who passed the invitation to the participants. A more targeted recruitment process was used for the stakeholders. For example, the Thai authorities were simply invited to participate in an interview by Suwinthawong at their office at their convenience. The interviews were conducted in either the Bangkok dialect or the Isan dialect of north-eastern Thailand – both of which are similar to the Lao language. Suwinthawong is a Thai national from Bangkok, and therefore she was able to conduct the interviews without an interpreter. At the end of every interview, the Lao women were offered 200 baht (approximately 7.50 AUD/4.50 GBP).

In India, the recruitment process was not so straightforward. The initial recruitment approach was that of an informal snowball approach through Hedwards's known – and trusted – network in India at the time. This approach was converted at the ethics stage into a less direct approach: posters were drafted in Tibetan, displaying the project's information and the researchers' contact details and inviting people to participate if they wanted to. As it is discussed in more detail in what follows, the latter approach had significant risks for the potential participants and the researcher, so on arrival the former approach was used. Since Hedwards was an Australian woman with no further language skills than English, the interviews were conducted with the assistance of an interpreter. In total, 12 interviews were conducted. At the end of every interview, participants were offered a 'khata'[2] and 250 INR (approximately 5 AUD) as a token of appreciation; only two participants accepted the money, while the others refused it and placed the 'khata' around Hedwards's neck instead.

Upon reflection on these experiences, the researchers highlighted two practical contextual factors in first accessing and then recruiting participants: the individual immigration status and the presence and role of different gatekeepers.

Immigration status

The notion of 'irregularity' as a participant's immigration status in a country was highlighted as a potential risk for recruiting participants in the respective ethics applications. This notion created concerns for the ethics committees that then led to specific research instructions for safe and ethical recruitment meant as a requirement of granting ethical approval. However, some of the assumptions that these instructions relied on acculturalised understandings of the notion of irregularity, which were not always applicable and had implications for conducting fieldwork.

For example, for the research in Thailand, the ethics committee suggested speaking to the authorities first in order to prevent any unintentional disclosure of information about undocumented migrant workers to the authorities. Given our understanding of the risks that irregular migrant workers face (Archavanitkul & Hall, 2011; Rukumnuaykit, 2009) this suggestion was understandable. While authorities largely turned a blind eye to the presence of undocumented Lao workers in Thailand, and their status was generally accepted by the local business community, interviews with stakeholders, including local border guards, indicated that women were technically at risk of being deported if they were caught. Yet it is important to note here that in many cases it was the local authorities that facilitated interviews with undocumented Lao women through their relationships with employers. While interviews did unfold in the way that the ethics committee suggested (albeit unintentionally), Suwinthawong's experience with recruitment highlights several cultural nuances, thus not only challenging some of the presumptions about the impact of the immigration status but also challenging some of the perceptions about how particular relationships can be manifested within different contexts, namely that of the authorities and irregular migrants (see Bonnin, 2010; Miller, 2004).

Comparatively, the influence of immigration status was both perceived and experienced differently by interviewees in India. In order to avoid any undue pressure regarding the use of a direct snowball approach, the latter was rejected by the ethics committee. In response to concerns raised about potential pressure to participate as a result of the direct approach, posters were made and translated into Tibetan, inviting people to contact the researcher if they wanted to participate. On arrival, the interpreter and locals advised that the posters presented risks for both participants and the researcher, as the research could be viewed as 'anti-Chinese'. This meant that both the researcher and broader community could be subject to surveillance by the local authorities, the consequences of which are explored in what follows. To mitigate this risk, a more informal snow-ball approach was adopted, with information about the research passed by the interpreter through informal and trusted community networks. While Tibetans who fled Tibet are able to naturalise in India and the risks of actual deportations to Tibet are minimal, participants and community members more broadly believed that participation in activities that could be considered 'anti-Chinese' could result in increased surveillance by informants living in the community. This was informed by the circulation of horror stories within the community about activists and their families in Tibet who were subject to harassment. Increased surveillance was also thought to have negative implications for the issuance of visa applications to return to Tibet, particularly for ex-political prisoners. For example, Dolma, a Buddhist nun and ex-political prisoner, specifically asked the interpreter if he trusted Hedwards and whether she could be a 'Chinese spy'. Regardless of the reasons that participants fled in the first place, the fact that they all left irregularly meant that their chances of getting permission to re-enter Tibet were low, but still they raised concerns about the possibility that their participation could exacerbate the risk of having their visa application denied and thus of being unable to return legally. For the participants in this research, it was the risks associated with their status that potentially prevented them from returning home, as opposed to the Lao workers (more broadly), who faced the risks of being deported back to their home as a result of their participation in the research.

While the impact of the participants' migration status was experienced differently by Hedwards and Suwinthawong, it highlights the importance of integrating and preparing for the the contextual features that can shape different relationships at different stages of the research project, and understanding the impact they can have on fieldwork. Both Suwinthawong and Hedwards had to navigate contextual features in relation to their participants' immigration status that were not necessarily foreseen by their respective ethics committees. The reference to the ethics committee is just one example that draws attention to the preconceptions and expectations that can shape the early stages of and preparation for a research project. In using the ethics committee as an example, however, these experiences provided a reference point so as to begin unbundling some of the authors' own expectations based on the preconceptions associated with the migration status and authorities.

This raises two issues that need to be considered in the early stages of the research process. The first is the importance of local knowledge and expertise of both the researcher and the local network. This consideration conveys the complexities associated with the navigation of the initial research stages with irregular migrants and the importance of examining the preconceptions and expectations via the combined experience of locals and researchers. The second draws attention to the way that power and positionality develop and shift throughout the early stage of the project and reiterates the importance of understanding the different relationships and hierarchies that can either complicate or facilitate research. In the experiences of the authors, the key features of their research were not anticipated. This, then, clearly shaped their early fieldwork experiences. The authors' experiences highlight an opportunity for more consultation with local representatives in the early preparation stages of fieldwork, including key ethics processes. Consultations with key stakeholders involved in the research at the early stages of the fieldwork preparation, including the formal ethics processes, are vital in ensuring that research standards are upheld. However, the authors' experiences highlight the benefits of incorporating the knowledge and expertise of local representatives in a more formalised manner, namely ensuring that the various research stages are both contextually grounded and sensitive.

Gatekeepers – local authorities, employers and the community

The second determinant factor of the recruitment process was the presence and role of gatekeepers. The gatekeepers manifested themselves in different ways in the two projects and had implications depending on where the gatekeeper was positioned in the different cultural power structures and their proximity to participants and the researcher. For example, during the research in Thailand, gatekeepers were identified as both employers and in-laws ('auntie') but also extended to actual authorities, including border police. As it will be explored in what follows, in Thailand the gatekeepers were both imminent and present during the interviews. Alternatively, in India they were not present, but their influence was well established at the table. In this study, the gatekeepers were the Chinese authorities. While they were not physically in the room, their presence existed within a well-established fear of the consequences associated with anti-Chinese activities.

Despite the fact that the members of the Chinese authorities in India were not physically present 'they were always at the table' (Barnett, 2010, p. 85). Robert Barnett explains this simply, stating that [interviews are] "always a three-way process in which [the Chinese Government] is sitting visibly or invisibly at the table, sometimes encouraging, sometimes threatening, sometimes enticing, sometimes intervening" (2010, p. 85). As mentioned, the risks associated with participation were perceived as imminent, in that the participants' political activism (in this case, the mere participation in research) was thought to be linked to their (in)ability to return to Tibet. Miller (2004) experienced similar issues with recruiting Afghani women living in the United States, explaining that their perceived fear of what would happen if they took an interview stopped many from participating. He explained that their husbands or in-laws, without actually knowing what the research was about, discouraged the women from participating: many women were so frightened by the anticipated displeasure which their participation might evoke that they simply declined to be interviewed (2004, p. 221). Some of the participants suggested that Hedwards could even be a 'Chinese spy', and those that made this suggestion often withheld a lot of detail regarding their personal experiences, opting rather to share a more generalised history of Tibetan experiences. While no one in this project declined to be interviewed, one did actually refuse to have the interview recorded through fear that the information could be used to have her returned to prison. In the Indian context, Hedwards's experience highlights the ways that gatekeepers can influence or shape various elements of the research process.

Hedwards's experience aligns with a more traditional view on the role of gatekeepers in social science research: as barriers to recruitment and engagement (Hett & Hett, 2013). As Bonnin (2010) found in her ethnographic work in Vietnam, however, this is not always the case; gatekeepers can also facilitate the research by helping to navigate the local complexities and power structures (see also Hett & Hett, 2013). This relates to Suwinthawong's experience in interviewing Lao irregular migrant workers in Thailand, where gatekeepers not only facilitated the research but also created a safe and comfortable environment for participants to share their stories. For example, in one case the researcher was introduced to both Waen,[3] a domestic worker, and her employer through the local authorities. The interview was then conducted at the presence of Waen's employer. Waen stated that she did not keep secrets from her employer, and she would prefer to be interviewed at the employer's house while the latter was present. Despite the fact that Suwinthawong was introduced as ajarn, which translates to 'lecturer' in Thai – a position held in high esteem within the community – a significant time investment had to be made in order to establish the rapport with Waen prior to undertaking the interview. Regardless, Suwinthawong was still a stranger, so the presence of her employer of ten years made her more comfortable. Alternatively, in an interview with a Lao shopkeeper, the worker specifically said she would rather do the interview without her employer, so Suwinthawong had to return to the restaurant after the employer had left. Despite this, authorities – be it the employer or the police – facilitated access to the Lao workers either via formal introductions or via referrals. Suwinthawong's experience challenges some of our preconceptions regarding the authorities in conducting research with irregular migrants.

The experiences with gatekeepers further develop our understanding of fieldwork by challenging our assumptions of who is in power in a research setting and how that can influence the research. Hedwards' experience involved gatekeepers, who manifested themselves as the Chinese government, and, despite not being in close proximity, created risks and thus barriers in recruitment and interviews as well. Despite the fact that Suwinthawong, as an academic, held a highly respected job title, the assumed power that accompanied that title held little weight in regard to recruitment. This power could be interpreted in two ways: as either a barrier or a means of pressure to participate resulting from the respect owed to academics within the community. Rather, it was the presence of or role of the gatekeepers that facilitated the interviews, as evidenced by the local authorities that facilitated recruitment or employers that created a comfortable environment in which to undertake the interview. The fact that Suwinthawong did not encounter any major issues with gatekeepers in recruiting participants challenges our preconceived understanding of the way that power influences the research process, given that it was not necessarily the power that accompanied her title that facilitated the recruitment process.

The authors' experiences draw attention to positionality as a much broader notion that needs to incorporate the impact of proximity. The need to account for the impact of proximity in the interpretation of the researcher's own positionality and the different power structures that exist during fieldwork is vital in responding to and understanding distinct and contextually specific nuances that can be manifested through different research stages. Further, positionality needs to extend to all stakeholders in the research process, including participants, the researcher and the gatekeepers. Therefore, as we progress through the different fieldwork processes, we need to create the space needed to recognise and adapt to the ways that the position and power of different actors can influence not only the power structures within an interview but also the ways they can shape the broader research experience.

Participation and engagement in an interview

On reflection, the experiences raised thus far highlighted an interesting consideration for our understanding of the role and position of the gatekeeper in research, particularly with irregular migrants. Further, as raised in the previous section, these experiences also illustrated how power and positionality shift and are differently manifested at different stages of the research. In the interviews in India, Hedwards was immediately put into an 'outsider' position and, in some cases, viewed as a threat to her participants' individual safety. Suwinthawong's experience, however, suggests that positionality is fluid and can be contextually specific.

Despite being perceived as holding an 'insider' position, in the interviews with Lao workers, Suwinthawong was still a 'stranger'. However, this position was not fixed. Despite the early presumptions that Suwinthawong was in a position of power due to her academic title, in the example of Waen, where there was a significant time investment prior to undertaking the interview, this position and power were challenged, as her presumed status of 'ajarn' was not the most influential position in the room. The fact that Waen required her employer to be present shifted the power hierarchy within that specific interview setting to the employer, who, in this context, could also be considered a gatekeeper. Alternatively, the women working in the restaurant did not care for Suwinthawong's status as a researcher; she looked and spoke Thai, so she was just like any other Thai person they engaged with on a daily basis. This shifted the workers into a different position, as they held the information which Suwinthawong was seeking. Suwinthawong's experience therefore illustrates the fluid nature of power and positionality among all stakeholders during fieldwork – the researcher's position and power shifted throughout interviews depending on who was being interviewed and who else was in the room.

The fluidity of Hedwards's positionality also had implications for the way in which interviews were conducted; however, it was more evident in the way the participants shared their stories. While a certain level of trust was established through the presence of the Tibetan interpreter, there was an element of suspicion towards Hedwards and the overall research project. Compared to interviews in Thailand, the participants in India questioned the research, the aims and outcomes, the anticipated benefits of the research for the Tibetan community and the safeguards set in place to protect their identity from the Chinese government. The questioning was encouraged by Hedwards, both before and after the interview, in an effort to create a level of ownership, in that it was *their* own personal story informing the research. Initially, it appeared that the types of questions they posed could be indicative of the way participants would share their stories; those that did not completely trust the researcher would not talk openly and would be less forthcoming, and those that did would be open and enthusiastic. However, this was not always the case. One participant, a layman referred to as 'Dorjee', interrogated the research and its aims and outcomes both before and after the (three-hour) interview. While he recognised the risks associated with participating and the 'presence' of the Chinese authorities, his answers were detailed, with vivid descriptions shared through an overtly enthusiastic and comfortable body language. Alternatively, those who maintained their suspicions presented a different narrative. For example, Dolma – a Buddhist nun who escaped Tibet after she was released from prison for being involved in political activism – refused to have her interview recorded, checked the notes at the end of the interview and watched the researcher with suspicion. While she participated in the interview, her answers were comparatively short, and Hedwards had the sense that many of the answers lacked detail or were not answered directly. Answers to questions regarding her actual border crossing or her experience with the authorities were limited, and she spoke about the collective experience of Tibetans more broadly.

The combined experience of Hedwards and Suwinthawong suggests that power, positionality and proximity are more complex and influential when considered within the practicalities of the actual research conduct: *who* holds the power, what is their position in relation to the research, the participants or the gatekeeper and, importantly, what implications does this dynamic have on how participants engage in research? Ultimately, the answer to this question was highly dependent on who was being interviewed, where and why.

Interpreting the silence – what is not said during interviews with irregular migrants

The implications of power and positionality relate to the final point of convergence between these two projects: the experience of silence within the participants' narratives. In some instances, silence was the unspoken, evidenced through sentences that were abruptly cut off or changed. In other instances, silence was effectively the language of convention, especially in Thailand, where practices that underpinned the relationship between businesses and police authority were so commonplace that no one thought to offer an explanation thereof. Where a question was asked, it was responded to with surprise for asking 'the obvious'. For example, in the interviews with Lao women working in restaurants, the questions were typically the same, and as a result they generated similar responses. The women were from Savannaket and grew up in poor farming families, so they were surprised when asked about why they decided to move to Mukdahan. They did not understand why the question even had to be asked, as it is something that a Thai citizen and a researcher should have already known. Their facial expressions and occasional laughter at the questions reiterated this; some laughed and stated 'you know this . . . I moved because I need money to support my family in Savannaket'. While financial hardship is well-understood as a driver for migration within the labour migration literature (Hugo, 2012), the expectation or assumed knowledge meant that the more personalised experiences were neglected.

The expectation or assumption of knowledge of the broader Tibetan history and experiences of the Tibetan participants was not only felt, it was rather obvious. For example, a key part of the interviews was to understand participants' reasons for leaving Tibet, which for the ex-political prisoners included questions about their experiences with authorities both in Tibet and while crossing the border. In Dolma's case, during the discussion about her experience with the authorities inside Tibet, she explained that it was obvious that she – as a Tibetan, a nun and an ex-political prisoner – had the same experience as everyone else and that collective narrative need not to be discussed. In the early stages of Dolma's interview, she explicitly stated that it was obvious she was tortured in prison and further added that if Hedwards was actually researching Tibet (and was not a spy), the questions about the experience of torture need not to be asked. Going beyond what is documented in the (albeit) limited research (see Marshall, 2000), informal conversations and observations in Dharamsala reiterated an assumed understanding of the experiences of ex-political prisoners during their time in prison in Tibet, largely that those who were politically active were more likely to be subject to severe beatings and torture (Marshall, 2000).

Silence was also present as unspoken words. During the interview with Dolma, when the conversation about the experience with authorities arose, she stopped speaking, and her eyes everted to the scars on her arms and face, thus suggesting that her experience could be explained without words. However, in the research in Thailand, silence did not always translate into negative experiences. During an interview with Noi, a domestic worker, questions about her work and her employer were often left unanswered. Instead, her aunt-in-law, who was also her employer, answered the questions, and Noi just nodded and smiled to the responses. There are multiple reasons that could explain Noi's silence; the fieldwork notes highlight that she was a shy lady and not necessarily comfortable with a researcher from Bangkok in the house. The look in Noi's eyes and the discreet smiles suggested that this made her feel a little awkward and that Suwinthawong was perceived as a stranger. Alternatively, women who were working in restaurants had greater experience in holding conversations with strangers, so the interview experience would be less intimidating. While it would be easy to conclude that those who disclosed fewer details or were less forthcoming (such as the domestic workers) were potentially experiencing some kind of exploitation or had negative experiences working in Mukdahan, observations from the field suggest otherwise. In the case of Noi, who was less forthcoming with responses to questions about her employer and her work, she demonstrated a genuine comfort with the fact that a family member was there to support her and help her through the interview. Burnham and Theodore (2012, p. 9) indicated that '[a domestic worker], especially a nanny or caregiver, may begin employment as a stranger, an outsider, but rapidly enters into an intimate relationship with the family that employs her'. This also resonated with Waen's situation, as there was a clear intimacy and comfort between her and her employer that challenged the negative connotations that could be associated with this silence.

Wajnryb explains in her research with the children of Holocaust survivors, 'there is something about the experience of trauma that defies communicability, that constrains the person involved in the trauma from using language to give a voice to the experience" (Wajnryb, 2001, p. 84). In the same way that Ani Dolma did not discuss the details of her experience in prison, Ngawang's story was infused with ambiguity and silence. In response to a question about why she left Tibet, the researcher was faced with an uncomfortable silence between Ngawang and the interpreter, both of whom stopped short of continuing the description of what would make her second prison experience worse. Given the language barriers between the participant and the interviewer, it could be expected that some details would be lost in translation. Despite this, silence was a mutual recognition of a clearly understood, if not articulated, potential harm. This harm was clearly regarded and so well known that it did not warrant words.

The unspoken shared understanding during several interviews with participants in India reinforced the idea that there was an assumed knowledge of the collective experience that would be translated into an understanding of the individual experience. For Tibetan participants, this was a threat of imprisonment, the authorities harassing their families or preventing them from ever returning to Tibet. For the Lao domestic workers in Thailand, there was an expectation that the researcher, as a Thai citizen, would understand and know beforehand why they left their homes in Laos, and therefore she should not have to ask the questions. These factors shaped the narrative; they shaped what information was shared and what was not. These experiences highlight the importance of looking beyond what is said and taking into account context and personal circumstance (see also Hett & Hett, 2013). Further to this, these factors can not only influence the way persons share their own story, but they also affect the way we understand them in the context of much broader migration experiences.

Conclusions – recruiting, engaging and interpreting stories of migration from the Global South

Based on the fieldwork experience of both Hedwards and Suwinthawong, this chapter argues that the context in which the research is undertaken needs to be a central feature in the fieldwork preparation, as the local realities can have practical implications for conducting, engaging people in, and then interpreting interviews.

The experiences of both researchers in this chapter highlight how within different local settings, the same presumed challenges – such as migration status or gatekeepers – can be manifested in contextually distinct ways. As a result, the preparation for fieldwork needs to incorporate local expertise and relevant researcher experiences. Where Hedwards's initial approach provided an additional layer of anonymity by publicising the research only within trusted networks, the more public approach suggested by the ethics committee arguably prioritised acculturalised presumptions of Hedwards's power and position within the community and the impact of migration status in this context, which ultimately created a range of risks for participants. By emphasising local consultation at the early stages of fieldwork preparation, including the ethics processes, doctoral students in particular would be far better placed to navigate unexpected cultural and contextual nuances that can and do shape fieldwork. This will further ensure that research standards are not only upheld but the research is grounded in participants' realities and can provide an opportunity for better engagement with and ownership of the research and outcomes.

Each project sought to map the impact of the border and the ways in which bordering practices emerge out of personal and lived experiences of border crossings; however, the social and political context meant that the individual stories were shaped and presented in distinct ways. By examining the features of participants' narratives, the fluidity of power and positionality and its implications for the way in which participants engage with the research and the way their stories are interpreted was revealed. The research in Thailand demonstrated how power within a research setting is fluid; at some points, power may lie in the hands of gatekeepers, at others, power returns to the hands of the researcher. Alternatively, for the interviews in India, power was held by the gatekeeper – the Chinese government. This meant navigating an authority with great power within the research setting that rendered complex and politicised the accessing of the participants' personal narratives. While there was insufficient space to dedicate to unravelling the power dynamics across both projects, it forced both researchers to look beyond what was actually said and to document what was not.

By examining presumptions associated with all stakeholders in the research process and their role in the facilitation of fieldwork, this chapter has shown that the local context and reality shapes different research processes at different times and for different stakeholders. It has argued that position and power are not static within the interview setting and that both concepts should expand beyond the researcher to include everyone involved, the participants as well as gatekeepers. The proximity of each of the stakeholders is also important and, as this chapter has shown, is also influential not only in accessing participants, but also in the way that the participants engage with the researcher and in the interpretation of their narrative. By examining these experiences in a more detailed way that goes beyond just the methodological or reflexive experience, we can begin to unbundle the lived experience – of both participants and the researcher – from the presumptions that often underpin research with irregular migrants. Finally, by emphasising the importance of how we as researchers capture this experience and what we capture, we can develop a more complex understanding of borders and border practices.

Notes

1 For the purpose of this chapter, irregular migration captures the migration of people who do not have explicit legal permission to cross a particular border or enter a specific territory. In this case, it includes undocumented workers and asylum seekers or refugees.
2 A 'khata' is a silk scarf given as a sign of the giver's goodwill and regard for the recipient. Participants were offered this and some rupees on the advice of the interpreter, who also had significant experience in coordinating and conducting research with academics and universities.
3 Pseudonyms were employed in both projects, and they are used here.

References

Ackerly, B., & True, J. (2008). Reflexivity in practice: Power and ethics in feminist research on international relations. *International Studies Review, 10*, 693–707.

Ackerly, B., & True, J. (2010). Back to the future: Feminist theory, activism and doing feminist research in an age of globalisation. *Women's Studies International Forum, 33*, 464–472.

Aléx, L., & Hammarström, A. (2008). Shifts in power during an interview situation: Methodological reflections inspired by Foucault and Bourdieu. *Nursing Inquiry, 15*(2), 169–176.

Archavanitkul, K., & Hall, A. (2011). *International migration in Thailand*. Bangkok: International Organization for Migration.

Barnett, R. (2010). Understated legacies: Uses of oral history and Tibetan studies. *Inner Asia, 12*, 63–93.

Bonnin, C. (2010). Navigating fieldwork politics, practicalities and ethics in the upland borders of northern Vietnam. *Asia-Pacific Viewpoint, 51*(2), 179–192.

Bosworth, M., & Guild, M. (2008). Governing through migration control. *British Journal of Criminology, 48*(6), 703–719.

Burnham, L., & Theodore, N. (2012). *Home economics: The invisible and unregulated world of domestic workers*. New York: National Domestic Workers Alliance.

Hett, G., & Hett, J. (2013). Ethics in intercultural research: Reflections on the challenges of conducting field research in a Syrian context. *Journal of Comparative International Education, 43*(4), 496–515.

Hudson, B. (2007). The criminalisation of migration. *Criminal Justice Matters, 70*(1), 35–36.

Hugo, G. (2012). International labour migration and migration policies in Southeast Asia. *Asian Journal of Social Science, 40*, 392–418.

Human Rights Watch. (2013, June 27). *They say we should be grateful*. Online. Retrieved September 20, 2017, from www.hrw.org/report/2013/06/27/they-say-we-should-be-grateful/mass-rehousing-and-relocation-programs-tibetan

Human Rights Watch. (2016a, January 18). *China: No end to Tibet surveillance program*. Online. Retrieved September 20, 2017, from www.hrw.org/news/2016/01/18/china-no-end-tibet-surveillance-program

Human Rights Watch. (2016b, May 22). *Relentless: Detention and prosecution of Tibetans under China's 'stability maintenance' campaign*. Online. Retrieved September 20, 2017, from www.hrw.org/report/2016/05/22/relentless-detention-and-prosecution-tibetans-under-chinas-stability-maintenance

Khosravi, S. (2009). Sweden: Detention and deportation of asylum seekers. *Race and Class*, *50*(4), 38–56.

Luanglatbandith, R., & Leuangkhamsing, S. (2016). Asian development outlook 2016: Asia's potential growth. *Asian Development Bank*. Retrieved September 20, 2017, from www.adb.org/sites/default/files/publication/182221/ado2016.pdf

Marshall, S. D. (2000). Rukhag 3: The nuns of Drapchi prison. *International Campaign for Tibet*. Retrieved September 20, 2017, from www.savetibet.org/rukhag-3-the-nuns-of-drapchi-prison/

Miller, K. E. (2004). Beyond the frontstage: Trust, access, and the relational context in research. *American Journal Psychology*, *33*(3/4), 271–227.

Phouxay, K. (2010). *Patterns of migration and socio-economic change in Lao PDR*. Sweden: Department of Social and Economic Geography, Umeå University.

Pickering, S., & Weber, L. (2006). *Borders, mobility and technologies of control*. Dordrecht, The Netherlands: Springer.

Rukumnuaykit, P. (2009). *A synthesis report on labour migration policies, management and immigration pressure in Thailand*. ILO/Japan Project on Managing Cross-Border Movement of Labour in Southeast Asia Regional Office for Asia and the Pacific, Thailand.

Wajnryb, R. (2001). *The silence: How tragedy shapes talk*. Australia: Allen & Unwin.

Weber, L. (2007). Policing the virtual border: Punitive preemption in Australian offshore migration control. *Social Justice*, *34*(2), 77–93.

World Bank. (2006). *Lao PDR: Rural and agriculture sector issues paper*. Online. Retrieved September 20, 2017, from http://documents.worldbank.org/curated/en/295881468300856900/pdf/375660LA0Rural1ctor0Issues01PUBLIC1.pdf

Chapter 8

Life and death in immigration detention

Dominic Aitken[1]

Introduction

Immigration detention in the UK has expanded rapidly since the turn of the millennium, yet immigration removal centres (IRCs) remain something of a mystery. How they are run, what they are like and whether they can be justified are difficult questions to answer (Bosworth, 2013; Costello, 2015). Few people are allowed inside them (Bosworth, 2012; Hall, 2012), and periodic controversies have made Home Office officials and centre managers reluctant to let outsiders in. Since the early 2000s there have been occasional rooftop protests, hunger strikes, riots and deaths (for an overview see Bosworth, 2014; Shaw, 2016). When these episodes are brought to our attention, a default state of secrecy is interrupted by a flash of negative publicity.

IRCs are, by any account, low-visibility spaces. They are usually located near airports or in parts of the country that are difficult to reach (Bosworth & Slade, 2014). It is easy to infer from this that IRCs are shielded from meaningful scrutiny and public accountability. Like many secure establishments, there seems to be something insular about IRCs, perhaps an air of defensiveness about what goes on inside them. But how reliable are these impressions? If all we have to go on are undercover recordings of shocking behaviour or partisan opinion pieces from across the political spectrum, we are unlikely to learn a great deal about IRCs. There are plenty of people who would like to know more about immigration detention, yet information and understanding are in short supply. So where should a relative of a detainee, a journalist, an academic, a Member of Parliament or a concerned citizen go to find out about the hidden world of detention? How are we to make sense of the sharp end of British immigration control?

This chapter addresses these questions by drawing on two research projects about immigration detention. In the first section I reflect on my experience as a research assistant working alongside Mary Bosworth on a study about IRC staff and their relationships with detainees. The project began with a period of observations during which we spoke to staff informally about their work and professional experience while also seeing their routine interactions with detainees. This research project was my first encounter with the British immigration detention estate, and the first section of this chapter draws on the observational data I gathered rather than the qualitative interviews we subsequently conducted with staff. I reflect more broadly on what it was like to enter an IRC and some of the methodological issues I encountered doing an exploratory research project on everyday life for staff and detainees. I argue in this section that IRCs are distinctive places in many ways and describe some of the peculiarities and problems of researching them, recounting details from the project. Many of the issues discussed are likely to affect any researchers interested in IRCs, for example the challenge of interpreting staff–detainee relationships, feelings of discomfort or guilt and the uncertainty and ambiguity of detention life more generally.

The second section describes my ongoing doctoral research into deaths in custody. This project has so far involved 50 interviews with individuals who prevent and investigate deaths in custody, particularly suicides in IRCs and prisons. These interviews have largely been with individuals located outside the four walls of detention and prison, for example elite interviews with senior coroners and members of expert panels on deaths in custody. I discuss the appeal and difficulties of taking a broad approach to understanding deaths in custody and suggest that there is much to be learned about detention from within and without.

Immigration removal centres

Academics strive for clarity, accuracy and rigour in their work (Liebling, 2011), but immigration detention often seems resistant to these standards. IRCs are hard to describe and difficult to understand (Bosworth, 2014). There is little information about them in the public domain, employees are encouraged not to speak about their work to outsiders and detainees are a politically weak group. These factors are compounded by a reluctance to allow outsiders in. But spending time inside detention does not always clarify matters. My impression that IRCs are elusive and confusing places was formed early on in a research project about IRC staff and their relationships with detainees, and it remained with me throughout. The primary purpose of this research was to understand staff experiences and tap into their perspectives on working in an IRC. But in the course of doing fieldwork we inevitably encountered many other aspects of detention life, which I reflect on in this section.

Changing places

IRCs contain a highly diverse and rapidly changing population. Diversity in detention is predictably racialised (Bosworth & Kellezi, 2014) and is one of the most striking features of entering an IRC, particularly if it is located in a part of the UK where the local population is predominantly white. The vast majority of detainees are ethnic minority men from the Global South, some of whom have lived in Britain for decades and face the prospect of deportation to a country they have not been to since childhood (Bosworth, 2014).

Official statistics confirm that around 3,000 people are in detention in the UK on any given day, while approximately 30,000 people pass through detention each year (Home Office, 2016). The number of people in detention tends to be represented statistically, but there is also a distinctive qualitative dimension to population turnover. IRCs constantly receive and release people, while a small number of individuals find themselves stuck for months or even years in the immigration estate (Griffiths, 2014; Turnbull, 2016).

Our research project took place in autumn 2015 at Heathrow IRC in West London.[2] Over the course of a few weeks we saw many detainees come and go, making everyday life in the centre seem transient and impersonal. In the early stages of research the constant movement of people and property was striking. It was hard to keep track of what was going on when almost every aspect of detention was new to me, not least the physical layout of the centre and the daily regime. I took detailed notes about the minutiae of the centre, the interactions I saw and what services were available to detainees. But the sheer novelty of detention meant I had little time to pause and reflect on what all this activity was for. The desire to understand what was happening and how things worked often obscured more fundamental questions about why people were being held in the first place. As far as possible, I tried to fill my fieldwork diary with accurate, detailed description of what I saw and heard, but also questions about the broader purposes and justification of detaining people in this manner.

My own feeling that the centre was a mixture of constant movement and numbing repetitiveness was echoed by the staff. As Rob from the security unit put it, 'It is 90% routine and 10% chaos'. Many others agreed, although they would tend to fixate on the chaos, offering dramatic accounts of how insecure and unpredictable the centre used to be. Their stories often recounted detainee violence and staff use of force, which prompted smirks from other detainee custody officers (DCOs) who recognised the scenarios. A young man like me was an ideal audience for these tales of machismo and authorised violence, but they also provided an opportunity for male staff to convey that they were embattled and demoralised. DCOs on more than one occasion confided in me that they were glad someone was 'taking an interest in us for once' or 'hearing our side of the story'. Staff were often appreciative that someone appeared interested in them, although we had no intentions of taking sides with staff rather than detainees, as we were interested in how both groups interacted with each other (Becker, 1967; Liebling, 2001).

As we became more familiar to staff, the research team became a sounding board for complaints about the private provider who ran the IRC. We noticed a marked disparity between how senior management talked about the centre and how operational staff felt, and it was difficult not to be affected by the constant flow of staff pessimism and their feelings of powerlessness. Describing the different private contractors who had run the centre over the years, Julia from healthcare said, 'Every time a new company takes over you think it's gonna get better and it gets worse'. She and others were dismayed that so many experienced staff had left and been replaced by younger employees on cheaper contracts. DCOs in particular expressed a generic sense of decline, with serious concerns about staffing levels, shift patterns and senior management support. These problems were especially acute for DCOs whose personal lives were also painful. For some, long hours were combined with domestic violence, divorce, ill health or family tragedy. Their testimonies made it clear that IRCs, like prisons (Liebling, 1999a; Jewkes, 2011; Crewe et al., 2014), are intensely emotional places for the detainees, staff and researchers who enter them.

To overcome these challenges, I reminded myself that researchers do not need to solve problems but to identify and understand them. Irrespective of whether we were present in the centre, detainees would suffer and members of staff would struggle. In this context, our aims were relatively modest and open ended. I was careful to explain that the research was not a form of monitoring or inspection and tried to make employees feel comfortable with my presence. By mentioning the themes of my discussions so far, such as staffing levels and relationships with detainees, employees often began to engage with me, voicing their opinions or dissenting from their colleagues. For myself, I wrote extensive notes each day and occasionally made short audio recordings when I left the centre. These allowed me to make sense of what I was witnessing as the research progressed and gave me a chance to express discomfort, confusion or frustration about detention without any adverse consequences. On days when both my supervisor and I were there together, conversations in the car back to Oxford allowed us to think through what we had seen and felt.

Staying put

While some individuals came and went every day, contributing to a sense that the IRC was almost unknowable, many detainees languished in their rooms for days on end, frustrated and withdrawn. Similarly, some detainees were held in less visible parts of the centre, such as the healthcare unit. These areas had a slower pace of life than elsewhere but were revealing in their own way. Over the course of a week I saw one detainee, Andriy, go from being argumentative with staff to being so sedated he could hardly speak. As I was doing healthcare observations, Andriy periodically walked up to the office door, looked blankly at staff and attempted to talk, occasionally muttering a few words or walking away, having said nothing.

Most members of staff were patient and sensitive with Andriy, recognising that he was heavily medicated and confused. However, one DCO, John, in mid-conversation with a colleague when Andriy approached them, was less tactful. Sensing that he was being interrupted for no good reason, John commanded Andriy, 'Speak up! Express yourself!' His remarks shocked me, although I stayed quiet in the corner of the staff office. Soon after Andriy had left, another DCO mocked him in his absence. This interaction soon led to disparaging remarks about other detainees, as Karen told her colleagues, 'We've got a psycho coming in today at 5.30'. Noticing my presence in the room and sensing my discomfort, another DCO, Ian, said defensively, 'You get hardened working in these places. Tougher sense of humour'.

A DCO, Harry, later came in to ask about Andriy:

'Does he know he's got a flight tomorrow?'
'He's being sectioned. He's not going on a flight'.
'Yeah but does he *know* he's got a flight?'
'I think so'.
'That'll do for me'.
'Feel free to go and talk to him'.
'I'm not stupid'.

Healthcare staff knew far more about Andriy than others elsewhere in the centre, but information about him had not been shared properly. Their main priority, it seemed, was to manage the 'risk' he presented by ensuring that he remained medicated and passive. Over the course of a few hours Andriy had been treated with patience and courtesy as well as cold indifference. Despite the variable quality of relationships staff had with him and other detainees, DCOs consistently described their work as 'caring for' detainees and 'looking after them while they are here'.

Another hidden space within detention is the segregation unit, often euphemistically called the 'care and separation' unit. One day I was taken to see Roshan, who was, according to staff, on a 'dirty protest'. When I arrived with two senior members of staff, Roshan was lying face down, depressed and reluctant to speak. His bed was covered in urine, and I was told that he had various physical health problems, having been deemed unfit to fly a month earlier. A senior member of staff, Richard, stood beside his bed saying, 'It's not gonna do you any good lying in bed all day. We're just trying to help you'.

Seeing situations like this, it was natural to wonder how Roshan came to be in detention in the first place, ending up in such a squalid, austere space. These moments brought into sharp relief how distant immigration decision makers were from the consequences of their actions. I found these sights upsetting and uncomfortable but felt unable to express such feelings to the middle-aged men showing me around. For them it was normal. Over the course of their careers, they had worked in difficult prisons or had been on duty during detention riots, so seeing Roshan in segregation had little emotional impact. However long he stayed in segregation, there would soon be someone to replace him. As I stood wondering whether I could ever become desensitised to the segregation environment, the duty manager was called to an incident elsewhere. We left the unit immediately, and I heard no more about Roshan.

Pain and suffering caused by detention are not always hidden, and researchers often have to confront them directly (e.g. Gerlach, this volume). During our research project, a DCO recommended that I speak to Tony, a new detainee who was finding life difficult. Tony told me the painful story of how he had been in prison before coming to immigration detention, losing his business along the way and nearly destroying his family life. I had asked him a few initial questions about what he thought of this centre compared to the last one he had been in. I asked about the food, internet access and the gym, but these questions seemed trivial. Tony soon began to speak uninterrupted for an hour and a half about his life and identity, becoming more animated as he described layer upon layer of hardship, all of which had culminated in his indefinite detention. When I left Tony and thanked him for his time, I returned to the staff on the wing, who could tell I seemed drained. 'Did he talk your ear off? Welcome to our world!' I was glad to have spoken to Tony, but I was overwhelmed by our conversation. Unlike detainees and staff, I was free to leave if I wanted. I did not have to sleep there or arrive home late and go in early the next day for another 13-hour shift. I was aware that my own freedom limited my understanding of the centre. At half past four that afternoon, shortly after speaking to Tony, I went home exhausted and knowing that his dispiriting story was one of many.

The individual stories of detainees and staff are reminders that IRCs are highly social environments. They require a constant flow of communication and rely on human relationships to function. But they are also complex bureaucracies replete with processes and paperwork (Bosworth, 2014). At times I had to feign interest in the details of IRC administration or watched as staff handed out toothbrushes, gave detainees paracetamol and helped them fill in forms. The staff–detainee interactions I saw tended to be very brief, often lasting no more than a few seconds. Whereas in prisons staff might be expected to form more meaningful professional relationships with inmates (e.g. Crawley, 2004; Crewe, Liebling, & Hulley, 2015), it was unclear what a word like 'rapport', popular in a culture of corporate management speak, meant in the short-termist detention context. The language used in the detention centre was often sanitised, and I came across many forms, posters and notices that referred to 'residents' and 'service delivery'. There was a stark contrast between such official language and the vivid, direct way that detainees (and some staff) spoke about detention.

This brief description of my experience going into an IRC highlights several important things about them and the research process more generally. Immigration detention is a racialised environment in which the global, national and local mix. The variety of languages spoken, religions observed and life experiences compressed into a small space is extraordinary. In academic research it is common to represent these facts statistically, but diversity also has a qualitative dimension. It is difficult to convey the sound of multiple languages echoing in a packed corridor or the confusion I felt speaking to a 'foreign national' detainee with a strong London accent.

With many people moving in and out of IRCs, they produce a great deal of interaction while remaining somewhat impersonal. Staff–detainee conversations tended to be brief and instrumental, although small gestures could make staff's administrative work more humane and personal. Making the effort to help someone contact their solicitor or taking the time to fetch a bottle of bleach for someone's room are not actions that are likely to be recorded or measured, but they are important acts of recognition (Bosworth & Slade, 2014). At the same time, much of the emotional intensity of detention is mediated by a mass of paperwork and procedure, which helps to rationalise a system that otherwise feels unpredictable and often questionable. I left detention feeling that I still did not understand it but resolved that this was not entirely due to my limitations as a researcher. Some of the uncertainty and confusion I felt reflected the nature of detention itself (Bosworth, 2014).

The IRC research project I have described was about everyday life in detention for staff and detainees. It focused on the routine aspects of IRCs rather than moments of high drama. There are, however, events in custody that prompt serious reflection about detention. In the next section I consider what happens when people die in custody and how deaths, which start as localised tragedies affecting a small number of people, become public concerns, opening up detention and imprisonment to the wider world.

Researching deaths in custody

I argued in the previous section that IRCs are opaque institutions, prone to myths and misconceptions. To researchers who are able to get inside them, detention centres frequently confuse and trouble us. With relatively little information available to the public on life inside IRCs, researchers have to make do with whatever fragments of experience and expertise we can find. Ethnographic and other qualitative methods are a particularly promising way of understanding IRCs (Hall, 2012; Bosworth, 2014), as they allow us to draw on existing theories and concepts while helping to generate new ideas. By spending extended periods of time with detainees and staff, qualitative research can help us understand everyday life in detention and contribute to informed criticism of IRCs. But if most people are unable to go into IRCs and talk directly to those who live and work there, how else might we understand them?

There are times when IRCs are subject to a degree of external scrutiny. The work of Her Majesty's Prisons Inspectorate is one example, where the inspection team can visit IRCs or prisons unannounced, go anywhere, speak to anyone and access a great deal of paperwork and confidential information. There are also ad hoc investigations following major incidents such as 'disturbances' or reviews into the state of immigration detention (Shaw, 2016). Deaths in IRCs also trigger formal investigations and, on occasion, prompt broader debates about the purposes and culture of immigration detention.

My doctoral research concerns responses to deaths in custody, focusing on suicides in prison and immigration detention. I have so far completed 50 semi-structured, qualitative interviews with coroners, lawyers, academics, reform groups, inspectors and investigators. Many of those I have spoken to only know the prison system, and they are often curious to know more about immigration detention. At present there is a limited amount of literature on deaths in IRCs, and much of the writing on this subject is critical of immigration control (Pirouet, 1994; Ryan, 1995; Athwal & Bourne, 2007; Athwal, 2015; Medical Justice, 2016). Deaths in detention are relatively rare compared to many prisons. Some IRCs have had no deaths, while others have had deaths from natural causes, suicides or other non-natural deaths. There are typically no more than two or three deaths per year in the immigration estate (Medical Justice, 2016), and with such a small number of cases it is difficult to establish trends or make generalisations about the statistical prevalence of the problem. A public official, Michael, who was familiar with both the prison and immigration estates, suggested to me that the biggest puzzle about IRCs is why there are so few deaths, given the vulnerability of the population and the widespread anxiety about deportation. Irrespective of how many deaths there are, suicide prevention and the management of vulnerable detainees are routine aspects of running IRCs.

My decision to research deaths in custody was influenced in part by research on the 'pains of imprisonment' (Sykes, 1958; Crewe, 2012), including prison suicides (Liebling, 1992; Liebling, 1999b; Liebling & Ludlow, 2016). There has been some recent public debate about the high number of suicides in prisons in England and Wales, and suicide rates are one of many overlapping problems in the penal system. Criminological research into prison suicide has often involved interviews with prisoners themselves (e.g. Liebling, 1992), but I decided to avoid this approach. Interviewing vulnerable prisoners and detainees would have been profoundly upsetting, and since I did not expect my research to improve prisoners' or detainees' lives, I felt it would have been unethical to ask so much of people for little in return. Moreover, there are other actors who are rarely discussed in the literature but who are central to understanding how deaths in custody are prevented and responded to, such as coroners, solicitors and reform groups. By interviewing a mixture of people inside and outside the system, I hope to place deaths in custody in their wider context.

My research began from the assumption that deaths are a profoundly important event in custody (Liebling, 2017), likely to provide broader insights into the world of immigration detention and imprisonment. They open up hidden sites and necessitate official investigations by the state, whose representatives assess whether processes were followed properly and if lessons can be learned. Deaths also raise a set of contentious political questions about the relationship between state power and vulnerable individuals, the right to life and duties of care (e.g. Harris, 2015). These theoretical issues are in some cases overlaid with suggestions of racial discrimination or debates about staff culture (Shaw & Coles, 2007; Athwal, 2015). Deaths in custody therefore invite us to reflect on many aspects of IRCs and prisons, including fundamental questions about care, power and inequality, as well as more practical questions about information sharing and organisational culture. The following section describes the process of conducting my own research on this issue and offers some methodological reflections along the way.

Sources and subjects

There is an abundance of written material on deaths in custody. The official policies on suicide and self-harm prevention are available for IRCs and prisons, as well as regular statistics compiled by the government. The Prisons and Probation Ombudsman (PPO) has an online database of its investigations into all deaths in IRCs, prisons, courts, approved premises and secure training centres since 2004, in addition to annual reports and thematic reviews.[3] Coroners, who hold inquests into all deaths in custody, are under a duty to issue a Prevention of Future Death report when concerns have been identified in a particular case. In addition to reports resulting from these two official investigative processes, there are many other sources in the public domain. The Independent Advisory Panel on Deaths in Custody, part of a three-tier Ministerial Council on Deaths in Custody, has done research that builds on the existing body of academic work on prison suicides conducted by criminologists (Liebling, 1992; Liebling, 1999b; Liebling & Ludlow, 2016), psychiatrists (Fazel et al., 2008, 2011) and psychologists (Towl & Crighton, 2017; Walker & Towl, 2016). Over the years, major reviews have also addressed deaths in custody, particularly suicides in prison (e.g. HMCIP, 1999; Harris, 2015). In short, deaths in custody provoke a great deal of commentary and analysis.

Written records have proven useful to me when researching deaths in detention and prison, but there are many limitations to these sources. Perhaps most importantly, investigators and coroners routinely find that official policy is not implemented in practice (e.g. PPO, 2014). There is broad agreement that the official suicide and self-harm policies and documents for prisons and IRCs are adequate. The problem, however, is that decision making about safety in custody is often context sensitive. Staff must use discretion and judgement to prevent deaths, and they are influenced by their occupational culture and the resources available to them.

As I began to interview those involved in PPO investigations and inquests, my impressions of these official processes started to change. The standard texts on coronial law, for example, stress that this legal process is inquisitorial rather than adversarial in nature (e.g. Matthews, 2014, pp. 7–10). An inquest is not about apportioning blame or drawing sweeping conclusions about the culture of an IRC or prison. Inquests are instead fact-finding exercises concerned with a narrow set of questions. In my interviews, however, a different picture has emerged. As an experienced barrister, Olivia, put it to me: 'I have never been in an Article 2 [right to life] inquest that is not adversarial and that's the end of it.

I cross-examine, and if I was stopped from cross-examining, I would complain. They are adversarial'.

Like the distinction between policy and practice, there is a difference between legal formality and how legal proceedings are carried out. It is only through interviewing those involved in the process that I have come to understand the role of conflict and emotion in inquests. Interviewees have characterised the coroner's court as a potentially combative environment, despite the inquisitorial status of the proceedings. A senior coroner, Robert, described prison death inquests by saying:

> The fiction in these cases is that it is inquisitorial. It's a mixture, really. You've got an adversarial element. And when you think of our duty in an Article 2 case – identifying the issues and seeing where mistakes have been made – it's difficult for a family's lawyer not to be just a touch adversarial because you need to get the evidence out. It's interesting, in my experience of a long inquest, you'll have the first day or two where there's sort of muscle-bulging and posturing by barristers. By day three, they've all settled down, realised that cooperation is rather better than open warfare, and you have a really good inquest.

The adversarial quality of some inquests is illustrated by how Sarah, a solicitor who represents bereaved families, spoke about government lawyers:

> I couldn't ever work for the [NHS] Trust or the prison. I mean, I just couldn't do that job and I don't know how a lot of people do that job given the instructions that they're given [about] how they should deal with inquests. You know, the fairly well-publicised cases of other interested parties turning up and deciding that they'll blame the deceased, that they'll blame family members of the deceased and that will be their tactics for a certain inquest. In essence, prison barristers . . . their role is to try and restrict the scope of the inquest as much as possible and to restrict criticism of their client and to ensure that the coroner doesn't make any Prevention of Future Death reports.

These conflict dynamics are an important part of understanding what inquests are like, but they also have methodological implications for my research. Few interviewees who represent bereaved families have recommended that I speak to government lawyers. There is a sense that only those on the side of the family can be trusted to tell the truth. Sonia, a solicitor who has dealt with many custodial inquests, described her experience with some government lawyers:

> Ideally the inquest process is supposed to be inquisitorial, there's not supposed to be any parties, any winners or losers, it's not supposed to attribute blame. But with state authorities, it doesn't work like that. They all

> individually lawyer up and it makes the whole process a lot more aggressive and contentious and difficult for families as well. I've noticed that the prison lawyers have become more and more aggressive lately and minimised the failings or any problems and issues within the prison. That's been really difficult.

When interviewees express anger, disgust or frustration to me about how a deceased person was portrayed in court or how the bereaved family was treated, it is a reminder of the seriousness of the subject matter. But it also hints at a more basic point about imprisonment and detention: they are fundamentally contested and controversial. Even dispassionate professionals who deal with inquests daily find themselves embroiled in the emotions and ethics of the issue. They cannot stand objectively outside their subject matter, and nor can I. Conflict and emotion are in this sense constitutive parts of deaths in custody. State investigations by the PPO and coroners attempt to keep emotions at a manageable distance, but in truth they can never be entirely removed.

Opening up

Researching deaths in custody has allowed me to understand aspects of detention and imprisonment that would otherwise remain hidden from view. An immigration lawyer, Clive, told me that he finds the IRC system confusing but that the aftermath of a death is uniquely illuminating:

> It's the only situation where there's that level of scrutiny, where you get to question all the different people. We bring a case for unlawful detention and it's against the Home Office. You might get a Home Office witness who may or may not have been involved in the decision making. But you never get custodial staff or healthcare. [An inquest] gets everyone together.

These comments chimed with my view that deaths invite reflection and scrutiny in a way that few other issues do. They provide a window into detention precisely because they are rare and unexpected. Yet Clive was refreshingly honest that he did not fully understand the system he was criticising. He spoke of how strange and exhausting inquests were compared to other legal work. As with immigration detention more generally, I have often felt that deaths in custody are an unknowable subject and that interviews can never capture the full emotional and ethical depth of the issue.

Many other interviewees have been frank about the limits of their knowledge and understanding. Linda, an experienced investigator of deaths in custody, reminded me that there is a great deal she does not see:

> It is necessary to say that we only ever see the most acute cases. And I absolutely am convinced that so much good work goes on in prison, but

we unfortunately never see it.... We do look at a very weird snapshot of cases.

These comments are important because it is easy for conversations about deaths to become relentlessly pessimistic. During interviews I have heard little about crises that were managed well or times when IRC or prison staff acted in a compassionate, professional way. Perhaps interviewees are unwilling to acknowledge these examples lest they be seen to be legitimising detention or shoring up state power. But it is nevertheless true that many serious problems in custody are solved early on and therefore never come to anyone's attention. On the rare occasion that deaths do occur, they are rarely the result of a single error or oversight. As a charity worker, Nicola, described it: 'Often when you look at the deaths, there are lots of little things that broke down. There isn't one massive failure that caused it'.

Responsibility for preventing deaths is supposed to be shared by everyone in custody in a multidisciplinary fashion, but in practice this can mean that no one feels personally responsible. Nicola went on, 'In detention, there are so many actors. It's complex, so they can hide behind each other'.

It is certainly true that things can go wrong in many ways in detention. But there is also reason to believe that suicide risk and vulnerability are influenced not only by what individual members of staff do but also by what detention is ultimately for. Being detained in the first place and the possibility of deportation cause a great deal of anxiety, yet they are beyond the scope of official investigations. Michael, the public official mentioned earlier, argued that:

> The problems weren't really created by the people in the detention centres, they were created by the people detaining.... To understand the problem you need to take a broad view of how the system as a whole is operating, rather than look very narrowly at individual behaviours, either of staff or of detainees.

These comments have led me to believe that deaths in custody ought to be approached as a systemic issue. They suggest that a wide lens is more desirable than a narrow focus. I have tried to use these observations as a guide to my research, generally believing that speaking to as broad a range of people as possible is the best approach. But with a congested field, I cannot speak to everyone. As several interviewees have noted, the sheer number of competing voices on deaths in custody makes it difficult to build consensus about how to address this issue. Between government, IRCs and prisons, trade unions, healthcare staff, investigators, inspectors, lawyers, academic experts, reform groups and journalists, there is a lot of room for disagreement. Some of those involved in the three-tier Ministerial Council on Deaths in Custody, which looks at deaths in prison, immigration detention and other settings, have described it as 'like wading through treacle'. Different government departments try to limit their responsibility, while professional organisations talk past one another. In doing my research I have tried to sample the wide array of voices on this issue, but there will be many I have missed: retired civil servants, prisoners locked in their cell for 23 hours a day or detainees who were deported the day before I entered an IRC. There is always a possibility that I will miss the real story by omitting one group or another.

With a slew of different players involved, my research project has felt less clearly defined than I had hoped. At times its lack of focus has made people unwilling to speak to me. One coroner told me he would not participate because my topic was too vague. A charity for detainees suggested I was approaching the issue from a 'Home Office perspective'. Some of those invited to interview have been uncomfortable with the subject matter, feeling that deaths are too serious an issue to be discussed with a stranger or worried that a meeting with me could create problems with the Home Office or an IRC centre manager. They usually asked not to be audio recorded. As I took down notes of their answers, they spoke quietly and remained guarded throughout the conversation.

Feeling at times that my research is too broad, I have occasionally been tempted to narrow its parameters. Perhaps I should focus on the internal life of IRCs and try to come up with technocratic solutions to particular problems, such as improving screening procedures for at-risk groups or suggesting ways to facilitate information sharing between detention centres. But such an approach would close off many of the most important questions about IRCs and prisons, such as the basic themes of power, inequality and accountability.

Interviewing a wide range of stakeholders has changed how I have conceptualised detention and imprisonment in the first place. My initial impression that IRCs and prisons are strictly bounded institutions, with a sharp distinction between those inside and those not, has been qualified. Separating inside and outside is not so simple, and deaths in custody illustrate the connections between the internal world of custody and its external surroundings. Those who work in IRCs enter and leave every day, just as some detainees arrive and others are released. Healthcare professionals, lawyers, translators, Home Office officials, charities, academics, priests, imams, artists, ambassadors and others all find themselves within and without. I have tried to make my research reflect a field that is varied and complex, influenced by the high politics of national sovereignty and border control as well as more localised discussions about resource allocation and staff culture in different establishments. As a matter of research methodology, my aim has been to find a middle ground between abstract social theory and more detailed institutional studies of life in detention or prison. Although this sometimes means that I have felt uncertain about the appropriate 'level of analysis', I remain convinced that sites of confinement should be seen as embedded in wider society, not as standalone institutions.

Conclusion

Researching IRCs is challenging. They are difficult to access in the first place, and there is always a chance that access, once granted, will be taken away. As I spent more time researching staff–detainee relationships in detention, I was perennially uncertain about the character and dynamics of IRCs. While IRCs are plainly embedded in the politics of asylum and migration and reflect global inequalities of various kinds, they also have a rich internal life that cannot be second-guessed using academic theory. There seems to be no substitute for the detail and texture of primary empirical research.

At the same time, getting inside detention is not the only thing that matters. As I have discovered through interviews on deaths in custody, detention and imprisonment are connected to the outside world in many ways. By maintaining a certain distance from IRCs, it has been easier to question their assumptions and challenge what many people believe about them. It has also lessened the considerable emotional toll of institutional research. When inside, it is natural to feel that what goes on is so complex that it is beyond anyone's control. Bureaucratic state power seems too entrenched to be challenged or reformed in any meaningful way. But that is a complacent attitude. Researching the inside and outside of detention can bring us closer to understanding how IRCs work and analysing them as institutions. Describing them carefully and honestly is essential if we want to provide informed, critical commentary on immigration detention.

Notes

1 I would like to thank the editors and Mary Bosworth for comments on an earlier draft of this chapter.
2 Heathrow IRC refers to two adjacent sites, Harmondsworth and Colnbrook. They were previously run by GEO and Serco, respectively, and came under the central management of Mitie Care & Custody in 2014. Although we spent time in both sites, the observational data used in this chapter is from Harmondsworth, the larger and older of the two centres.
3 Deaths during or following police contact are investigated separately by the Independent Police Complaints Commission (see Baker, 2016).

References

Athwal, H. (2015). 'I don't have a life to live': Deaths and UK detention. *Race & Class, 56*(3), 50–68.
Athwal, H., & Bourne, J. (2007). Driven to despair: Asylum deaths in the UK. *Race & Class, 48*(4), 106–114.
Baker, D. (2016). *Deaths after police contact: Constructing accountability in the 21st century*. London: Palgrave Macmillan.
Becker, H. (1967). Whose side are we on? *Social Problems, 14*(3), 239–247.
Bosworth, M. (2012). Subjectivity and identity in detention: Punishment and society in a global age. *Theoretical Criminology, 16*(2), 123–140.

Bosworth, M. (2013). Can immigration detention centres be legitimate? Understanding confinement in a global world. In K. F. Aas & M. Bosworth (Eds.), *The borders of punishment: Migration, citizenship, and social exclusion.* Oxford: Oxford University Press.

Bosworth, M. (2014). *Inside immigration detention.* Oxford: Oxford University Press.

Bosworth, M., & Kellezi, B. (2014). Citizenship and belonging in a women's immigration detention centre. In C. Phillips & C. Webster (Eds.), *New directions in race, ethnicity and crime.* Abingdon: Routledge.

Bosworth, M., & Slade, G. (2014). In search of recognition: Gender and staff-detainee relations in a British immigration detention centre. *Punishment & Society, 16*(2), 169–186.

Costello, C. (2015). Immigration detention: The grounds beneath our feet. *Current Legal Problems, 68*(1), 143–177.

Crawley, E. (2004). *Doing prison work: The public and private lives of prison officers.* Cullompton: Willan.

Crewe, B. (2012). Depth, weight, tightness: Revisiting the pains of imprisonment. *Punishment & Society, 11*(5), 509–529.

Crewe, B., Liebling, A., & Hulley, S. (2015). Staff-prisoner relationships, staff professionalism, and the use of authority in public- and private-sector prisons. *Law & Social Inquiry, 40,* 309–344.

Crewe, B., Warr, J., Bennett, P., & Smith, A. (2014). The emotional geography of prison life. *Theoretical Criminology, 18*(1), 56–74.

Fazel, S., Cartwright, J., Noman-Nott, A., & Hawton, K. (2008). Suicide in prisoners: A systematic review of risk factors. *Journal of Clinical Psychiatry, 69,* 1721–1731.

Fazel, S., Grann, M., Kling, B., & Hawton, K. (2011). Prison suicide in 12 countries: An ecological study of 861 suicides during 2003–2007. *Social Psychiatry and Psychiatric Epidemiology, 46,* 191–195.

Griffiths, M. (2014). Out of time: The temporal uncertainties of refused asylum seekers and immigration detainees. *Journal of Ethnic and Migration Studies, 40*(12), 1991–2009.

Hall, A. (2012). *Border watch: Cultures of immigration, detention and control.* London: Pluto.

Harris, T. (2015). *Changing prisons, saving lives: Report of the independent review into self-inflicted deaths in custody of 18–24 year olds.* London: Ministry of Justice.

HMCIP. (1999). *Suicide is everyone's concern: A thematic review by HM chief inspectorate of prisons for England and Wales.* London: Home Office.

Home Office. (2016). *National statistics: Detention. Immigration statistics January to March 2016.* Online. Retrieved June 15, 2017, from www.gov.uk/government/publications/immigration-statistics-january-to-march-2016/detention

Jewkes, Y. (2011). Autoethnography and emotion as intellectual resources: Doing prison research differently. *Qualitative Inquiry, 18*(1), 63–75.

Liebling, A. (1992). *Suicides in prison.* London: Routledge.

Liebling, A. (1999a). Doing research in prison: Breaking the silence? *Theoretical Criminology, 3*(2), 147–173.

Liebling, A. (1999b). Prison suicide and prisoner coping. In M. Tonry & J. Petersilia (Eds.), *Crime and justice* (Vol. 26). Chicago, IL: University of Chicago Press.

Liebling, A. (2001). Whose side are we on? Theory, practice and allegiances in prisons research. *British Journal of Criminology, 41*(3), 472–484.

Liebling, A. (2011). Being a criminologist: Investigation as a lifestyle and living. In M. Bosworth & C. Hoyle (Eds.), *What is criminology?* Oxford: Oxford University Press.

Liebling, A. (2017). The meaning of ending life in prison. *Journal of Correctional Health Care, 23*(1), 20–31.

Liebling, A., & Ludlow, A. (2016). Suicide, distress and the quality of prison life. In Y. Jewkes, B. Crewe, & J. Bennett (Eds.), *Handbook on prisons* (2nd ed.). London: Routledge.

Matthews, P. (2014). *Jervis on the office and duties of coroners: With forms and precedents* (13th ed.). London: Sweet & Maxwell.

Medical Justice. (2016). *Death in immigration detention: 2000–2015*. Online. Retrieved June 15, 2017, from www.medicaljustice.org.uk/wp-content/uploads/2016/09/MJ_death_in_immigration_detention__FINAL_WEB-1.pdf

Pirouet, L. (1994). Suicide and attempted suicide of asylum seekers detained by the UK. In A. Liebling & T. Ward (Eds.), *Deaths in custody: International perspectives*. London: Whiting & Birch.

PPO. (2014). *Learning from PPO investigations: Self-inflicted deaths of prisoners on ACCT*. Online. Retrieved August 8, 2017, from www.ppo.gov.uk/wp-content/uploads/2014/07/ACCT_thematic_final_web.pdf

Ryan, M. (1995). *Lobbying from below: INQUEST in defence of civil liberties*. London: UCL Press.

Shaw, H., & Coles, D. (2007). *Unlocking the truth: Families' experiences of the investigation of deaths in custody*. London: INQUEST.

Shaw, S. (2016). *Review into the welfare in detention of vulnerable persons*. London: HMSO.

Sykes, G. (1958). *The society of captives: A study of a maximum security prison*. Princeton, NJ: Princeton University Press.

Towl, G., & Crighton, D. (2017). *Suicide in prisons: Prisoners' lives matter*. Hampshire: Waterside Press.

Turnbull, S. (2016). 'Stuck in the middle': Waiting and uncertainty in immigration detention. *Time & Society*, 25(1), 61–79.

Walker, T., & Towl, G. (2016). *Preventing self-injury and suicide in women's prisons*. Hampshire: Waterside Press.

Chapter 9

Making sense of the shifting 'field'

Ethical and practical considerations in researching life after immigration detention

Sarah Turnbull

Introduction

> I've missed and avoided lots of calls from [Brent]. I speak to him today, although with his accent and the connection it's hard to catch everything he says. He's in [the Caribbean]. He says he's living in the bush above the houses in the city, eating mangos off the trees. He says his mind isn't working well, that he's been off his medication (antidepressants?) and that he's feeling down. [Brent] talks about his friends abandoning him, that he can't trust anyone. He begs me not to stop taking his calls. [Brent] sounds really down. He says his niece (or his niece's friend?) was killed recently. He says his mom needs him to help her as she's getting old and her place is falling apart but he can't even take care of himself. He says he thinks he'd be better off in prison. [Brent] talks about trying to stay positive and hopes that god will take care of him and give him a second chance. He says he can't believe how he wasn't given a chance to prepare to leave the UK, just made to go from detention.... It's hard to know what to say to [Brent], so I say that I'm sorry he's going through this, that I hope things get better soon. What else can I say?
> —(Fieldnotes, 2 March 2015)

This excerpt from my fieldnotes followed a telephone conversation with a research participant who had been deported to the Caribbean and was left destitute, suffering both the loss of his life in the United Kingdom (UK) after ten years of residence and his new, dire situation in the Caribbean island of his birth. It hints at some of the ethical, methodological, and practical challenges of doing follow-up research with individuals who have been released from detention into the UK or forcibly removed, as in Brent's case. More specifically, in addition to revealing a bit about what life after deportation was like for him, the excerpt evinces my reaction as a researcher: my emotional distress and fatigue, the poor telephone connection, my concern as to his vulnerability, and my feelings of helplessness at not knowing what to say.

With some notable exceptions, criminologists have tended to play down the importance of the difficulties of doing research and our chosen methodologies in our publications or conferences (see, inter alia, Bosworth & Kellezi, 2017;

Phillips & Earle, 2010; Phillips, 2012; Lumsden & Winter, 2014; Wakeman, 2014). Other disciplinary fields, particularly those that draw on qualitative, feminist, and antiracist epistemologies and methodologies, are far more nuanced and critical in terms of these issues, tackling concerns around power, positionality, reflexivity, identity, representation, and so forth (e.g. Coutin & Vogel, 2016; Faria & Mollett, 2016; England, 1994; Jazeel & McFarlane, 2010). Yet such conversations and dialogues are important for criminology, particularly for moving us beyond simplistic, positivist, disembodied accounts of research methodologies that disregard the complexities and messiness of projects involving human beings and the highly politicised and emotionally difficult environments in which much of this work takes place. Such contexts necessitate an openness to speak to both the challenges and opportunities of research, how we put ethics into practice 'on the ground' when we are in 'the field' (Darling, 2014), and how our identities and positionalities shape academic knowledge production (McCorkel & Myers, 2003; Jazeel & McFarlane, 2010; Wakeman, 2014).

The aim of this chapter is to offer a critical discussion of and reflection upon some of the challenges and opportunities of doing community-based and remote (i.e. via telephone and new media) follow-up research as part of a larger study of immigration detention and deportation in the UK. I draw on my experiences of conducting follow-up research with women and men that I first met during fieldwork in four immigration removal centres (IRCs) in the UK (see Turnbull, 2016, 2018; Turnbull & Hasselberg, 2017; Bosworth & Turnbull, 2015) and who were subsequently released, either into the British community or returned to another country. Undertaking research with a follow-up component required establishing solid relationships with participants during the in-detention phase of the fieldwork so that they would continue past release and into daily life, whether this was in the UK or abroad. As this chapter will illustrate, building – and then maintaining – such relationships, however, was challenging because it required balancing the research aims with ethical concerns, logistical challenges, and the 'intimacies' that frequently accompany these interpersonal relationships, in navigating across various gender, racial, cultural, religious, national, and linguistic differences.

This chapter considers the following questions: How do researcher–participant relationships, with their attendant power relations and positionalities, play out when researching life after immigration detention? How, if at all, can sustainable and ethical relationships be forged and maintained over time to allow for a follow-up research component? I do not aim to offer solutions to these questions or the challenges of ethics, emotions, or interpersonal relationships but rather to give critical consideration to the messiness of such research and encourage ongoing dialogue and discussion. By 'messiness' I mean the contradictions, difficulties, opportunities, and emotions that inhere in the process of doing social science research.

A word on 'the field' of research is first necessary. Immigration detention and deportation are highly politicised policies and practices. Research access to study immigration detention is extremely limited if not precluded entirely

(Bosworth, 2014; Maillet, Mountz, & Williams, 2017). This research project was conducted during a time in which the broader political context was explicitly focused on creating a 'hostile environment' for migrants (Jones et al., 2015). Additionally, those who are subject to detention and deportation are, for the most part, marginalised in terms of their legal standing, racial and ethnic identities, and socioeconomic status. Immigration detention itself also produces vulnerability, exacerbating pre-existing conditions and/or creating new ones (e.g. mental or physical health issues; see Bosworth, 2016). This marginality and vulnerability typically continues once detention formally ends through release to the community on temporary admission or immigration bail or deportation to another country. For those who remain, the daily, lived experience of 'deportability' (De Genova, 2002) is difficult, as their lives remain precarious and uncertain (see, e.g., Williams, 2015; Hasselberg, 2016; Turnbull, 2016). Those who have been deported face a variety of challenges, ranging from being returned destitute to war-torn countries (e.g. Schuster & Majidi, 2013) to experiencing the stigmatisation of their migration failures (e.g. Golash-Boza, 2015).

However, following Maillet and colleagues (2017, p. 929), it is important to complicate notions of vulnerability, recognising that 'people enter and exit varying degrees of vulnerability and precarity at different times and in different places.' This conceptualisation includes the researcher in addition to the research participants (Maillet, Mountz, & Williams, 2017; Drozdzewski & Dominey-Howes, 2015). As Darling (2014, p. 211) astutely observes, '[c]ontext and positionality are always shifting beneath our feet as research develops, relationships grow and recede and the lives of those we work with move on around us.' The field of research is dynamic and changing, necessitating decisions and choices that influence the research project and the data that are gathered and analysed. Research is much messier than most methodology books allow us to believe. This messiness brings with it challenges but also affords opportunities for innovation, critical reflection, and advancing knowledge and understanding. In the context of the emerging field of the criminology of mobility (Aas & Bosworth, 2013) and the highly politicised nature of immigration control, such conversations are timely and important.

This chapter is organised into three main sections. The first provides some background information about the methods and data upon which the chapter is based. The second section outlines three interrelated challenges – indicative of the messiness of social research – that I encountered during the follow-up phase of the study. In the third section, I further situate the challenges in terms of my affective experiences as researcher while also identifying opportunities that research on life after immigration detention may afford.

Method and data: understanding life after detention

One of the goals of my research was to understand what happens to people once they leave immigration detention. I primarily used qualitative interviewing to develop a rich account of participants' post-detention lives. I also attempted to include a visual research strategy called 'photo-voice' which involved the distribution of digital cameras to a sample of participants as or once they left detention. The aim with photo-voice was to offer insight into how detention impacts individuals upon their return 'home' (in the UK or in another country) using a different medium to capture and express such experiences (see, e.g., Wang, Cash, & Powers, 2000; Fitzgibbon & Stengel, 2017). The follow-up interviews focused on how participants were coping with their situations and daily life after detention, how they experienced release or deportation, how they felt about the UK based on their experiences of detention and release or deportation, and their hopes for the future. As I detail more in what follows, I used social media to keep in touch with participants and as a potential source of data.

The majority of participants were men ($n = 15$, compared to $n = 6$ women) and most were in their twenties and thirties. Their countries of origin were located primarily in South Asia and Africa as well as the Caribbean, Middle East, and South America. The UK-based participants were in the community on immigration bail or temporary admission while awaiting determination of their immigration cases – most of which involved asylum applications or appeals against deportation under the European Convention on Human Rights. Among those who were expelled from the UK, the vast majority were administratively removed, meaning that their removal was for administrative rather than criminal reasons.[1]

In practical terms, I maintained contact with participants to carry out the follow-up research by using a variety of means. The primary mechanisms were email, telephone, and text message, but I also used social media platforms like Skype, Facebook, and LinkedIn. I found it prudent to be available on multiple platforms, so this meant using my research telephone and having publicly oriented Facebook and LinkedIn profiles. Using social media to carry out the research and drawing on visual methods like photo-voice were part of my methodological approach, which aimed to be 'innovative' and generate new techniques for connecting with difficult to reach and marginalised populations.

The challenges of follow-up research

In what follows, I detail three interrelated challenges I encountered whilst conducting follow-up research with former detainees: ethical, logistical, and the researcher–participant relationship.

Ethical dilemmas and challenges

Bosworth (2014), Bosworth and Kellezi (2017), and Maillet, Mountz, and Williams (2017) have considered some of the ethical challenges of undertaking fieldwork in immigration detention centres. Much more has been written about ethical issues in research with refugees and asylum seekers (Darling, 2014;

Block et al., 2012; Hugman, Bartolomei, & Pittaway, 2011a) and migrants more generally (Coutin & Vogel, 2016). Some scholars have argued that the vulnerabilities of certain migrants are so great that researchers must go beyond the trope of 'do no harm' in order to protect participants and forge ethical research relationships (MacKenzie, McDowell, & Pittaway, 2007; Hugman, Pittaway, & Bartolomei, 2011b).

In terms of ethical concerns, I found that detention and its aftermath created conditions of vulnerability for participants. Even after release, most suffered from some form of psychological distress associated with the experience of confinement, which was then compounded by the uncertainty related to the impending outcomes of their immigration cases or their experiences of deportation. These factors and circumstances raise important ethical considerations as to how much and what to ask of participants. It also requires trying to find a balance between care and empathy with the research goals, while at the same time not infantilising people through the label of vulnerability (Maillet, Mountz, & Williams, 2017) nor giving them false expectations about my reasons for following up with them (e.g. that I could offer legal or other forms of assistance). It was not always easy to find or maintain such a balance.

Unfortunately, research goals do not always fit nicely to the reality of researching a difficult subject within a marginalised population. For instance, I was unable to undertake the photo-voice component of the research because nearly all of the participants were not able to contribute photos as would have been conducive to the research goals in terms of producing 'data.' Most informants did not return my emails, texts, or phone calls about their photographs. One participant told me that he did not want to document his life after deportation because it felt too personal for him and he was concerned at being portrayed as a powerless 'victim' of the UK immigration system. Such difficulties in pursuing this particular research method often led me to question what the point of the project was, for when many participants were just trying to survive and I could not do anything to help them, other than be someone to talk to and offer a small honorarium of £15 for their participation.

Reaching out to participants to follow up with them sometimes felt awful, raising ethical dilemmas when their replies yielded upsetting or troubling information. For example, I received the following email back from Chris (early 20s, deported to South Asia) after I had approached him with the goal of setting up a follow-up interview:

> Hi Sarah :)
> Thanks for your concern and the email. Just living my life and facing new problems every new day as life so hard for me ATM [at the moment]. Away from family can't go to them can't see them often this life is not less than a hell for me. Don't know what to do and hard to survive as I don't have job even wanted to do but I can't :(

> I don't know what will British government will get to send me back I just asked from them my life nothing else [sad face emojis] now I don't have place to live oh my god tbh [to be honest] Sarah if life is going to treat me like this better I commit suicide I don't wanna live in this world like this :(
>
> [Chris] (email, 18 September 2014)

This email made me question how far to push the research relationship and for what ultimate goal, especially when I was thousands of kilometres away and unable to offer any real support or assistance. Who could I have contacted for help if Chris was really suicidal? Was I (re)traumatising him by asking him what his life was like after being deported from the UK? The formal mechanisms put in place by university ethics review boards or the guidance provided by academic associations tend not to cover these sorts of remote research encounters, necessitating instead what Guillemin and Gillam (2004) call 'ethics in practice.' This means making 'on-the-ground' decisions that uphold ethical commitments as best as possible. In this case, I could only reply to Chris's email to encourage him to take care of himself and seek help if he was distressed, while deciding not to pursue a follow-up interview. As with Brent, I did not know what to say.

The logistics of communicating across time and space

For the follow-up research with UK-based participants, the logistical challenges of geographic distance were more easily overcome, requiring longer train journeys and a rare overnight stay at a hotel. The benefit of such research trips allowed, at first, for some snowball sampling so that I was able to interview former detainees who I had not first met during my fieldwork at the four IRCs. The logistical challenges of time were somewhat more difficult to contend with, as this required drawing on the relationships that I had made 'inside' before we lost touch once participants were 'outside.' This involved allowing informants enough time to 'adjust' to life after detention while respecting their emotional and practical needs, such as decompressing after often long periods of detention (and occasionally imprisonment), finding shelter and food, figuring out new routines, reporting to the Home Office, and so forth.

The remote follow-up research was difficult to carry out in other ways. Depending on where people ended up, some did not have access to the internet and/or it was expensive to make and receive calls. For instance, several interviews and conversations held over Skype or the telephone suffered from patchy, unreliable connections. Social media helped somewhat, but there are also issues of boundaries, including the line between research and personal relationships and the location of 'the field' (Luh Sin, 2015). For instance, like Luh Sin (2015), through 'friending' participants on Facebook, I was provided access to their lives in ways they perhaps had not imagined nor to which had they consented. Although convenient in many regards, the use of social media may make boundaries of researcher–participant relationships blurrier, even as I used professional (not personal) accounts in order to present my researcher 'front.'[2]

As with the in-detention fieldwork, my gender (in its intersection with my race, age, nationality, sexuality, and ability) also became a 'logistical issue' (see Billo & Hiemstra, 2013, p. 323) during the follow-up research, shaping how I conducted the fieldwork. For instance, in addition to confirming the usual safeguards, it required managing the researcher–participant relationship in an attempt to ensure that research trips within the UK and the follow-up correspondence were not misinterpreted by participants as anything beyond the research and that my expression of empathy or concern was part of the researcher–participant relationship. As I next show, managing these relationships was especially challenging.

The messy boundaries of the researcher–participant relationship

Qualitative methods, like interviews and participant observation, 'rely heavily upon interpersonal encounters; the very interaction between researcher and informant creates data' (Maillet, Mountz, & Williams, 2017, p. 942). Following up with participants requires that such interpersonal encounters continue to occur over time and geographic distance in order to build and maintain the researcher–participant relationship. Through the act of creating relationships and following up with my informants, a key challenge was continually drawing and redrawing the (artificial) boundaries around 'researcher' and 'participant' (Fraser & Puwar, 2008) as well as being cognisant of the attendant 'asymmetrical power relations' (Maillet, Mountz, & Williams, 2017, p. 928). Yet various 'research intimacies' (Fraser & Puwar, 2008) accompany these relationships, requiring navigation across gender, racial, cultural, religious, national, and linguistic differences (e.g. Phillips & Earle, 2010; Phillips, 2012) while getting to know the participants through the project. Such research also demanded a certain degree of reciprocity such that I also had to give something of myself, whether this was about my interests, hobbies, or family life (Darling, 2014). Darling (2014, p. 204) terms these sorts of issues 'emotional entanglements,' highlighting the both affective and challenging nature of research relationships and the fieldwork experience.

I learned that for some participants who were very marginalised and distressed, I remained one person who remembered them and would answer their texts, calls, or emails. This often occurred in a context in which they had lost friendships and family relationships through their detention and, in some cases, their deportation. For several informants, I was their only remaining connection to the UK that was still in communication with them. In talking about detention, release, and/or deportation, I was also someone who could understand, often better than their friends and family, what detention was like and the impacts it had had on their lives. This frequently occurred for male participants who did not want to look 'weak' in front of their (female) partners or families. With such researcher–participant relationships, my role was often one of witness to their loss and suffering.

In other instances, participants looked to me for help out of their predicaments, but there was nothing I could practically do to help them other than to be someone they could talk to – a witness – which connects back to key ethical considerations and the research goals, as the project was not intended to (nor could it) provide practical assistance. At times it was difficult for me to balance my empathy and desire to interact ethically with participants and treat them with care and respect while collecting 'data' in the context of a time-sensitive research project.

So in reaching out to people to follow-up, I had to draw on and continually build relationships with people whilst being mindful of all of these challenges. I was not always successful, and several of these relationships caused me a lot of (di)stress. For instance, in the excerpt that follows of a chat on Facebook Messenger with Eshan (early 20s, South Asia), I was trying to find out how things were going for him as he waited in the UK community for a resolution to his immigration case. I had met him previously for an in-person follow-up interview but used Facebook Messenger to maintain contact.

ME: How are things going?
ESHAN: Just ok
ME: What's happening?
ESHAN: Miss you
ME: Can you say what's happening for you?
ESHAN: Nothing
ME: Are you still living at the same place in London?
ESHAN: Yes. do you miss me Sarah?
(chat via Facebook Messenger, 3 June 2014)

Through this exchange, I was frustrated at Eshan's attempt to make me answer his question ('do you miss me?') because it veered the conversation out of my comfort zone and away from the 'ideal' (not messy) researcher–participant relationship I was trying to maintain. His question invoked intimacy and recognition, revealing how gender, heteronormativity, and sexuality are interwoven in such research relationships, even as we may try to deny or minimise them (see Kaspar & Landolt, 2016). I did not want to hurt his feelings by answering the question ('no, I do not'), even as I could appreciate and understand what I interpreted as his request to be recognised. At the same time, I felt burnt out and lacked the emotional and intellectual energy to deal with the situation by addressing his comments directly. I have no doubt that researchers face similar responses when trying to 'recruit' and 'retain' participants. However, we rarely talk about the gendered and sexualised aspects of fieldwork, especially in criminology, perhaps because they are embarrassing, difficult to articulate, or do not fit with positivist constructions of 'the field' and research itself as if it is 'a linear, pristine, ordered process' (Valentine, 2001, p. 43). It is often not easy to address the gendered and sexualised dimensions of research, as this risks appearing weak, inappropriate, or simply unable to professionally handle the complexities of fieldwork (Billo & Hiemstra, 2013; Kaspar & Landolt, 2016).

As the follow-up research progressed, my role as researcher was forgotten or conveniently ignored by some participants. It required me to reassert my researcher positionality while some tried to bend the not-so-clear boundaries of the researcher–participant relationship in the direction of 'friend' or potential 'love interest,' with me trying to steer my position back towards 'friendly researcher.' The 'emotional entanglements' (Darling, 2014) of such relationships were particularly difficult to navigate across various lines of difference (e.g. gender, culture, education, and language) while being respectful of people's feelings and trying to capture the intricacies and messiness of research relationships. It was hard, for instance, to explain that I could care about a participant as an empathetic human being and not just for the sake of the research. Such entanglements led me to end two researcher–participant relationships with male participants because I felt I could no longer ethically manage them.

Like Darling (2014, p. 208), I was also unprepared for participants' expectations of me as a 'privileged citizen' (albeit Canadian, not British) who could possibly effect change through my social and cultural capital. I had been cognisant of my positionality (i.e. white, English-speaking, heterosexual, able-bodied woman) as I entered and worked in 'the field,' but not in relation to what I could be expected to do to 'help.' Such requests ranged from the extreme (e.g. a proposal of marriage to help resolve the participant's lack of regularised status; an appeal for a £500 loan), which I declined, to the more mundane (e.g. guidance on Canada's immigration system), which I did my best to assist. Such expectations and requests were challenging to deal with on an emotional level yet were also revealing of the entanglements that characterise researcher–participant relationships and their unequal relations of power. They were, however, a good reminder that such 'relationships are continually negotiated during fieldwork' (McCorkel & Myers, 2003, p. 204), particularly those that are formed and maintained over time.

Overcoming challenges, identifying opportunities

In addition to the interconnected challenges of ethics, logistics, and interpersonal relationships, the follow-up research itself was emotionally difficult for me, eliciting feelings of sadness, anger, guilt, shame, and anxiety. It was hard to manage participants' stories of suffering, loss, depression, hardship, suicidal ideation, anger, and injustice. Put simply, I became personally affected by participants' lived experiences of border control. It took some time and distance before I could recognise and respect their resilience and agency, seeing them as human beings in their entirety rather than solely in terms of suffering and loss. As others have argued, it is important to identify and attend to the emotional implications of research (Darling, 2014; Elmhirst, 2012; Bosworth & Kellezi, 2017; Billo & Hiemstra, 2013; Wakeman, 2014). Darling (2014, p. 205) argues that 'emotional engagement must be considered as central in the *practice* of research.' Emotions thus are not peripheral but shape the choices we make and how we engage with 'the field' (Darling, 2014; Wakeman, 2014).

Importantly, concern around vicarious trauma while undertaking social science research is garnering increased attention (see Gerlach, this volume; Drozdzewski & Dominey-Howes, 2015). After completing 149 days of in-detention fieldwork over the course of one year, I had experienced vicarious traumatisation and was emotionally and intellectually fatigued. However, at the time, I was not yet aware of the deep impacts of the first phase of the research and had already started the follow-up component in an attempt to maintain the research relationships I had established with former detainees before the complications of time and geographic distance got in the way. I also did not expect how going through my data – the interview transcripts and my fieldnotes – for analysis and writing-up would bring up challenging emotions and feelings again, affecting me once more.

As Billo and Hiemstra (2013, p. 322) argue, 'a researcher must be better at reconciling any fieldwork ideal with the reality of what you can personally do and what is sustainable for you.' Being reflexive thus requires attending to one's 'own needs, abilities, and emotions' and recognising that 'the material constellations encountered in the field can also influence a researcher's positionality' (Billo & Hiemstra, 2013, p. 322). Working through such challenges requires identifying and talking about them. This is not mere self-indulgence but an important aspect for making sense of the data and how the researcher's own subjectivity and positionality shape the research and the production of knowledge. Indeed, the recognition of research and research relationships as situated and embedded 'facilitates the emergence of more nuanced understandings of the realities of everyday lives and practice[s]' (Case & Haines, 2014, p. 59).

With the difficulties of fieldwork come opportunities for understanding the intricate workings of criminal justice and penal power in an era of mass mobility. Even as the follow-up fieldwork was challenging, it has provided a glimpse into the lived experiences of life after immigration detention and the emotional and interpersonal impacts of border control in contemporary Britain. My own experience of upset at participants' situations and stories also illuminates how oppressive and trying these forms of state power are to contend with. The fact that certain methods (i.e. photo-voice) did not 'work' as expected provides important information as to the limits of what can reasonably be expected of research participants, particularly those in situations characterised by significant uncertainty, precarity, and/or hardship.

The use of social media to maintain research relationships proved useful, although much more thought needs to be paid to the benefits and limitations of new forms of communication and engagement in relation to research methodologies and ethics (Luh Sin, 2015). Although social media platforms like Facebook open up new possibilities for conducting research with increasingly mobile research populations, it is possible that they may also intensify the likelihood of misunderstandings or misdirection in researcher–participant relationships, such as in the Messenger chat with Eshan discussed earlier. This may be the case especially if, as I suggest, these platforms are more likely to invite greater intimacy or expressions of emotion than more 'traditional' methods like semi-structured interviews in person or over the telephone. Consequently, as I have learned, in the rush to use 'innovative' methods as part of time-sensitive research projects, the ethical and practical implications of social media should be given adequate consideration, especially in advance of their use.

Concluding thoughts

This chapter offered a critical discussion of and reflection upon some of the challenges and opportunities of doing community-based and remote follow-up research with former immigration detainees about life after detention. In particular, it highlighted issues of ethics, logistics, and researcher–participant relationships as three key, interconnected challenges that shaped the collection of data and my own interactions with and experience of 'the field.' Such challenges point to the inherent messiness of the research process and the importance of attending to the emotional and interpersonal difficulties that accompany fieldwork. I concur with Bosworth (2014) and Maillet, Mountz, and Williams (2017) that such research on border control is important even as it is often difficult to undertake. However, it is important for researchers to think critically about what can reasonably be asked (or expected) of participants whose lives are increasingly precarious through state efforts to (im)mobilise and expel.

At the time of writing, I am still working on the analysis and writing up of my research. As such, I continue to grapple with these issues and others that I have not had the space to discuss here, such as whiteness, the possibility of feminist and anti-racist research praxis in criminological research on detention and deportation, and the ethics of presenting participants' stories of suffering and loss (see Coutin & Vogel, 2016). I hope this chapter offers something useful for researchers who are exploring related issues and employing similar methodologies.

Acknowledgements

I would like to thank the women and men who participated in this research project and shared their thoughts and experiences with me. I also thank the Home Office and IRC centre managers for granting research access. This work was generously supported by Mary Bosworth's European Research Council Starting Grant (no. 313362). Thanks to Ines Hasselberg, Alpa Parmar, Synnøve

Økland Jahnsen, Rebecca Powell and Andriani Fili for reading and commenting on earlier drafts of this chapter.

Notes

1 Under UK law, administrative removal and deportation are separate legal processes and categories, although both involve the expulsion of individuals to another country and restrictions on re-entry (ranging from 1 year to 10 years' duration). Deportation applies specifically to individuals who are subject to expulsion due to their criminal convictions. However, in this chapter, deportation is used throughout to denote the forced removal of a migrant from a state's territory.
2 On the other hand, using a professional Facebook account, for example, often felt disingenuous to participants who shared their personal profiles with me (see also Luh Sin, 2015). This is not to say that participants are not capable of being savvy users of social media but rather that seemingly simple acts of 'friending' (by either making or accepting friend requests) participants are not without ethical considerations nor reflective of asymmetrical relations of power.

References

Aas, K. F., & Bosworth, M. (Eds.). (2013). *The borders of punishment: Migration, citizenship, and social exclusion*. Oxford: Oxford University Press.
Billo, E., & Hiemstra, N. (2013). Mediating messiness: Expanding ideas of flexibility, reflexivity, and embodiment in fieldwork. *Gender, Place & Culture, 20*, 313–328.
Block, K., Warr, D., Gibbs, L., & Riggs, E. (2012). Addressing ethical and methodological challenges in research with refugee-background young people: Reflections from the field. *Journal of Refugee Studies, 26*, 69–87.
Bosworth, M. (2014). *Inside immigration detention*. Oxford: Oxford University Press.
Bosworth, M. (2016). Mental health in immigration detention: A literature review. *Criminal Justice, Borders and Citizenship Research Paper Series*. Retrieved March 6, 2016, from http://ssrn.com/abstract=2732892
Bosworth, M., & Kellezi, B. (2017). Doing research in immigration removal centres: Ethics, emotions and impact. *Criminology and Criminal Justice, 17*, 121–137.
Bosworth, M., & Turnbull, S. (2015). Immigration detention and the expansion of penal power in the United Kingdom. In K. Reiter & A. Koenig (Eds.), *Extreme punishment: Comparative studies in detention, incarceration and solitary confinement* (pp. 50–67). London: Palgrave Macmillan.
Case, S., & Haines, K. (2014). Reflective friend research: The relational aspects of social scientific research. In K. Lumsden & A. Winter (Eds.), *Reflexivity in criminological research: Experiences with the powerful and the powerless* (pp. 58–74). Basingstoke: Palgrave Macmillan.
Coutin, S. B., & Vogel, E. (2016). Migrant narratives and ethnographic tropes: Navigating tragedy, creating possibilities. *Journal of Contemporary Ethnography, 45*, 631–644.
Darling, J. (2014). Emotions, encounters and expectations: The uncertain ethics of 'the field'. *Journal of Human Rights Practice, 6*, 201–212.
De Genova, N. P. (2002). Migrant 'illegality' and deportability in everyday life. *Annual Review of Anthropology, 31*, 419–447.
Drozdzewski, D., & Dominey-Howes, D. (2015). Research and trauma: Understanding the impact of traumatic content and places on the researcher. *Emotion, Space and Society, 17*, 17–21.

Elmhirst, R. (2012). Methodological dilemmas in migration research in Asia: Research design, omissions and strategic erasures. *Area*, *44*, 274–281.

England, K. (1994). Getting personal: Reflexivity, positionality, and feminist research. *The Professional Geographer*, *46*, 80–89.

Faria, C., & Mollett, S. (2016). Critical feminist reflexivity and the politics of whiteness in the 'field'. *Gender, Place & Culture*, *23*, 79–93.

Fitzgibbon, W., & Stengel, C. (2017). Women's voices made visible: Photovoice in visual criminology. *Punishment & Society*, epub before print March 28, 2017. doi:10.1177/1462474517700137.

Fraser, M., & Puwar, N. (2008). Introduction: Intimacy in research. *History of the Human Sciences*, *21*, 1–16.

Golash-Boza, T. (2015). *Deported: Immigrant policing, disposable labor, and global capitalism*. New York: New York University Press.

Guillemin, M., & Gillam, L. (2004). Ethics, reflexivity, and 'ethically important moments' in research. *Qualitative Inquiry*, *10*, 261–280.

Hasselberg, I. (2016). *Enduring uncertainty: Deportation, punishment and the everyday life*. Oxford: Berghahn.

Hugman, R., Bartolomei, L., & Pittaway, E. (2011a). Human agency and the meaning of informed consent: Reflections on research with refugees. *Journal of Refugee Studies*, *24*, 655–671.

Hugman, R., Pittaway, E., & Bartolomei, L. (2011b). When 'do no harm' is not enough: The ethics of research with refugees and other vulnerable groups. *British Journal of Social Work*, *41*, 1271–1287.

Jazeel, T., & McFarlane, C. (2010). The limits of responsibility: A postcolonial politics of academic knowledge production. *Transactions of the Institute of British Geographers*, *35*, 109–124.

Jones, H., Bhattacharyya, G., Davies, W., Dhaliwal, S., Forkert, K., Gunaratnam, Y., Jackson, E., & Saltus, R. (2015). *Go home: Mapping the unfolding controversy of home office immigration campaigns*. Warwick: University of Warwick.

Kaspar, H., & Landolt, S. (2016). Flirting in the field: Shifting positionalities and power relations in innocuous sexualisations of research encounters. *Gender, Place & Culture*, *23*, 107–119.

Luh Sin, H. (2015). 'You're not doing work, you're on Facebook!': Ethics of encountering the field through social media. *The Professional Geographer*, *67*, 676–685.

Lumsden, K., & Winter, A. (Eds.). (2014). *Reflexivity in criminological research: Experiences with the powerful and the powerless*. Basingstoke: Palgrave Macmillan.

MacKenzie, C., McDowell, C., & Pittaway, E. (2007). Beyond 'do no harm': The challenge of constructing ethical relationships in refugee research. *Journal of Refugee Studies*, *20*, 299–319.

Maillet, P., Mountz, A., & Williams, K. (2017). Researching migration and enforcement in obscured places: Practical, ethical and methodological challenges to fieldwork. *Social & Cultural Geography*, *18*, 927–950.

McCorkel, J. A., & Myers, K. (2003). What difference does difference make? Position and privilege in the field. *Qualitative Sociology*, *26*, 199–231.

Phillips, C. (2012). *The multicultural prison: Ethnicity, masculinity, and social relations among prisoners*. Oxford: Oxford University Press.

Phillips, C., & Earle, R. (2010). Reading difference differently? Identity, epistemology and prison ethnography. *British Journal of Criminology*, *50*, 360–378.

Schuster, L., & Majidi, N. (2013). What happens post-deportation? The experience of deported Afghans. *Migration Studies, 1*, 221–240.

Turnbull, S. (2016). 'Stuck in the middle': Waiting and uncertainty in immigration detention. *Time & Society, 25*, 61–79.

Turnbull, S. (2018). Starting again: Life after deportation from the United Kingdom. In S. Khosravi (Ed.), *After deportation: Ethnographic perspectives* (pp. 37–61). Basingstoke: Palgrave Macmillan.

Turnbull, S., & Hasselberg, I. (2017). From prison to detention: The carceral trajectories of foreign-national prisoners in the United Kingdom. *Punishment & Society, 19*, 135–154.

Valentine, G. (2001). At the drawing board: Developing a research design. In M. Limb & C. Dwyer (Eds.), *Qualitative methodologies for geographers: Issues and debates* (pp. 41–54). London: Hodder Arnold.

Wakeman, S. (2014). Fieldwork, biography and emotion: Doing criminological autoethnography. *British Journal of Criminology, 54*, 705–721.

Wang, C., Cash, J., & Powers, L. (2000). Who knows the streets as well as the homeless? Promoting personal and community action through photovoice. *Health Promotion Practice, 1*, 81–89.

Williams, L. (2015). From immigration detention to destitution. *Criminal Justice Matters, 99*, 12–13.

Part 3

The politics of positionality, ethics and emotions

Chapter 10

Researching vulnerable women
Sharing distress and the risk of secondary and vicarious trauma

Alice Gerlach

I have a favourite cartoon called *The Awkward Yeti*. The cartoonist depicts the internal dialogue of its main character, a large blue yeti, through his organs, such as the brain and the heart. The storylines generally show the sensible Brain reining in the whimsical Heart. In one of these cartoons the following scene is sketched:

BRAIN: You can't make EVERYONE happy, Heart. Why do you try?
HEART: When people aren't happy, I'M not happy, so I have to try!
BRAIN: This never turns out well for you.

In a single frame this cartoon captures beautifully the complex relationship between the heart and the brain that the academics in the field of border control must navigate. Researchers in this area regularly speak with people who have crossed borders and who are often entangled with immigration enforcement agencies across the world. The participants we encounter in this field are frequently vulnerable, angry and sad and have suffered considerable emotional or physical hardship and trauma. Our job is to ask them to share their stories so that we can make sense of how borders and people who come into contact with them can be understood. Our findings add to an increasing body of interesting and important work. Yet there is also a growing side effect of this field of study as researchers absorb the emotions of their subjects. It is this aspect, which leads to the phenomena of secondary or vicarious trauma.

'Secondary' and 'vicarious' trauma are often used interchangeably in academic literature, even though they refer to different outcomes, not always discrete, for the individual involved. Secondary trauma refers to the experience of taking on the emotional symptoms presented by others. These symptoms align closely to post-traumatic stress disorder (PTSD) and include intrusive thoughts, severe anxiety and difficulties in sleeping, including nightmares. Vicarious trauma, alternatively, signals a change in mind-set. Those who suffer from vicarious trauma view the world in a different and more negative way than in the past. The two issues are not mutually exclusive, and individuals may experience symptoms associated with either or both.

Secondary and vicarious trauma are recognised in the fields of psychology, humanitarian work and other caring professions (see for example: Baird & Kracen, 2006; Bober & Regehr, 2006; Bride, Hatcher, & Humble, 2009; Bride, 2007; Spring, Carlton, & Clark, 2011). However, they are often overlooked in qualitative literature from the academic social sciences. As a result, qualitative researchers are typically expected to cope with less support than their non-academic counterparts working with similar populations. In this chapter I explore the risks of conducting research on border control and the consequences of secondary or vicarious trauma before offering suggestions for the management of symptoms. Where possible I use my own experiences of interviewing women who had spent time in immigration detention in the UK and those who were removed to Jamaica to illustrate. The data I draw on include interviews with 76 women who were either in immigration detention at the time we met or had been removed to Jamaica or released to the UK following their incarceration. All interviews took place between January 2014 and 2015.

Secondary trauma

Secondary trauma occurs when a person experiences symptoms caused by exposure to trauma as a result of interaction with another individual who has suffered from trauma (Canfield, 2005). Literature regarding this phenomenon is most often found in social care, especially regarding professionals working with traumatised populations such as trauma therapists, counsellors, psychologists and social workers (see, for example, Bonach & Heckert, 2012; Bride, 2007; Bride Hatcher, & Humble, 2009; Canfield, 2005). In these professions individuals are regularly exposed to the traumatic events of others and are often responsible for helping clients to resolve problems by revisiting experiences that have been particularly painful for the individual.

Individuals suffering from secondary trauma experience symptoms which would normally be described as post-traumatic stress disorder (PTSD). Symptoms commonly include difficulties in falling or remaining asleep, nightmares, intrusive thoughts and flashbacks and difficulties with relationships (Baird & Kracen, 2006; Bober & Regehr, 2006; Canfield, 2005). In my own work I was particularly bothered by intrusive thoughts which developed after an interview with a woman in immigration detention in the United Kingdom. Chrissie[1] had fled from Kenya – her home country – after she and her family had become targets of a local militia. The penultimate turn of events that led to her departure from Kenya was the death of her husband and son. During her interview Chrissie described to me in a sentence the moment her husband was beheaded by a soldier. The interview with Chrissie was difficult for a number of reasons, but that one sentence kept replaying in my mind in the days and weeks that followed the interview. It would creep in unexpectedly when I was working or trying to sleep or just in mid-conversations with friends or colleagues. As I recalled her account, I felt intense emotions and physical symptoms such as sweaty palms and a fast-beating heart. I had never experienced such things before.

Vicarious trauma

Vicarious trauma occurs when an individual's mind-set shifts to one in which they view the world in a different and more negative way than in the past (McCann & Pearlman, 1990). This shift changes how individuals feel about themselves, the others and the world around them. In their founding article on vicarious trauma, the psychologists Lisa McCann and Laurie Pearlman (1990) highlight a number of areas in which psychologists' schemas alter when vicariously traumatised, such as trust, power, safety and esteem. Each of these schemas is nuanced, and the impact on an individual can vary due to their own predispositions towards the relative importance they place on their own safety or how they trust others, for example. However, all shifts in their frames of understanding follow the same pattern, whereby underlying assumptions are fundamentally changed for the worse.

Take safety as an example. I spent two months living in Kingston, Jamaica, as part of my fieldwork, to explore the experiences of women removed from the United Kingdom. I lived within the safety of the University of the West Indies compound in a secure apartment. However, the more women I interviewed from less safe areas of downtown Kingston, and the more stories I heard of their unstable living conditions, guns and fears for safety, the more I questioned my own sense of security. While there are risks in living in Kingston, whilst there, I felt that my sense of anxiety even in my own apartment was disproportionate and enduring; for my anxiety followed me back to the relatively safe streets of Oxford in the UK. I am an enthusiastic cyclist, and when commuting to work on my bike after my return, a driver started beeping his car horn and slowed alongside me. I was afraid, so I sped up and ignored him. With my heart pounding I eventually pulled over to the side of the road to get away. At this point the driver yelled something to me out his window, which I was unable to discern, and went on his way. It was only when I went to secure my bike at the office that I realised my lock had fallen from my basket. The man in the car was just trying to tell me I had dropped it on the road. Prior to my experiences in Jamaica I would have been more likely to look and see what the driver wanted, assess the situation and decide what to do. My instinct had altered. I responded with fear rather than curiosity.

The prevalence of secondary and vicarious trauma in research on border control

Border control is intrinsically emotive. Research subjects have often suffered emotional or physical hardship and trauma, and many are vulnerable and live a precarious existence. Looking through emerging border control literature, the prevalent themes of exclusion (Anderson, Gibney, & Paoletti, 2011; Bloch & Schuster, 2005; Collyer, 2012; Morris, 2002; Peutz, 2006; Schuster & Majidi, 2013), punishment (Bosworth, 2012, 2011; Golash-Boza, 2015; Phelps, 2009) criminalisation (Bosworth, 2014; Khosravi, 2009; Oberoi & Taylor Nicholson, 2013; Silverman & Massa, 2012) and psychological distress (Robjant, Robbins, & Senior, 2009; Steel et al., 2011) are common. These themes are part of what makes border control research important, but they also take their toll on researchers. We are not impervious to the hardships faced by others. I came to expect heart-wrenching stories. I was aware that undertaking research in this area would be difficult from past work experience in prisons and detention centres and from discussions with my supervisor. However, I did not expect the sheer volume of misery that emerged/was evident during the interviews. After concluding a year of research including nearly 80 participants, I could name only one or two women who had not suffered from extreme hardship either before, during or after their meeting with border controls in the UK. Their stories included rape, trafficking, domestic violence and entrenched poverty.

While some social scientists have documented the difficulties they faced when collecting sensitive or emotive data (Darlington & Scott, 2002; Dickson-Swift James, Kippen, & Liamputtong, 2007; Lofland, 2006; Warr, 2004), they do not label their reactions as secondary or vicarious trauma. Though not labelled as such, the impact of secondary and vicarious trauma can already be found in research on border control. In her book on immigration detention in the UK, Mary Bosworth recounts the emotional impact of interviews in immigration detention:

> While the research was ongoing and for months after it ended, I suffered from insomnia, bad dreams, palpitations, breathlessness, tears, and dizziness. It took about one year to be able to read the fieldnotes and transcripts without a sense of rising anxiety, sick to my stomach.
> (Mary Bosworth, 2014, p. 84)

It is easy to see in the quote here the symptoms of secondary trauma described earlier.

The devil is in the details

Researchers in border studies are at risk of secondary and vicarious trauma as much as psychologists and humanitarian workers. Researchers in border studies encounter a population that is more likely to have suffered trauma than the general population. Like counsellors or psychologists, researchers will often sit and listen to the stories of their participants, who will describe in vivid detail traumatic events and journeys. The traumatic detail is often not the subject of the interview; however, so much of the context surrounding border control is related to these events that it is often difficult to avoid.

In my own research with women in immigration detention I deliberately avoided probing into their backgrounds, partially in a bid to avoid upsetting them and partially to protect my own well-being. Avoidance of painful subjects was effective in some cases, but sometimes women wanted to discuss their trauma and despair. At the time of my fieldwork, there was no counselling or psychological support available for women in the detention centre I was based in, and several women declared I was the first person that took time to listen to their stories. Mary Bosworth and Blerina Kellezi (2016) found the women in their study were equally grateful for the humanising attention they offered as researchers. Given the importance women granted to the interaction between researcher and participant in the space of immigration detention, I was not willing to stop them in the middle of a detailed description of trauma to ask what they thought of theoretical constructs of dignity, which was the focus of my research, for example.

Transcription and analysis

Researchers will often transcribe qualitative interviews verbatim, listening to the stories for a second time, more slowly and with more time to ruminate on the details of the story. This is followed by an in-depth analysis alongside countless other similarly traumatic interviews. Some research has been conducted into the act of social science transcription, in which individuals describe the transcription and analysis process of their research as particularly emotionally draining, with some professional transcribers reporting sleep disorders and emotional fatigue from the work (Darlington & Scott, 2002; Gregory Cynthia, & Phillips, 1997; Warr, 2004). As I moved closer to transcribing Chrissie's interview which had caused me so much anxiety, I began to suffer from increased apprehension of how I would cope with listening to the details again.[2] Chrissie's interview was not the only transcription which I found difficult. Many others inspired in me strong and unexpected emotional responses ranging from anger to tears. Indeed, I reacted more strongly when I heard the conversation a second time than I had during the interviews, during which I had maintained a less emotional response, which served to support the women through their pain. I also feel that controlling my emotions during an interview preserves a sense of professionalism, which I believe is important in the relationship between researcher and interviewee.

Trauma affected my analysis and writing in two distinct ways. Coding required me to re-read the interviews once again, thoroughly, to develop the themes meant to be used in writing. I experienced similar emotional fatigue as with transcribing, and, at times, I needed to take time away from the process because I felt especially low, delaying an already long process. I also experienced an aspect of desensitisation when writing. I was discussing the theme of extreme hardship, and the suggestion of historical suicidal ideation was raised by more than one participant.

I had not realised how blasé I had become about the subject until I received comments from a colleague on a draft chapter. To illustrate the stress felt by women who had been returned to Jamaica, I had included a quote in which a mother described she was feeling so low she thought of killing herself and her two children. I had given the quote little extra thought; however, my colleague was disturbed by it. He commented that I had neglected to comment on the seriousness of the participants' deliberations: 'can't help feeling that you need to give more of your own assessment of this to avoid readers thinking you're straightforwardly sympathetic to someone contemplating child murder because she's stressed.' He was right, and I was conscious after this of the potential of vicarious trauma to shift my sense of what constituted shocking behaviour.

Secondary and vicarious trauma awareness

People who perform roles related to assisting with traumatised populations are usually made aware of the impacts of secondary and vicarious trauma and given assistance to limit the effect on their own person and to deal with symptoms when they occur (Bober & Regehr, 2006). In this study by Bober and Reghr, the participants who were aware of the possibility of secondary traumatisation and who believed in the impact of such a condition were more likely to seek assistance from supervisors and other colleagues. In turn, these participants were assisted by speaking through troubling cases with managers and other colleagues and displayed fewer symptoms of trauma than individuals who did not have support. Academics and students are not, typically, provided with such support, and this can lead to an increased risk of symptoms related to the phenomena. Further, much academic research is solitary. It involves long periods of time away from friends and family and in conditions that are different to what researchers are used to and are often uncomfortable with. In this type of environment researchers may not have ready access to supervision and support. During my own research I was rarely in the same city as my supervisor, and when visiting Jamaica the time difference made Skype calls hard to schedule. I was living away from my husband and had long evenings alone with little to do to distract me from my work.

How does secondary or vicarious trauma impact research?

Symptoms of secondary or vicarious trauma do not exist independently, nor do they allow the sufferer to act as they did before the symptoms developed. Symptoms are more than likely to have an impact on the professional and personal life of the researcher. The clinical social worker Julie Canfield (2005) suggests that there are two types of reaction to vicarious trauma, constrictive reactions and intrusive reactions. Constrictive reactions are referred to by Canfield as actions like avoidance, scepticism towards clients and numbing to traumatic events. Intrusive actions refer to overstepping boundaries, such as becoming a 'rescuer.'

Constrictive reactions

The constrictive reactions as described by Canfield (2005) can have an impact on the researcher's ability to complete their study and limit desire to conduct further research. Avoidance was apparent in the quote of Bosworth (2014), cited earlier, in which she referred to an inability to read the transcriptions and field notes from her time in immigration detention. I too have felt the desire to avoid conducting interviews. Towards the end of my fieldwork there was one woman, Karmel, who had agreed to an interview. Two prior attempts to meet had been cancelled for reasons beyond my control, but she continued to express a desire to talk to me. She was the last interview of my study, and I felt nothing but dread in the days leading to it. I did not want to conduct another interview, and I only turned up on the set day because I felt I would let Karmel down if I did not give her the opportunity to tell her story. Finally, when I arrived for the interview, Karmel was upset, as she had been made to move by the Home Office the day before. I was not willing to interview her while she was upset, and she agreed it would be best not to. I was leaving the country for six weeks the following weekend and had come to the end of my period of fieldwork, so the interview was not rearranged. I left the meeting feeling relieved that I did not have to conduct another interview but at the same time guilty because I knew I did not want to speak to any more women about their stories. A combination of guilt and happiness or excitement is common in social science research (Dickson-Swift et al., 2007; Finch, 1984; Lofland, 2006; Oakley, 1981), but this felt like I was avoiding work, and it was deeply unsettling. Developing a desire to avoid working on the subject is one of the challenges that researchers face in the current era of mass mobility. If secondary or vicarious trauma reactions are not managed within the field and academics move on to other subjects, a lack of speciality and depth in the remaining literature is likely to occur.

Intrusive reactions

The intrusive reactions described by Canfield (2005) are related to clinicians who become too involved in their patients' problems and overstep professional boundaries to help them. One pertinent difference between academics and care professions is that the role of the care professional is to help the individual work through their trauma and recover from related symptoms, whereas academics tend to collect the stories of participants for research aims. Helping patients can be a rewarding position (McCann & Pearlman, 1990), and it has been shown that an additional phenomenon of vicarious post-traumatic growth can occur in therapists (Arnold, Calhoun, Tedeschi, & Cann, 2005). This growth is largely the outcome of witnessing clients making sense of their trauma and beginning to overcome their symptoms (Arnold et al., 2005; Hernández, Gangsei, & Engstrom, 2007). Academics do not have the emotional return described in these studies. While academic research is of value in understanding the lives of individuals who encounter border controls and the potential for policy or other impact is high, the real-time outcomes can be frustratingly slow.

People who are interviewed during the course of research are often on their way to somewhere else, and even if they are in a position to remain in contact, the reality of time and space makes this impractical. There are many women who shared emotive stories with me which I have no doubt will remain in my mind for a long time; however, I am unlikely to ever learn what happened next to the participants in the study. Policy changes that may come from said research are also unlikely to help the women who offered their time for the study.

Overstepping boundaries is particularly complicated when it comes to academia regardless of the secondary or vicarious trauma–induced reactions. The risks of becoming emotionally involved or attached to research participants are well documented, predominantly those associated with the personal safety and well-being of researchers (Campbell, 2002; Dickson-Swift et al., 2007; Duncombe & Jessop, 2012; Finch, 1984; James & Platzer, 1999; Jamieson, 2000; Mitchell & Irvine, 2008; Oakley, 1981; Rowling, 1999). The injurious mix of limited emotional return combined with pessimistic schemas about the potential for research participants to find help elsewhere in a harsh reality puts researchers of border control at further risk of overstepping boundaries. In my own research I felt I was controlled when it came to remaining within the margins I had set myself; however, my resolve was regularly challenged.

What can be done to support social scientists?

In their definition of vicarious trauma, McCann and Pearlman (1990) suggest that the therapists' vicarious trauma should be viewed as the normal reaction to working with traumatised populations, in a similar way that PTSD is considered a standard reaction to a traumatic event. I propose that social scientists' vicarious or secondary traumas should be viewed in a similar way and that comparable precautions should be taken when embarking on research with potentially traumatised victims as those taken by health care professionals.

Effective supervision and support

Adequate supervision is a preventative factor against risk of secondary or vicarious trauma. In their review of vicarious resistance Hernandez-Wolfe et al. (2015) found evidence that supervision is a preventative factor against secondary trauma. Alternatively, Gil and Weinberg (2015) present statistical data which suggest that social workers who lack regular supervision are more likely to suffer from secondary trauma symptoms. During my own time in the field, I found the support offered by my supervisor invaluable. All the interviews

I undertook were completed somewhere else than the city in which I resided at the time, and for a long period I was also not in the same country as my supervisor. However, we were in constant email contact, with the option to Skype, if needed. My supervisor is experienced in the field of border control herself and was aware of the impact the research could have. I was thus warned in advance of the risks and was told it was okay to leave the field if I felt it was getting too much. Knowing it was normal to feel emotional, upset or else was important. In their investigation of qualitative researchers collecting sensitive data, Johnson and Clarke (2003) found that researchers were reluctant in reporting their need for support to supervisors out of fear of being perceived as weak or deficient in their ability to conduct research. Being aware of secondary and vicarious trauma and being able to normalise all symptoms and manage them allowed me to balance conducting the research and my own mental health.

I was also able to utilise formative workshops on the impact of secondary trauma within my university. Professional support groups are highlighted by McCann and Pearlman (1990) as an important source for health care professionals. Within these groups, individuals can draw on support from individuals who understand and appreciate the impact of distressing material and provide a place where professionals can unburden themselves alongside other persons in a similar capacity. Through these groups I was able to build a network with academics of a similar standing and discuss our reactions to the material and how it impacted our research. I particularly learned from a colleague who was undergoing similar issues related to the avoidance of transcriptions and analysis, and we were able to support each other when we came across particularly harrowing pieces of narrative. Through email we sent snippets of information in confidence and received feedback on how awful the narrative was. For example, during a discussion on how long coding was taking us both, I wrote 'I'm coding too – it is taking me longer than it should, but sometimes I just don't want to read another word.' Later in the emails there were also supportive texts such as 'no wonder you're feeling slumpy,' helping to legitimise and recognise constrictive reactions to the traumatic material. This was important to me in order to normalise the feelings stirred during the transcription process and limit the experience of isolation.

Ethical boundaries

The dilemma of crossing ethical boundaries as part of an intrusive reaction to secondary or vicarious trauma is a difficult one to manage, and will depend on the researcher's own experience and philosophical leanings. Literature regarding ethics in qualitative research is vast and varied (see, for example, Bosworth & Kellezi, 2016; Duncombe & Jessop, 2012; Finch, 1984; James & Platzer, 1999; Jamieson, 2000), and researchers must define their own boundaries. My research received ethics clearance through the University of Oxford's Central University Research Ethics Committee (CUREC). The review was thorough, as the women in my study were, without doubt, vulnerable. However, the focus of the clearance was on the ways to support and mitigate the harms of disclosure and trauma for participants. The ethical boundaries that concern this chapter are those related to crossing relationship boundaries. When in Jamaica, I interviewed several women who were having difficulty in finding food for themselves and their families. In one such interview Cassandra had brought her eight-year-old child along as she had no one else to care for her, and no money to send her to school. As in the cartoon described in the introduction above, my heart wanted to help in some way, but my brain knew that giving more than what was prescribed in the pre-agreed incentive would cross an ethical boundary. My brain won, and I settled with offering the girl a drink from the café as I do with any interviewees to help build rapport. I felt awful afterwards, and still do, but I stand by my decision, because crossing this threshold was something I had decided against beforehand. I know colleagues in border control research would have given extra attention to the child, and both decisions would be neither wrong nor right. The important point is to make these decisions before the research is conducted and understand the consequences of violating these for reasons of personal well-being.

Self-care and time

Taking time to care for your own mental health needs when conducting research is important. Self-care refers to ensuring that your time conducting research is balanced with positive leisure activities, healthy eating and exercise and has been found to be of use in social science research generally (Campbell, 2002; James & Platzer, 1999; Mitchell & Irvine, 2008; Rowling, 1999) as well as for care professionals (McCann & Pearlman, 1990). During my own time conducting troubling research I focused on running as a means of stress relief. I found it was an effective tool, though I regularly had to fight the urge to lie down and stare at the wall instead. When I was unable to run I found myself uncharacteristically watching a certain American teen drama which involved persistent enthusiastic singing and dancing. Apart from exercise and trashy television I systematically avoided the news, especially anything relating to migration, and stopped looking at my Twitter feed. I found that doing so made me feel either disproportionately angry or upset, and I was unable to shift these emotions easily.

The time an individual spends supporting trauma victims has been found to have a strong statistically predictive effect on secondary or vicarious stress (Bober & Regehr, 2006; Gil & Weinberg, 2015). While the statistics linking time with trauma material and secondary or vicarious stress are related to health care workers such as trauma psychologists, care support workers and the like, I suggest that the same principles can be applied to work with trauma-related research material. Spacing out interviews could be one method to achieve this aim, along with leaving ample time to transcribe interviews.

Conclusion

Academics and students of border control are at risk of secondary and vicarious trauma, just like psychologists and care workers dealing with traumatised patients. Both groups may regularly encounter victims of trauma and delve into some of the bleakest aspects of the human condition repeatedly and in gross detail. The care professionals, however, have recognised the phenomena, and thus measures have been taken in these professions to help people who care for trauma survivors to manage their symptoms of secondary and vicarious trauma while academics – in their majority – have not.

The field of border control and social sciences more generally can learn from their trauma care counterparts. There are measures that can be taken to minimise the impact of secondary or vicarious trauma. However, trauma must first be accepted as a normal reaction in research conducted with traumatised populations. Researchers should not feel weak or neglect their emotions as non-legitimate and important factors of the research process.

I propose that vicarious or secondary trauma in social scientists should be viewed in a similar way as in the care professions, where it is normalised as a logical reaction to their work. With this in mind, comparable precautions should be taken when embarking on research with potentially traumatised victims as health care professionals would do. Further, research should also be undertaken to explore the impact secondary and vicarious trauma can have on social science researchers and indicate profession-specific practices to ensure the well-being of individuals in this field.

In another comic of *The Awkward Yeti*, Heart is depicted lying, beaten, on the floor of a boxing ring, while Brain is encouraging it: 'It's not over Heart. GET. UP.', to which Heart responds: 'I will, just give me like five minutes.' By utilising methods of care for ourselves as researchers we can ensure that the impacts of secondary or vicarious trauma are temporary. So then, we can ensure that academics and students will be able to continue the important and interesting work in the growing area of border control.

Notes

1 Names have been changed to protect the identity of respondents.
2 Thankfully, when I came to transcribe the interview I discovered the sentence had been articulated when the recorder was paused, Chrissie had become upset and I had stopped the interview. She must have confided this information during the time I spent with her in the minutes after.

References

Anderson, B., Gibney, M. J., & Paoletti, E. (2011). Citizenship, deportation and the boundaries of belonging. *Citizenship Studies*, *15*(5), 547–563.
Arnold, D., Calhoun, L. G., Tedeschi, R. G., & Cann, A. (2005). Vicarious posttraumatic growth. *Journal of Humanistic Psychology*, *45*(2), 239–263.

Baird, K., & Kracen, A. C. (2006). Vicarious traumatization and secondary traumatic stress: A research synthesis. *Counselling Psychology Quarterly*, *19*(2), 181–188.

Bloch, A., & Schuster, L. (2005). At the extremes of exclusion: Deportation, detention and dispersal. *Ethnic and Racial Studies*, *28*(3), 491–512.

Bober, T., & Regehr, C. (2006). Strategies for reducing secondary or vicarious trauma: Do they work? *Brief Treatment and Crisis Intervention*, *6*(1), 1–9.

Bonach, K., & Heckert, A. (2012). Predictors of secondary traumatic stress among children's advocacy center forensic interviewers. *Journal of Child Sexual Abuse*, *21*(3), 295–314.

Bosworth, M. (2011). Deportation, detention and foreign-national prisoners in England and Wales. *Citizenship Studies*, *15*(5), 583–595.

Bosworth, M. (2012). Subjectivity and identity in detention: Punishment and society in a global age. *Theoretical Criminology*, *16*(2), 123–140.

Bosworth, M. (2014). *Inside immigration detention*. Oxford: Oxford University Press.

Bosworth, M., & Kellezi, B. (2016). Doing research in immigration removal centres: Ethics, emotions and impact. *Criminology and Criminal Justice*, 1–17.

Bride, B. (2007). Prevalence of secondary traumatic stress among social workers. *Social Work*, *52*(1), 63–70.

Bride, B. E., Hatcher, S. S., & Humble, M. N. (2009). Trauma training, trauma practices, and secondary traumatic stress among substance abuse counselors. *Traumatology*, *15*(2), 96–105.

Campbell, R. (2002). *Emotionally involved: The impact of researching rape*. London: Routledge.

Canfield, J. (2005). Secondary traumatization, burnout, and vicarious traumatization. *Smith College Studies in Social Work*, *75*(2), 81–101.

Collyer, M. (2012). Deportation and the micropolitics of exclusion: The rise of removals from the UK to Sri Lanka. *Geopolitics*, *17*(2), 276–292.

Darlington, Y., & Scott, D. (2002). *Qualitative research in practice: Stories from the field*. Buckingham: Open University Press.

Dickson-Swift, V., James, E. L., Kippen, S., & Liamputtong, P. (2007). Doing sensitive research: What challenges do qualitative researchers face? *Qualitative Research*, *7*(3), 327–353.

Duncombe, J., & Jessop, J. (2012). Doing rapport and the ethics or 'faking friendship'. In T. Miller, M. Birch, M. Mauthner, & J. Jessop (Eds.), *Ethics in qualitative research* (2nd ed., pp. 108–121). London: SAGE Publications.

Finch, J. (1984). 'It's great to have someone to talk to': The ethics and politics of interviewing women'. In C. Bell & H. Roberts (Eds.), *Social researching: Politics, problems, practice* (pp. 70–87). London: Routledge & Kegan Paul.

Gil, S., & Weinberg, M. (2015). Secondary trauma among social workers treating trauma clients: The role of coping strategies and internal resources. *International Social Work*, *58*(4), 551–561.

Golash-Boza, T. M. (2015). *Deported: Immigration policing, disposable labour, and global capitalism*. New York and London: New York University Press.

Gregory, D., Cynthia, R., & Phillips, L. (1997). Beyond textual perfection: Transcribers as vulnerable persons. *Qualitative Health Research*, *7*(2), 294–300.

Hernández, P., Gangsei, D., & Engstrom, D. (2007). Vicarious resilience: A new concept in work with those who survive trauma. *Family Process*, *46*(2), 229–241.

Hernandez-Wolfe, P., Killian, K., Engstrom, D., & Gangsei, D. (2015). Vicarious resilience, vicarious trauma, and awareness of equity in trauma work. *Journal of Humanistic Psychology*, *55*(552), 153–172.

James, T., & Platzer, H. (1999). Ethical considerations in qualitative research with vulnerable groups: Exploring lesbians' and gay men's experiences of health care – a personal perspective. *Nursing Ethics*, *6*(1), 73–81.

Jamieson, J. (2000). Danger in fieldwork on crime. In G. Lee-Treweek & S. Linkogle (Eds.), *Danger in the field: Risk and ethics in social Research*. London: Routledge.

Johnson, B., & Clarke, J. M. (2003). Collecting sensitive data: The impact on researchers. *Qualitative Health Research, 13*(3), 421–434.

Khosravi, S. (2009). Sweden: Detention and deportation of asylum seekers. *Race & Class, 50*(4), 38–56.

Lofland, J. (2006). *Analyzing social settings: A guide to qualitative observation and analysis* (4th ed.). Belmont, CA: Wadsworth/Thomson Learning Publication.

McCann, L., & Pearlman, L. (1990). Vicarious traumatization: A framework for understanding tile psychological effects of working with victims. *Journal of Traumatic Stress, 3*(1), 131–149.

Mitchell, W., & Irvine, A. (2008). I'm okay, you're okay? Reflections on the well-being and ethical requirements of researchers and research participants in conducting qualitative fieldwork interviews. *International Journal of Qualitative Methods, 7*(4), 31–44.

Morris, L. (2002). Britain's asylum and immigration regime: The shifting contours of rights. *Journal of Ethnic and Migration Studies, 28*(3), 409–425.

Oakley, A. (1981). Interviewing women: A contradiction in terms. In H. Roberts (Ed.), *Doing feminist research* (pp. 30–61). London and Boston, MA: Routledge & Kegan Paul.

Oberoi, P., & Taylor-Nicholson, E. (2013). The enemy at the gates: International borders, migration and human rights. *Laws, 2*(3), 169–186.

Peutz, N. (2006). Embarking on an anthropology of removal. *Current Anthropology, 47*(2), 217–241.

Phelps, J. (2009, January). *Detained lives: The real cost of indefinite immigration detention*. London: Detainee Support Group.

Robjant, K., Robbins, I., & Senior, V. (2009). Psychological distress amongst immigration detainees: A cross-sectional questionnaire study. *The British Journal of Clinical Psychology/ the British Psychological Society, 48*(Pt 3), 275–286.

Rowling, L. (1999). Being in, being out, being with: Affect and the role of the qualitative researcher in loss and grief research. *Mortality, 4*(2), 167–181.

Schuster, L., & Majidi, N. (2013). What happens post-deportation? The experience of deported Afghans. *Migration Studies, 1*(2), 221–240.

Silverman, S. J., & Massa, E. (2012). Why immigration detention is unique. *Population, Space and Place, 18*(6), 677–686.

Spring, G., Carlton, C., & Clark, J. (2011). Secondary traumatic stress and burnout in child welfare workers: A comparative analysis of occupational distress across professional groups. *Child Welfare, 90*(6), 149–168.

Steel, Z., Momartin, S., Silove, D., Coello, M., Aroche, J., & Tay, K. W. (2011). Two year psychosocial and mental health outcomes for refugees subjected to restrictive or supportive immigration policies. *Social Science and Medicine, 72*(7), 1149–1156.

Warr, D. J. (2004). Stories in the flesh and voices in the head: Reflections on the context and impact of research with disadvantaged populations. *Qualitative Health Research, 14*(4), 578–587.

Chapter 11

In the absence of sympathy
Serious criminal offenders and the impact of border control measures

Rebecca Powell and Marie Segrave

Introduction

In Australia, as in other parts of the world, convicted offenders may be deported following a period of incarceration, according to restrictive migration policies that are generally supported by governments and the public (for example, see Kaufman, 2015; Golash-Boza, 2015). In order to understand this policy better, and its implications for justice, we conducted a small research project over a two-year period (2012–2014) with 15 non-citizens who had been convicted of serious criminal offences and were awaiting deportation. We also interviewed 20 advocates who worked with them. In this chapter, drawing on this material, we focus on the role of sympathy[1] in research and policy. While we sought to highlight the variable enforcement and targeting of border controls in the criminal deportation process, we found those we interviewed to be challenging. We discovered their advocates often did as well. Our experiences suggest that attempts to restructure the border regime in favour of a human rights–based approach to visa cancellations for long-term residents who are convicted non-citizens may have to occur in the absence of sympathy.

Adopting a sympathetic position assisted us in building rapport and trust with convicted non-citizens. We wanted to hear their stories, and we were concerned about their deportation irrespective of their criminal conviction(s). Yet we often found their accounts of their criminal actions upsetting. Advocates for criminal non-citizens spoke of similar difficulties in providing assistance and support. By drawing on interviews with advocates as well as our experiences of interviewing convicted non-citizens we seek to share the challenges we faced in our research.

The articulation and recognition of sympathy was not part of the research design. However, as our work progressed we came to recognise and be troubled by the impact of our emotional responses to our research participants. While our feelings did not disrupt the broader aim of the research, they alerted us to the importance of exposing and grappling with the challenges of conducting borders research with an unsympathetic group. In this chapter we share our experiences in the field not to dwell on our emotions but in a bid to understand the role of sympathy in border control research.

Background: criminal deportation in Australia

Political justification and popular support for criminal deportation sits within the broader discourses of 'pre-empting' (McCulloch & Wilson, 2016) and 'exporting' risk (Weber & Pickering, 2012), according to which removing convicted non-citizens from Australia protects the community from future harm. Visa cancellation decision making against convicted non-citizens emphasises the future risk they present to the Australian community because of their criminal status as a major justification for their removal (see Ministerial Direction No. 65).[2] In this climate, the stories of those who have been or are awaiting deportation and who have already served their prison sentence are rarely heard. Where they are presented, it is not often from a sympathetic viewpoint (although see Grewcock, 2014).

In Australia, the precarious position of non-citizens, including those with a valid visa or permanent residency status, has increased since the 1990s following various amendments to the character test under the Migration Act 1958 that have expanded the powers of the Immigration Minister to cancel or refuse a convicted non-citizen's visa (see Grewcock, 2014). The most recent amendment to s501 occurred in December 2014 and included mandatory visa cancellation for non-citizens who had been sentenced to a prison term of 12 months or more.[3] Non-citizens are subject to the character test as a result of criminal conviction. Failing this test will put them on a pathway towards deportation regardless of the length of time they have been residents in Australia or the strength of their family and community ties. This development has been symptomatic of the increasing merging of immigration law with criminal law. As described within the emerging 'crimmigration' scholarship, 'crime control objectives' increasingly 'define the terms of... exclusion' for non-citizens (Aas, 2011, p. 342; see also Stumpf, 2006; Aas, 2014).

We know little about those subject to these migration restrictions, either in terms of the sum of those deported annually under s501 or their experience of the process of expulsion.[4] Our research sought to fill this gap by paying particular attention to those who had lived in Australia for most of their lives.[5] We sought to speak to those who work with and advocate for this group,[6] as well as to convicted non-citizen detainees themselves. In conducting this research, we had two primary goals: to understand better the impact of the border regime on individuals and the community and to effect policy change.

Research methodology: considering a sympathetic approach

In approaching this group of non-citizens with compassion, we sought deliberately to counter the 'you don't belong here' attitude of the Australian government towards convicted non-citizens and particularly those with serious criminal convictions (see Australian Government Ministers quoted in Cooper, 2015; Doran, 2015). Our ethical stance was influenced by the growing body of work on how gendered and racialised prejudice shapes the treatment of non-citizens (cf. Segrave & Powell, 2015). Much of that work is focused on situations involving non-citizens who have experienced some form of exploitation. In contrast, individuals subject to adverse s501 decisions are viewed not as 'victims' but as criminals and persons of risk to the community. Therefore, they do not evoke sympathy amongst wider political and public circles. Advocates and researchers also struggle to acknowledge their plight.

Our research design was informed by feminist and critical research methodologies that emphasise building rapport to 'give relatively powerless people a voice to express their standpoints'. Like others, we are committed to research that seeks to promote social justice and produce 'knowledge that informs and promotes positive social change' (Chesney-Lind & Morash, 2013, pp. 288, 294). The focus of the analysis offered here builds on the 'emotion work' that has come to the fore in reflexive accounts of feminist and critical criminological research (see Kilty, Felices-Luna, & Fabian, 2014; Fabian, 2014; Hannem, 2014).

While sympathy is, arguably, not required at all in feminist research, acknowledging fellow feelings connects researchers to the stories of individuals, families and communities they study. In this regard, our research focused on exposing how the Australian border regime undermines the justice system for convicted non-citizens and how removal adversely affects them, their families and the community. Serious offenders awaiting deportation, we pointed out, have often lived much of their lives in Australia and have served their sentence. Their expulsion from Australia feels like an additional punishment.

The challenges of positionality in conducting research with the unsympathetic

There is a body of reflexive research scholarship dedicated to the challenges and realities of working with and for serious criminal offenders who commit sexual and physical offences (see, for example Waldram, 2007; Liebling, 2001; Cowburn, 2007; Schlosser, 2008; Looser, 2007; Crewe & Ievins, 2015). However, we know little about the realities of researching offenders who are subject to migration laws that result in their detention and deportation after serving a prison sentence (although see Bosworth, 2011, 2014; Bosworth & Kaufman, 2013; Turnbull & Hasselberg 2017; Hasselberg, 2016; Kaufman, 2015; Achermann, 2013). In the Australian context, other than work by Mike Grewcock (2014), there is none at all.

Within the field of sociology, there has been a significant debate around the positioning of the researcher and the research subject, with Loic Wacquant famously deriding colleagues for seeking to 'attract sympathy' for the 'plight' of subjects. Such feelings, he argues, are counter to the role of ethnographers (see Wacquant, 2002, p. 1470, also the replies from Anderson, 2002; Duneier, 2002). For Wacquant, acknowledging our feelings means that rigorous social analysis is substituted by a sympathetic and moralistic description of subjects' accounts of their lives.

Our research sought to understand the experience of participants awaiting deportation in order to trace the impact and experience of border control measures that govern criminal deportation. Like ethnographic research, our methodology brought,

> investigators and the subjects of their inquiries into close contact interactionally and, in many studies, emotionally . . . and that investigators [aim to] get close to their subject matter and strive to understand it through the lived experience and perspectives of critical actors.
>
> (Shover, 2012, p. 140)

Is it possible, we ask, to separate the personal experience from the broader analysis, both in the immediate setting of doing research (i.e. when sitting in a room interviewing a research participant) and in the analytical and dissemination setting in which research findings are analysed and written up? In this context, there is a fine line between advocacy for individuals (which Waquant was criticising) for a fairer border enforcement system and the opportunity for analysis to offer a broader critique of bordering practices. We explore this predicament by considering the research experience itself, laying out our emotions and experiences that are often hidden behind the analysis.

It is clear that the interviewee can command considerable control through the telling of their personal narrative (see, for example, Looser, 2007; England, 1994; Pillow, 2003; Watt, 2007). The researcher must navigate a delicate power dynamic in order to build rapport. In semi-structured interviews, the focus must be simultaneously trained on the immediate discussion with an eye to the broader conversation. While the discussion can move towards and away from the main focus, this should not happen randomly. The researcher hopes the conversation will seem natural and thus needs to be open to where the conversation goes, yet at the same time, he or she must also be able to steer it gently back to the topic of the research project if the participant roams too far.

Such an approach to interviewing has consequences (Dickson-Swift et al., 2007; Liebling, 2001). For example, the researcher may inhibit reactions to disturbing statements and appear non-judgmental (with a view to the participants rather than his/her own welfare) in response to opinions or experiences that may be distasteful, objectionable and/or offensive (Cowburn, 2007). Drawing on our own experience, we offer a reflexive review of such situations as they arose, of how they were managed and the broader consequences of this research for advancing a critical border criminological agenda.

The research design

We conducted semi-structured interviews with eight s501 convicted non-citizens in Villawood Immigration Detention Centre in Sydney, New South Wales, and seven in Maribyrnong Immigration Detention Centre in Melbourne,

Victoria. Twenty further interviews were conducted with stakeholder groups in Sydney, Melbourne and Perth, including community-based law firms and other legal practitioners, NGOs and activist groups who support s501 cases.

In our research design and ethics approval application, we focused on potential risks to participants, even though we anticipated this would be minimal in most cases. Our ethics application emphasised immigration-related processes and experiences with little consideration for the offences committed, and our interview schedule reflected this set of assumptions. We also set out plans to interview how advocates and lawyers campaigned for those subject to s501 cancellation.

Informed by a feminist and critical research agenda, our research approach was founded upon close human interaction. As Chesney-Lind and Morash state:

> to challenge damaging policies and advance those that protect the less powerful, feminist criminologists often collaborate with and carefully listen to the people they study. Additionally, they collaborate with advocates to ensure that theoretical discoveries are translated into program and policy action.
>
> (Chesney-Lind & Morash, 2013, p. 294)

We sat in private rooms with detainees, developing rapport and creating openness to allow for stories and experiences to be shared (see also Hubbard et al., 2001 and the work of Bosworth, 2014). In so doing, we hoped we could advocate for social change based on empirical work (Mason & Stubbs, 2012).

However, such an approach led to moments of considerable discomfort. At times we felt unsafe. We also felt unsympathetic. We were particularly troubled when our participants described their offences in graphic detail. We were also disturbed to learn that advocates essentially ranked the sympathetic potential of individual cases.

Our experiences, which illuminate the reality of border research, resonate with other qualitative research. On the one hand, it is unsurprising that convicted non-citizens are complex people. Yet, as researchers focusing on the impacts of the border regime, we must reckon with our own and others' judgement against serious and/or disturbing criminal activity revealed in the research process. This can be tricky when our ultimate research goal is to deliver our findings to a challenging audience already deaf to the counter-arguments against the increasing use of s501 for deportation.

Experiences from the field

We now draw on two examples to illuminate the challenges of engaging sympathy when researching convicted non-citizens. The first is taken from an interview conducted by Segrave with an s501 deportee, and the second relates to the experience of Powell from her interviews with advocates who represented and supported convicted non-citizens in s501 removal order appeals. In the first instance, we highlight Marie's discomfort about the offending background of the participant and the immediate and ongoing challenge of this realisation as the interview progressed and beyond. The second example from Rebecca's experience draws on the practical, daily judgements of advocates and legal practitioners who exercise discretion regarding which cases to pursue based on the determination of the offence's severity.

Interviewing a sex offender: Segrave's experience

This section begins with the very first interview Segrave conducted in Maribyrnong Immigration Detention Centre (MIDC) in Melbourne, Australia, with Terry,[7] a hospitable man with a Yorkshire accent, who was around 60 years old. He was keen to be involved in the research project, so this was considered an 'easy' interview. While Terry was in charge of the conversation, he was responsive to the opening questions and was happy to be prompted to expand on some details. It felt, as an ideal semi-structured interview should, like a conversation that was flowing.

From the start, Terry referred to his situation as 'unfair'. He felt his conviction was an act of 'discrimination'. He had been in Australia for over 40 years, and though he had applied for citizenship, he had chosen not to attend a citizenship ceremony, unaware it was a necessary final step to becoming a citizen. He was married and had children and grandchildren in Australia. Although the research focus was on deportation, the impact of which would be significant for his family, it was immediately clear that Terry's motivation in participating in the research was to exonerate himself as a way of justifying his appeal against deportation:

> I committed crimes, sex offences but no sexual penetration or anything like that, it was just touching. And exposure, but I am being classed as a paedophile, by the judge, although I had a criminal psychologist which was Dr XXXX ... and [he] tried to put that to the Court that it was just one of these things.

This statement was unexpected. Until that point, Marie had had no idea of Terry's offence. His dismissal of his offences as simply 'one of those things' shifted the power dynamic and balance of the interview, not least because in that moment Terry clearly became a deportee for whom the researcher knew there would be very limited sympathy. 'The nature of this disclosure shifted the focus of the interview to Terry's criminality and also revealed two different agendas: for Segrave to better understand the impact of deportation and punishment beyond imprisonment to detention and deportation, while for the participant to be seen as victimised by the criminal justice system and migration system'.

The way forward was not immediately clear: Segrave did not want to hear more about his offences. Not only did she find the crimes upsetting, but Terry's account of them was not relevant for the research focus. She was particularly troubled by his attempts to deny their seriousness and impact. Yet, it was clear that Terry's attempt to exonerate himself and minimise his actions was a key part of why he was participating in the project. To make such matters 'out of bounds' would have ended the interaction. As a result, Marie could only try to acknowledge what Terry said without endorsing or encouraging this focus while constantly attempting to shift the conversation back to the remit of the project.

Over and over again, however, Terry veered the conversation back to his offences and his poor treatment by the criminal justice system. Segrave knew nothing of his offending background, and it felt compromising to listen to these justifications, in part because she knew nothing of the crimes to which he was referring and in part because it seemed he wanted her to be on 'his side' in relation to how he viewed these crimes. She did not want to take sides, yet before he disclosed his offence, she had been in many ways on 'his side'; compassionate about his experiences of the threat of deportation. Later on he began arguing that his offence could account for the Ministerial decision cancelling his visa:

> [The] Minister has to sign off. And you can guarantee they have got rubber stamp ... [Y]ou don't know who you dealing with in Immigration because see my file consisted of 115 pages and I had about 15 different signatures, which meant 15 people handled it, now they have all got different ideas. Any of them for example may have been against paedophiles or people like me.

In sharing these excerpts, we hope in part to recognise that the design of a research project can be naïve, and as a result, researchers may be unprepared for what participants reveal. This is not news, however. In designing a project focused on s501 visa cancellations and the impact of the criminal justice and the border regime on convicted non-citizens, we simply failed to prepare for this kind of interview experience. Over the course of the project, we encountered other examples, including highly violent offenders who similarly justified their actions. However, the point of this story is not simply one of research design. Rather, we deploy it here to highlight that our own sympathy to those subject to deportation practices can be challenged. It demonstrates how, in the interview process, the balance of power can be compromised in those moments of discomfort experienced by the researchers as it tips towards the convicted non-citizen during their narratives of their criminal offending. Ultimately, such interviews present challenges to the broader project of advocating for s501 deportees.

In the context of researching border control against convicted non-citizens, Terry's story and experience are not being undervalued here, but we hear them knowing that a case such as this one must be treated carefully or his story, if we publish them without care, could be used to reinforce the necessity of the strict use of s501 to deport such offenders. In the analysis of these data, we do not refer to this aspect of the conversation, as our focus is the utilisation of deportation: it remains under the surface of the analysis as a research experience rather than as an experience that impacted our broader analysis. We now turn to examining the ways in which advocates can make value judgments in their s501 caseload about who is more or less sympathetic every day and the impact of those judgments on convicted non-citizens whom they seek to represent.

Interviewing the stakeholder: Powell's experience

In Powell's interviews with legal practitioner stakeholders who support and advocate for s501 convicted non-citizens, participants spoke of the difficulties they faced in working with potential s501 clients and deciding which cases to accept. They appeared to operate a sliding sympathy scale towards this client group, which in various ways reflected our experience as researchers. Stakeholders could sympathise with their s501 clients over their deportation fate, but at times, their compassion was strained due to their clients' serious criminal offending. Such matters influenced their caseload decisions, which were compounded by limited staffing resources. Powell observed a great degree of sympathy from most of the interviewees towards their client group and a strong commitment to giving a voice to this otherwise marginalised and politically contested group. As one interviewee said:

> You list the things that our client had done, and nine people out of ten out in the general public would say, 'We don't want them here, get rid of them'. So there's ... our clients ... just don't have anybody, they don't have a voice. They don't have anybody to stand up for them and say, 'That's wrong. They should be allowed to stay'. They just don't.
>
> [ASS17]

Visa cancellation decisions are reviewed by the Administrative Appeal Tribunal (AAT) in Australia, where legal advocates have the opportunity to represent and defend s501 clients. In a system that favors the removal of convicted non-citizens who do not pass the character test under s501,[8] interviewing stakeholders for this research project showed that there is room for advocacy and defense of their right to a fair criminal justice process that accompanies the review of the decision to cancel their visa.

> Our role ... is about process and making sure that people get a chance to have their say and to put those things in their favour properly forward ... it's really important that people have an opportunity to put forward every last skerrick of evidence for consideration by a decision-maker before a power as profound as removal is exercised.
>
> [AMS18]

During reviews of cancellation decisions at the AAT, human rights–based considerations and personal circumstances of the individual including ties to the Australian community, length of residence, family and minor children and rehabilitation efforts are considered. The visa cancellation decision-making process and decisional review system, however, are weighted towards constructing the convicted non-citizen as a risk to the Australian community, which often trumps the personal circumstances of the individuals and their ties to Australia. With experience and knowledge of this discretionary imbalance, legal practitioners will often weigh up taking on an s501 case in regards to its potential for success based on an assessment of the seriousness of convicted non-citizens' crime/s against their ties to Australia. The additional burden of limited staffing and resources for advocate groups (Timms, 2016; Community Law Australia, 2016) alongside their view to the broader political reality in which some offenders have committed crimes too heinous and serious to warrant any sympathy, informed decisions about which cases stakeholders took on

> even though they might have been young adults [at the time of the offence], they have done some pretty gross stuff, some pretty serious stuff, and we won't take them on.
> [APS7]

> We also refuse quite a few applications.... The offences have been too bad.
> [ASS17]

These attitudes reveal and represent the moral position of some stakeholders and their sympathy towards serious convicted non-citizens. Such matters inevitably influence professional assessments of whether to support these clients in the AAT review of the Minister's decision to cancel their visa or not. The challenge for us is to write about this without sitting in judgment of these professional decisions that are clearly influenced by certain circumstances. We seek to develop and provide an understanding of the challenges advocacy groups experience in s501 cases in regards to upholding fairness in deportation practices for an unsympathetic group.

Conclusion: moving the agenda forward

In this chapter, we have sought to recognise that in advocating for equality, fairness and rights, we must be prepared to advocate, at times, for people for whom we and others will have little sympathy. As border researchers, we tried to separate the unsympathetic (serious criminality) from the appealing (the impact of Australia's border control on long-term residents who are convicted non-citizens subject to s501) as a means to engage with our research group in order to develop understandings of the Australian criminal deportation process. We note that as researchers we may feel an emotional response that may be unsympathetic, such as outrage, anger and disgust just as professionals who advocate for convicted non-citizens similarly make decisions about their clientele in part informed by a judgement of the person and their crime/s. Yet we try to continue the interviews and, in so doing, remain focused on the broader aim of the research whilst in some circumstances, as in the experience with Terry, we seek to gain some control (not always successfully) back in the interview focus.

We are in a position to give this marginalised group a voice (England, 1994) and to use the information we gather to advocate for their rights. We hope to promote due process and reveal the increasing entanglement of criminal justice and border regimes, at the disadvantage of those we may least want to protect. Although convicted non-citizens are sometimes challenging research participants, regardless of their crimes, they allow us to better understand the complexity and strength of the moral arguments for strong border controls alongside the harsh conditions they experience. Because of their long-term residence, their contributions and ties to the Australia community, they are valued as people who deserve fairness in balancing risk with considerations of their human rights in the visa cancellation decision-making process. Our research on criminal deportations from Australia provides a more nuanced account of this particular aspect of Australian border control. It sheds light on the injustices of this process for a largely unsympathetic research group, which therefore opens up avenues for sympathy towards this group when the impact of border control on their human rights is considered.

Notes

1 We define sympathy as per the Oxford Living Dictionary: 'feelings of pity and sorrow for someone else's misfortune' (https://en.oxforddictionaries.com/definition/sympathy), which we recognise here as enabling a different understanding and perspective on practices such as border control, in that it aids to recognise that despite the rhetoric of border enforcement, sympathy can not only evoke a feeling but a change in the support for social policy and, therefore, a platform for change.
2 The construction of convicted non-citizens as a risk to the Australian community is being explored in a PhD research project currently being undertaken by Rebecca Powell.
3 The s501 character test has been tightened in recent decades (Grewcock, 2011; Rimmer, 2008). Recent changes to the Migration Act in December 2014 led to the strengthening of s501 with the introduction of a mandatory visa cancellation clause for those convicted with a 12-month prison sentence or more. Alongside s501, visa cancellation decision-making guidelines set out in Ministerial Direction No. 65 reduced the significance and decisional weight against cancellation given to length of residence in Australia (including long-term permanent residents) and family ties in Australia of the convicted non-citizens subject to s501. The government claimed that these amendments strengthened 'the thresholds for visa cancellation on the basis of criminality and risk' (DIBP, 2015, p. 159). Further, the government stated that, '[T]hese changes reflect the Government's position that travelling to, and remaining in, Australia is a privilege, not a right, and that any non-citizen who would seek to do us harm or who chooses to breach the law or who fails to uphold the behavioral standards expected by the Australian community should

expect to be refused entry or have their visa cancelled' (DIBP, 2015, p. 159). These changes have occurred after the research that is the focus of this chapter.
4 These data are provided by the Australian government, Department of Immigration and Border Protection Annual Reports. Removal categories include monitored departures from the community, voluntary and involuntary removals from immigration detention and the return of transferees from Regional Processing Centres; see www.border.gov.au/about/reports-publications/reports/annual. For the most recent reporting year 2014–2015, there was a total of 588 visa cancellation decisions made by the Immigration Minister or his delegate and 16,026 removals from Australia. It is also important to note that there is a time lag between visa cancellations and removals from Australia which differs for each individual case.
5 See, for example, the case of Stefan Nystrom, who arrived in Australia when he was 27 days old and was deported to Sweden when he was 32 years old in 2006, where he did not speak the language and had no family or other support, and Andrew Moore who arrived in Australia when he was 11 and was deported to the UK in 2009 when he was 32 years old and died within days of his arrival (Grewcock, 2011, 2014).
6 For this research we sought to interview men and women, who are separated in detention centres. However, the limited period of access and a shifting leadership attitude towards supporting this research resulted in that researchers only had access to wings within two detention centres that were for men. That said, within the scope of this practice men are far more likely to be deported in this context than women, reflecting more broadly the differential offending rate between men and women regardless of whether they are citizens.
7 A pseudonym.
8 *Migration Act 1958*, Section 501, Refusal or cancellation of visa on character grounds. Available at, www.austlii.edu.au/cgi-bin/viewdoc/au/legis/cth/consol_act/ma1958118/s501.html [Accessed 23 August 2017].

References

Aas, K. F. (2011). 'Crimmigration' bodies and bona fide travellers: Surveillance, citizenship and global governance. *Theoretical Criminology*, 15(3), 341–356.
Aas, K. F. (2014). Bordered penality: Precarious membership and abnormal justice. *Punishment & Society*, 16(5), 520–541.
Achermann, C. (2013). Excluding the unwanted: Dealing with foreign-national offenders in Switzerland. In A. Ilker & S. Rosenberger (Eds.), *Politik der Inklusion und Exklusion* (pp. 91–109). Vienna: Vienna University Press.
Anderson, E. (2002). The ideologically driven critique. *American Journal of Sociology*, 107(6), 1533–1550.
Bosworth, M. (2011). Deportation, detention and foreign national prisoners in England and Wales. *Citizenship Studies*, 15(5), 583–595.
Bosworth, M. (2014). *Inside immigration detention: Foreigners in a carceral age*. Oxford: Oxford University Press.
Bosworth, M., & Kaufman, E. (2013). Prison and national identity: Citizenship, punishment and the sovereign state. In D. Scott (Ed.), *Why prison?* Cambridge: Cambridge University Press.
Chesney-Lind, M., & Morash, M. (2013). Transformative feminist criminology: A critical re-thinking of a discipline. *Critical Criminology*, 21(3), 287–304.
Community Law Australia. (2016, May 3). *Budget cuts to legal assistance services hit vulnerable hardest*. Online. Retrieved January 3, 2017, from www. community lawaustralia.org.au/budget-cuts-to-legal-assistance-services-hit-vulnerable-hardest/

Cooper, H. (2015, October 16). This is the reason Malcolm Turnbull's getting a less than kiwi friendly welcome. *ABC News*. Online. Retrieved September 14, 2016, from www.abc.net.au/7.30/content/2015/s4333535.htm

Cowburn, M. (2007). Men researching men in prison: The challenges for pro-feminist research. *The Howard Journal, 46*(3), 276–288.

Crewe, B., & Ievins, A. (2015). Closeness, distance and honesty in prison ethnography. In D. H. Drake et al. (Eds.), *The Palgrave handbook of prison ethnography* (pp. 124–142). London: Palgrave Macmillan.

Department of Immigration and Border Protection (DIBP). (2015). *Annual report 2014–2015*. Australian Government. Online. Retrieved November 27, 2016, from www.border.gov.au/ReportsandPublications/Documents/annual-reports/DIBP-Annual-Report-2014-15.pdf

Dickson-Swift, V., James, E. L., Kippen, S., & Liamputtong, P. (2007). Doing sensitive research: What challenges do qualitative researchers face? *Qualitative Research, 7*(3), 327–353.

Doran, M. (2015, September 25). NZ PM to speak to Malcolm Turnbull about citizens held in Australian detention centres. *ABC News*. Online. Retrieved October 10, 2016, from www.abc.net.au/news/2015-09-25/nz-pm-'concerned'-over-citizens-in-australian-detention/6805192

Duneier, M. (2002). What kind of combat sport is sociology? *American Journal of Sociology, 107*(6), 1551–1576.

England, K. V. L. (1994). Getting personal: Reflexivity, positionality and feminist research. *Women in the Field, 46*(1), 80–89.

Fabian, S. C. (2014). Reconciling the irreconcilable: Resolving emotionality and research responsibility when working for the traumatizer. In J. M. Kilty, M. Felices-Luna, & S. C. Fabian (Eds.), *Demarginalizing voices: Commitment, emotion, and action in qualitative research*. Vancouver: UBC Press.

Golash-Boza, T. M. (2015). *Deported: Immigration policing, disposable labour and global capitalism*. New York: NYU Press.

Grewcock, M. (2011). Punishment, deportation and parole: The detention and removal of former prisoners under section 501 Migration Act 1958. *The Australian and New Zealand Journal of Criminology, 44*(1), 56–73.

Grewcock, M. (2014). Reinventing 'the stain' – bad character and criminal deportation in contemporary Australia. In S. Pickering & J. Ham (Eds.), *Routledge handbook on crime and international migration* (pp. 121–138). Abingdon: Routledge.

Hannem, S. (2014). Grappling with reflexivity and the role of emotion in criminological analysis. In J. M. Kilty, M. Felices-Luna, & S. C. Fabian (Eds.), *Demarginalizing voices: Commitment, emotion, and action in qualitative research* (pp. 267–285). Vancouver: UBC Press.

Hasselberg, I. (2016). *Enduring uncertainty: Deportation, punishment and everyday life*. New York: Berghahn Books.

Hubbard, G., Beckett-Milburn, K., & Kemmer, D. (2001). Working with emotion: Issues for the researcher in fieldwork and teamwork. *International Journal of Social Research Methodology, 4*(2), 119–137.

Kaufmann, E. (2015). *Punish and expel: Border control, nationalism, and the new purpose of the prison*. Oxford: Oxford University Press.

Kilty, J. M., Felices-Luna, M., & Fabian, S. C. (2014). *Demarginalizing voices: Commitment, emotion and action in qualitative research*. Vancouver: UBC Press.

Liebling, A. (2001). Whose side are we on? Theory, practice and allegiances in prison research. *British Journal of Criminology, 41*, 472–484.

Looser, D. (2007). Lexicography on the inside: Doing time in every New Zealand prison. *International Journal of Lexicography*, *17*(1), 69–87.

Mason, G., & Stubbs, J. (2012). Feminist approaches to criminological research. In D. Gadd, S. Karstedt, & S. Mesner (Eds.), *The Sage handbook of criminological research methods* (pp. 486–499). London: SAGE Publications.

McCulloch, J., & Wilson, D. J. (2016). *Pre-emption, precaution and the future*. Abingdon: Routledge.

Ministerial Direction No. 65 to the *Migration Act 1958*, Direction under Section 499, Visa refusal and cancellation under s501 and revocation of a mandatory cancellation of a visa under s501CA. Online. Retrieved January 3, 2017, from www.border.gov.au/visas/Documents/ministerial-direction-65.pdf

Pickering, S., & Weber, L. (2006). Borders, mobility and technologies of control. In S. Pickering & L. Weber (Eds.), *Borders, mobility and technologies of control* (pp. 1–19). Dordrecht, The Netherlands: Springer.

Pillow, W. (2003). Confession, catharsis or cure? Rethinking the uses of reflexivity as methodological power in qualitative research. *International Journal of Qualitative Studies in Education*, *16*(2), 175-196.

Pittaway, E., Bartolomei, L., & Hugman, R. (2010). 'Stop stealing our stories': The ethics of research with vulnerable groups. *Journal of Human Rights Practice*, *2*(2), 229–251.

Rimmer, S. H. (2008, October). *The dangers of character tests: Dr Haneef and other cautionary tales*. Discussion Paper No. 101, The Australia Institute. Online. Retrieved September 16, 2016, from www.tai.org.au/sites/defualt/files/DP101_7.pdf

Schlosser, J. A. (2008). Issues in navigating inmates: Navigating the methodological landmines of prison research. *Qualitative Inquiry*, *14*(8), 1500–1525.

Segrave, M., & Powell, R. (2015). Victimisation, citizenship and gender: Interrogating state responses. In D. Wilson & S. Ross (Eds.), *Crime, victims and policy: International contexts, local experiences* (pp. 53–83). Hampshire, UK: Palgrave Macmillan.

Shover, N. (2012). Ethnographic methods in criminological research: Rationale, reprise and warning. *American Journal of Criminal Justice*, *37*(2), 139–145.

Stumpf, J. (2006). The crimmigration crisis: Immigrants, crime and sovereign power. *American University Law Review*, *56*, 367–419.

Timms, P. (2016, May 16). Legal aid matters: Lack of government funding 'destroying lives', law council says. *ABC News*. Online. Retrieved January 3, 2017, from www.abc.net.au/news/2016-05-16/law-council-of-australia-launches-legal-aid-matters-campaign/7417094

Turnbull, S., & Hasselberg, I. (2017). From prison to detention: The carceral trajectories of foreign-national prisoners in the United Kingdom, *Punishment and Society*, *19*(2), 135–154.

Wacquant, L. (2002). Review: Scrutinizing the street: Poverty, morality, and the pitfalls of urban ethnography. *American Journal of Sociology*, *107*(6), 1468–1532.

Waldram, J. B. (2007). Everybody has a story: Listening to imprisoned sexual offenders. *Qualitative Health Research*, *17*(7), 963–970.

Watt, D. (2007). On becoming a qualitative researcher: The value of reflexivity. *The Qualitative Report*, *12*(1), 82–101.

Weber, L., & Pickering, S. (2012). Exporting risk, deporting non-citizens. In F. Pakes (Ed.), *Globalisation and the challenge to criminology*. London: Routledge.

Chapter 12

Reflexivity and theorizing
Conceptualizing the police role in migration control

Helene O. I. Gundhus[1]

Introduction

In order to understand how control and security works, participant observation of those with power to define security agendas is an important vantage point. By using participatory observation together with interviews in a project on migration policing in Norway at different organizations and locations, we sought to gain proximity to police practices and occupational culture norms, values and professional ethos. To do so required access to study the field and willingness from the actors in the field to be researched. In this chapter I reflect on doing such research and look at how the positionality of the researcher might open up for new analytical insights about the practices of migration policing.

My research post during the project was at the Norwegian Police University College. This adds a particular layer to the reflection of the power dynamics within this research project, since this educational institution is part of the police. Nevertheless, researchers based there are supposed to have full academic freedom.[2] It was precisely because of my research position that I was particularly interested in mapping the policing field as a site where knowledge–power discourses take place in Foucauldian terms. Specifically, I was interested in understanding how the professionalisation discourse influences the police's role in society within the field of policing migration (Gundhus, 2017).

In discussing proximity relations between researched and researcher I reveal how theoretical approaches and theory provide pivotal sensitizing concepts for research in the practice field.[3] How level of access impacts the production of knowledge will, in this light, become secondary to questions about how to use the approach as a productive point of departure for analysis. The question will then be: when you find your research caught up in the cross-fire of competing moral and political agendas, how can you actively make use of these struggles on the production of knowledge, and to what ends?

The chapter follows four paths. I first provide the context of the study by describing the shifts in policing migration in Norway. I then move on to discuss the concept of positionality and how researchers negotiate proximity. In the third section I present empirical findings illustrating the challenges police officers, working with migration control and particularly deportation, experience and how these tensions affect the positioning of the researcher. In the last section I conclude with discussing how to deal with experiences of discomfort and competing moral and political agendas by moving and navigating between different research sites and concepts.

Multi-sited: researching policing migration in Norway

As a member of a multi-sited research project on the policing of migration in Norway, called 'Transnational policing, tasks, organization and professionalization', I experienced certain challenges in getting access, negotiating trust, and analyzing the field's complexities and tensions. The project constitutes a sub-project within the main project 'Crime Control in the Borderlands of Europe', headed by Katja Franko, carried out from 2012–2016 (University of Oslo, 2018).[4]

The project's overall objective was to map and examine the changing demands for knowledge within the police raised by international cooperation when it comes to policing diversity in a global society; how does globalization contribute to the changing nature of police professionalism, the development of novel work methods and standards, and professional and organizational cultures? The approach was built on the notion that globalization takes place *inside* the national rather than just over it, and the aim has been to explore the 'mundane globalization' – not just police working for international organizations but the internationalisation of everyday tasks of policing and their dynamical intertwining. Policing in itself is increasingly a global phenomenon, transgressing traditional boundaries of the nation-state (Bowling & Sheptycki, 2012). To capture what Sassen (2007) has coined as 'multiscalar nature of globalization processes' within the policing context, a broad range of sites was studied, from the Ministry of Justice and Public Security, Norwegian Police Directorate, and Norwegian Police University College to units with specialized competence, such as the National Police Immigration Service and National Criminal Investigation Service (KRIPOS). We also interviewed officers with experience in Frontex operations, Frontex personnel in Warsaw, and officers working at a local police station in Oslo that has a special co-operation with Romanian police, as well as the Organised Crime Unit in the Oslo police district.

In total the researchers conducted 70 qualitative in-depth interviews with police staff over a two-year period, from 2012 to 2014. Staff worked at a variety of levels in the institutions under review, and at different locations. They ranged from guest officers participating at ground level in cross-national police operations in the Mediterranean to interviews with top managers at national and European headquarters and communication unit desk workers at the Norwegian Criminal Investigation Service. We also observed meetings aimed to share experiences and best practices from the field.

Emerging and contested field of policing

Policing migration has been a priority in Norway over the last five years, particularly since the perceived refugee crisis during the summer of 2015, which put it at the top of the political, public, and police agendas. Two of the sites studied, the Norwegian Police Directorate and the Police Immigration Service, have for the last five years sought to normalize the use of immigration law as a crime control tool and to facilitate more effective identity checks of foreigners within the Norwegian border. Their aim has been both to improve the effectiveness of special agencies and to link their practices to core crime-fighting police activities (Franko & Mohn, 2015). In Norway, as elsewhere in Europe and the United States (see, inter alia, Aas, 2014; Leun, 2003; Stumpf, 2006: Weber & Bowling, 2008; Weber, 2013), immigration law is increasingly used in tandem with criminal law, as a tool for both crime fighting and migration control (POD, 2014a, b). The trend is a result of an increased political focus on mass mobility and security and of changes in European policy, domestic criminal justice systems, and, particularly, police leadership (Franko & Mohn, 2015). By deportation, the police prevent crime from recurring. This development, which is often referred to as a 'crimmigration'[5] process, is partly related to the intensified criminalization of immigration-related conduct, particularly illegal entry and re-entry, as well as to the progressive convergence and mutual support of criminal law and administrative immigration enforcement.

The National Police Immigration Service (NPIS) is the main domestic immigration law enforcement body tasked with migration policing and the key agency responsible for registering all asylum applications and verifying the identities of asylum seekers, as well as for coordinating and executing forced returns. There has been a substantial growth in the number of immigration police specialists in the NPIS over the last decade, from 135 in 2004 to 950 in 2016. The growth is closely connected to the political priorities mentioned earlier and the related increase in deportation orders based on removal orders/expulsion (from 190 in 2002 to 2,500 in 2014) (Franko & Mohn, 2015).[6] The NPIS cannot forcibly return a person to his or her country of origin without verifying and documenting their identity. In the many cases in which identifying documentation is absent, they rely on various methods developed by what interviewees describe as 'creative thinking'. By this they mean discretion concerning when to use criminal or immigration law, depending on the citizenship status of the non-citizens (third-world national or EEC citizen), their connection to Norway, and the possibility of deporting them (see also Aas, 2014). NPIS officers, who lack power to prosecute criminal cases, use coercive measures available from immigration law. These include arrest and remand in custody and seizure and search of a foreign citizen's personal belongings or dwelling, as well as traditional police methods like surveillance and the tracking of a person's network.

Although restrictive immigration policies introduced by the Ministry of Justice have been welcomed by the majority of the Norwegian population, this has been criticized within the public debate in Norway (Gundhus, 2017). Detention of children at the Immigration Police closed detention centre at Trandum and deportation of children who have lived for many years in Norway have been controversial, debated, and questioned in Parliament (Eriksen, 2017; Ugelvik, 2016). As a result, police often describe external pressures from the political level, police management, researchers, and the public. For instance, interviewees experienced pressure from above to produce removal orders and expulsion to increase the numbers of deportations and talked about ambivalence regarding performing the job. Moreover, the management of the Police Immigration Service also described being researched as challenging because external criticism has created both internal turmoil and pressure.[7] Nonetheless, the police have taken our research results seriously, including critical aspects, and we have been invited to numerous seminars and conferences to talk about the findings.

Positionality as an analytical concept

The research design was developed to give more voice to police officers' experiences of policing in the age of mass mobility in order to unveil the connections between the police practitioners' worldview and the operation of migration policing in practice. Taking account of their views of everyday life and the mundane within their work can be difficult. Researchers must trace meaning across different sites while grasping the multiplicity of meanings or the multivocality of situations. The research was therefore designed to capture nuances in the respondents' everyday world. Like other studies of culture and practice fields, it sought to explore actors' logic, rationalizations, characterized by ambiguity, contradictions, doubts, and conflicts, including ambivalence and doubt in reaction to the policies that they were implementing (Fassin, 2011, p. 245).

Traditionally methodological reflections related to qualitative research of the police have been discussed in terms of the researcher's positionality, that is, being an insider or outsider to the institution and/or academic or practitioner within the police (Brown, 1996). This chapter will further add to these methodological reflections on the insider/outsider aspect by looking deeper into the concept of positionality (Buegner & Mireanu, 2015). As mentioned in the introduction, the question is not how to reduce the impact of positionality in the research process or to analyze how the social position in the field may have impacted the fieldwork processes. Recent discussion on reflexivity and research effects also points to certain limits that difference in social position might have on the data production process (Damsa & Ugelvik, 2017). The aim of this chapter is rather to discuss what the tensions and dynamics produced among the researcher, the researched, and the topic explored might tell about the field and how negotiations of proximity may open up new analytical insights.

Analyzing empirical data requires analytical terms and translation of the field (Callon, 1986). Van Maanen's (1979) divide between first-order and second-order terms is useful to illuminate the process. First-order concepts are the terms and descriptions used by the participants. Second-order concepts are the theories or theoretical concepts used or created by the researcher. In the process of making first-order concepts into second-order ones, the researcher more or less creates analytical distance from the actors' point of view. Researching the global impact on policing indispensably requires such a break, since global processes are not tangible but need to be framed in a theoretical context so as to be understood (Sassen, 2007).

However, since the analytical approach of this project consisted of analyzing migration security and control as processes within mundane policing, such practices are interpreted as speech and performative acts. But involving humans in the research, by studying practices, implicates amplifying the voice and subjectivity to the entities involved. Moreover, getting closer to the practice field might challenge the researchers' experienced latitude for being critical towards the actors being researched. As Buegner and Mireanu (2015, p. 123) point out: "Methodology is the movement from the world to academic practice (and back) by which, to use a Latourian expression, the world is *mobilized*" [emphasis in the original]. Such translation may also be experienced by the researched as a breach of trust in the relationship between the researcher and the researched. This is common in ethnographic research but appears more prominently when the researched's internal logic and rationalities are questioned by the researcher, and as we will see, the researcher experiences discomfort with the practices they promoted thereof.

Hence, unlike traditional representations of proximity as an objectivity problem (see also Alvesson & Sköldberg, 2009), the claim of this chapter is that proximity has been fruitful to balance access, trust, discomfort, and the critical dimensions of the project. As it will be further explored, issues discussed in the interviews, such as professionalism and human rights, became central objects of the study, which served in navigating between closeness and distance.

Negotiation in the field

The topics under exploration, professionalism and standardization, were helpful in getting access to the field. Access was negotiated formally and informally. Securing formal access to the field was the easiest part of the research process. It was considered and approved by the Council of Confidentiality and Research, the Norwegian Police Directorate, and Norwegian Social Science Data Services (NSD) relatively quickly, within 5 months.

The second step towards approaching the field was, in line with the ethical research guidelines for doing police research at the Norwegian Police University College (Bjørgo & Myhrer, 2015), to send letters to police chiefs in the districts to ask for permission to use their employees' working time to participate in the research. Positive responses were received from all chief managers, giving us the contact details of key informants. Information meetings were arranged, and key contacts were established. However, the process was dependent on researchers calling and pushing forward the formal requests using informal networks. Finally, contact details and emails of volunteers who would like to participate in the project were sent to us. Formal access was therefore marked by elements of both informal and personal initiatives.

Getting inside the field and starting interviewing revealed that the specialists within the police saw themselves as change makers inside the police, framing deportation as a more rational and smarter way to combat crime. As one police officer argued:

> I see no reason why we should use a lot of money to put them in prison here, when we can fly them out. Because I can see that this is what is being done now, and I do not understand why. They do 10 or 12 years inside and continue just as before. Then we can send them to Kurdistan instead.
> (OPD2)

These arguments and justifications were quite different from my own preconceptions about deportation, which I assumed was more about implementing policies and enforcing immigration laws. The interviewees also revealed much more diversity in justifications and legitimations than expected, ranging from accounts claiming it as better ways to punish the perpetrators, as in the preceding quote, to ambivalence towards joint use of immigration and criminal law. Crimmigration processes within the Norwegian police were also considered as progressive, 'creative', 'using opportunities', and 'doing smart' policing. Yet this narrative is not in line with notions of appropriate police work among police in general – catching criminals – and rather is seen as morally dubious. Hence, those interviewed saw the possibility of being heard as an opportunity to be understood.

For example, applying criminal and immigration law to enhance deportation were highlighted by the migration police specialist in the field as 'innovative' policing, as this interview with a police prosecutor makes clear:

> First of all, this is a system where we follow the cases from A to Z. We start the cases, we apprehend, we prepare them for detention – and in our cases most of them they stay in pre-trial detention until they are ready for court. But we are not finished yet until they are sentenced and then deported. These cases are very special because all interviews and all work is done through an interpreter, and there are some special guidelines when one is doing these types of cases. . . . And, as I said, we imprison quite a lot of them. They are not detained only once. Detention is often prolonged again and again. They stay in pre-trial detention until their court hearing, because of the danger of absconding, right. If you let go of them, they disappear out of the country. So there is quite a lot of work for lawyers in this.
> (MAJ4)

This way of doing policing is portrayed as creative, innovative, and successful because it increases the deportation of criminals and is met with applause from the Police Directorate. In contrast to these positive connotations, researchers have criticized the practice for being disproportionate in selection of cases, random, arbitrary, and lacking safeguarding mechanisms as in criminal code cases (Aas, 2014; Gundhus, 2016). These different approaches to the same phenomena reveal clear gaps between our views of this practice.

An illustration of ambivalence in the field is how to deal with the politics of compassion. As Aas and I (2014) have argued elsewhere, participating in Frontex operations in the Mediterranean can be interpreted as mobilization of the political utility of compassion. Policing humanitarian borderlands may communicate engagement by actually responding to the perceived refugee crises. It is not unilaterally signalling security politics aimed at fending off the unwanted poor from the Global South. There are obviously humanitarian reasons for governing precarious lives; however, the language of compassion, empathy, and assistance is in a way replacing the language of injustice and rights (Fassin, 2011). By doing policing in humanitarian borderlands, the distinction between help and control is further intertwined (Aas & Gundhus, 2014). The ability to create fantasies of goodness and moral community on the part of the helpers, in this context the guest officers, gives humanitarianism a remarkable consensual force and is affecting the self-presentation of this work. However, this vocabulary of suffering and responsibility to protect both "serves to qualify the issues involved and to reason about choices made" (Fassin, 2011, p. 2). On the other side, the alarming picture of drowned refugees also releases resources to attack the bad guys within this illicit trade, the human smugglers and traffickers, and further militarize the border. There are, therefore, several aspects that contradict the police work as being innovative and progressive and raise moral issues with the practices.

Partly because of the ambivalence and ambiguities in the practice field, during the first phase of the research I was overwhelmed by a feeling of power inferiority. In such an environment there is a danger of becoming co-opted, with a lack of the necessary distinction between researcher and researched (Zehfuss, 2012). Participation may easily become 'complicity' towards the political reality under scrutiny. This is especially important when doing empirical research within political battlefields such as mass mobility control, where global disparities are vast, and the police enforce political decisions to achieve targets determined by police and political processes (Gundhus, 2017).

Dealing with discomfort/complicity

Looking into the methodology literature, particularly on migration, security, and international relations, it is not unusual for researchers to experience ethical and moral discomfort in being co-opted and losing critical distance in a contested field of research (Salter & Mutlu, 2013). Researchers might also contribute to and increased securitization, or even produce it, when getting involved in security practices (Aradau et al., 2015). To deal with co-option, moral obligations, and discomfort, an analytical break from empirical data is necessary. In the following, drawing on my experiences, I will suggest different ways of dealing with this.

Creating distance and finding common space between the researcher and the world inhabited by the researched may be an important step towards understanding the field, especially when studying the meaning produced in the field. Navigating between different practices and academic 'worlds' are making dissonance between the academic world and the world of fieldwork. More important, by making these tensions into an object of study, they do promote distance (Buegner & Mireanu, 2015). However, gaining a distant view to make space for critique may be accomplished with or without the recognition and subjectivity of actors in the field. As Fassin (2011) discusses, there are two ways of framing empirical research in which human subjects are involved. One is to translate what the actors in the field know better than us as a means to deal with the world (sense making). The other is to unveil what the actors cannot see. In this context, ideology is understood as a layer concealing the 'reality' (the objective world), and research questions aim to portray different types of illusions making them blind. This highlights different understandings of critical research, with long traditions of epistemological and ontological controversies. By starting with the actors' point of view and researching the micro level of interaction and relations, the first perspective aims to translate the actors' meaningful processes and subjectivity. The other perspective aims to unveil the ideology. Here the analysis point of departure is from the external, and the actors involved become more extras than subjects. In this context an obvious way of following such an approach would be to apply a thesis-driven analysis from the top down and stop there. An exterior analysis of the police as a proxy for the securitization of migration would illustrate the said position.

However, it is possible to go beyond that duality, as Fassin (2011) claims, and avoid reproducing the traditional dualism between translation and unveiling. This is also his understanding of critique; criticism must be produced on the basis of studies which assume that individuals have agency and that groups are formed and opposed to each other, and have conflicting interests. Fassin argues for the advantages of an empirical material based on the actor's point of view for taking actors' logic and rationalizations, characterized by ambiguity, contradictions, doubts, and conflicts, seriously. As he put it, "By facing the actors and the facts, which resist all attempts at reduction, critique must precisely give an account of this irreducibility" (Fassin, 2011, p. 247). His term for a research position that is able to reformulate duality is 'on edge', because it can: "''Reveal what agents cannot see at the same time as translating what they know better than we do" (Fassin, 2011, p. 245). This way of framing a strategy for gaining distance is close to Buegner and Mireanu's (2015) argument about turning tensions between the researcher and the researched into an object of the study. They argue for analyzing antagonisms as objects of study rather than objects of assessment.

To sum up so far, gaining distance in this research project has been attempted by making epistemological breaks with the actors' narratives and point of view by framing the data through theoretical conceptions. Moreover, analyzing antagonisms in the field, for instance the tensions between the specialists within migration police and the traditional police occupational culture approaches in framing crime and crime control, as study objects rather than objects of assessments, has also been helpful in the process. An analytical break inherent in the research design is informed by theoretical approaches within criminology and globalization theory, suggesting that, today and in previous historic epochs, mobility is not only *controlled* by the state and policing actors but also *produced* by them as a strategy for expanding and reasserting state sovereignty.

Policing is not only becoming a global phenomenon but is also shaped by and shaping globalization (Gundhus & Franko, 2016). One way of producing an analytical break is not to take for granted the police story about their mission by unveiling hidden structures. This was done by challenging the customary approach of examining mobility as a problem to state sovereignty and as a burdensome task for the police and other institutions of governance. However, such a top-down theoretical approach may also be refuted by the researched as suppressing their own life-world. In this project this was attempted to be avoided by balancing what people in the practice field cannot see with recognizing what they know better. Study of cultures as fields of practice explores the actors' logic, rationalizations, which are often characterized by ambiguity, contradictions, doubts and conflicts, including ambivalence and doubt in reaction to the policies that they implement (Fassin, 2011, p. 245), in this case the ambivalence in implementing and enforcing the policies.

In this study the discourse about professionalism and political utility of compassion mentioned earlier might then function as sensitizing concepts bringing forth new reflections among the researched, as well as new research insights. Observed changes in conceptualizing professionalism were met with research questions like: Why is it important? How is the professionalism discourse functioning as a means of establishing legitimacy? What is it with empathy and compassion, making it into a political utility? Empathy is an important aspect of police education in Norway and emphasizes the process of refining the police students' social competence (Bloksgaard & Prieur, 2016), but what does it mean in this context?

Moving between different 'worlds', in this study the Police University College, the University of Oslo, and the police service, makes it possible to actively create space by becoming aware of how the demands of recognition tempt our practices of knowledge production. Acknowledging the subjectivity of the interviewees and preventing the researched from feeling inferior and estranged in the scientific analysis are key in this process. Listening, showing interest, and being present in the field were met with positive response despite the use of discomforting topics and our critical stance towards the police practice and their aims and ways of acting. Likewise, incorporating into the methodological approach a sensitivity to the fact that scholars are as much subject and product of this world as the objects and subjects we study is an assumption for gaining distance to the world we inhabit but also proximity to the researched.

Conclusion: recognizing police agency

This discussion of proximity relations between the researched and the researcher has revealed how theoretical approaches and theory provide pivotal sensitizing concepts for research to get the necessary distance to go beyond a top down and thesis-driven analysis. Analyzing different antagonism and dynamics as objects to study provides sensitizing concepts which help to orient the interest by guiding data collection and writing process. The ontological and basic assumptions about how the world is, and methodological choices on how to study things so that particular ontology materializes, work together, and are impossible to distinguish from each other. This approach raises questions like: Which problems do we want to reconstruct in using which sensitizing concepts? Which links do we want to strengthen towards whom or what? How do we move and translate and thereby produce realities? How do we as researchers avoid producing increased control?

In general, the approach outlined in this chapter stress the need to be close to the problems, to the practices and the actions and objects that constitute them, through for example participatory observation and other methods requiring proximity. It requires us to think through proximity and how it can be negotiated successfully. Tension is expected to arise when actors are involved in reforms and projects and experience themselves as 'vibrant souls' dedicated to make things better, being progressive and striving to influence a rather stubborn traditional and conservative police institution. Although the aim of the project under study here is not, as Bourdieu (1999) suggests, to reveal the objective conditions behind the interviewees' misery, thinking about the tension between structural frameworks and ensuring the actors' point of view have been reflected upon throughout the research project. Since the processes examined in the project are practiced by practitioners striving for recognition of their work and efforts, it becomes crucial how the object of study is analyzed and the participants in the project are involved in the study.

In contrast to criminology researchers in Australia (see Powell and Segrave; Cochrane, this volume) and Canada (Hannah-Moffatt, 2011), Norwegian researchers of the criminal justice apparatus in general do not experience many problems with acquiring access (Finstad, 2000; Gundhus, 2013; Ugelvik, 2014).[8] Critical research on the police is in general perceived as beneficial by the research society. The police are also going through different types of reforms, partly because of the new police district structures and reactions to the criticism of the police in the wake of how the police handled the terrorist attack on 22 July, 2011[9] (Gundhus, 2017).

Likewise, as this research supports, it is possible to do critical police research without being banned, excluded, and neutralized as an arrogant academic or research activist. In this research project it is my opinion that this is prevented by recognizing the actors' subjectivity in the field of practice. The experience supports Fassin's (2011) argument that taking the actors' situation seriously by doing practice research based on proximity, and thereby not reducing them to marionettes and objects, strengthens the practice field's reception of criticism. Numerous invitations to researchers in the project team Crime Control at the Borders of Europe to present findings, for different audiences in the field of practice, supports this. However, this is not to argue that proximity and treating the researched as subjects are sufficient for such a relation, but it may indicate that it is an important precondition.

Critical research may flourish if the research reformulates the traditional duality between translating or unveiling by recognizing that it involves both of them: Actors cannot see all, but they carry knowledge that must be translated in order to cross the threshold of just an individual experience. Involving actors' reflexivity also renders the logic in the field more understandable and intelligible. Equally important to strengthen the practice field's reception for criticism is a critique that includes us as researchers and does not leave the social scientist alone outside the world.

Notes

1 I am grateful to the editors, Johanne Yttri Dahl and Katja Franko, for their helpful comments and suggestions.
2 The Norwegian Police University College offers a bachelor's degree in police studies, two master's degree programs in police science, and post-graduate studies, built on knowledge based teaching. In addition it has a research department with approximately 25 police researchers employed.
3 By sensitizing concepts I mean the role of concepts in social science to sensitize perceptions when applying theory in ways that clarify and develop conceptual understanding (see also Liebling, 2011). By applying such concepts it is possible to change the perceptual world by questioning 'taken for granted' assumptions and meaning mobilized by practitioners. Doing that is affected by the proximity to the field, since the sensitizing concepts are depending on obtaining thick knowledge about what is happening at site.
4 Researchers who participated in the sub-project team by conducting interviews on migration policing have been Katja Franko (project leader), Helene O. I. Gundhus, Synnøve Jahnsen, Sigmund Book Mohn, and Annette Vestby.
5 Stumpf (2006) first coined the term 'crimmigration' to describe the merger of immigration law and criminal law in both substance and procedure. However, Aas (2011, p. 332), introduced a broader perspective on crimmigration as intertwinement of crime control and migration control, which also includes the social context of crimmigration on issues relating to crime and migration and processes connected to it.
6 Expulsion here means re-entry ban; removal is administrative. Deportation order also includes asylum rejections.
7 This was highlighted by the assistant chief of National Police Immigration Service at the Leverhulme Trust Network, seminar in Oslo, June 2015.

8 There is an interesting discussion on criticizing part of the research on Scandinavian exceptionalism for being too benevolent in the interpretation of the more repressive part of the criminal justice apparatus (see e.g. Barker, 2012; Smith, 2012; Ugelvik & Dullum, 2012). How this influences access to research the criminal justice system is an interesting topic to explore but goes beyond the scope of this chapter.
9 The deadliest attack in Norway since World War II was the 2011 Norway attacks, referred to as 22 July. It consists of two sequential terrorist attacks by Anders Behring Breivik against that executive government quarter of Norway and a Worker's Youth League (AUF)–run summer camp. The attacks claimed a total of 77 lives.

References

Aas, K. F. (2011). Crimmigrant bodies and bona fide travelers: Surveillance, citizenship and governance. *Theoretical Criminology*, 15(3), 331–346.
Aas, K. F. (2014). Bordered penality: Precarious membership and abnormal justice. *Punishment and Society*, 16(5), 520–541. Aas, K. F., & Gundhus, H. O. I. (2014). Policing humanitarian borderlands: Frontex, human rights and the precariousness of life. *British Journal of Criminology*, 55, 1–18.
Alvesson, M., & Sköldberg, K. (2009). *Reflexive methodology: New vistas for qualitative research*. London: SAGE Publications.
Aradau, C., Huysmans, J., Neal, A., & Voelkner, N. (2015). *Critical security methods: New frameworks for analysis*. London: Routledge.
Barker, V. (2012). Nordic exceptionalism revisited: Explaining the paradox of a Janus-face penal regime. *Theoretical Criminology*, 17(1), 5–21.
Bjørgo, T., & Myhrer, T-G. (2015). *Forskningsetisk veileder for Politihøgskolen*. Oslo: PHS.
Bloksgaard, L., & Prieur, A. I. (2016). Den professionelt empatiske politibetjent: politistuderendes håndtering af følelser i arbejdet. *Dansk Sociologi*, 27(3–4), 107–127.
Bourdieu, P. (1999). *The weight of the world: Social suffering in contemporary society*. Cambridge: Polity Press.
Bowling, B., & Sheptycki, J. (2012). *Global policing*. London: SAGE Publications.
Brown, J. (1996). Police research: Some critical issues. In F. Leishman, B. Loveday, & S. P. Savage (Eds.), *Core issues in policing* (pp. 177–190). Harlow: Longman.
Buegner, C., & Mireanu, M. (2015). Proximity. In C. Aradau, J. Huysmans, A. Neal, & N. Voelkner (Eds.), *Critical security methods: New frameworks for analysis* (pp. 118–141). London: Routledge.
Callon, M. (1986). Some elements of a sociology of translation: Domestication of scallops and the fishermen of St Brieuc Bay. In J. Law (Ed.), *Power, action and belief*. London: Routledge.
Damsa, D., & Ugelvik, T. (2017). A difference that makes a difference? Reflexivity and researcher effects in an all-foreign prison. *International Journal of Qualitative Research*, 16, 1–10.
Eriksen, L. (2017). *Målenes tvetydighet -målstyring og kriminalitetsbekjempelse i Politiets Utlendingsenhet*. Oslo: Politihøgskolen.
Fassin, D. (2011). *Humanitarian reason: A moral history of the present*. Berkeley, Los Angeles, CA and London: University of California Press.
Finstad, L. (2000). *Politiblikket*. Oslo: Pax.
Franko, K., & Mohn, S. B. (2015). Utvisning som straff? Om grensesnittet mellom strafferett og utlendingskontroll. *Tidsskrift for strafferett*, 2, 153–176.
Gundhus, H. I. O. (2013). Experience or knowledge? Perspectives on new knowledge regimes and control of police professionalism. *Policing: Journal of Theory and Practice*, 7(2), 178–194.

Gundhus, H. I. O. (2016). Å målstyre skjønnsutøvelse: profesjonalisering av politiets utlendingskontroll. *Sosiologi i dag, 46*(1), 54–81.
Gundhus, H. I. O. (2017). Discretion as an obstacle: Police culture, change and governance in a Norwegian context. *Policing: Journal of Theory and Practice, 11*(3), 258–272.
Gundhus, H. I. O., & Franko, K. (2016). Global policing and mobility: Identity, territory, sovereignty. In B. Bradford, B. Jauregui, I. Loader, & J. Steinberg (Eds.), *SAGE handbook of global policing*. London: SAGE Publications.
Hannah-Moffatt, K. (2011). Criminological cliques: Narrowing dialogues, institutional protectionism, and the next generation. In M. Bosworth & C. Hoyle (Eds.), *What is criminology*. Oxford: Oxford University press.
Leun, J. P. van der (2003). *Looking for loopholes: Processes of incorporation of illegal immigrants in the Netherlands*. Amsterdam: Amsterdam University Press.
Liebling, A. (2011). Being a criminologist: Investigation as a lifestyle and living. In M. Bosworth & C. Hoyle (Eds.), *What is criminology*. Oxford: Oxford University press.
POD. (2014a). *Evaluering av returarbeidet i politiet: Delrapport 1 – ressursbruk i perioden 2009–2013*. Oslo: Politidirektoratet.
POD. (2014b). *Evaluering av returarbeidet i politiet: Delrapport II – effekten av retur*. Oslo: Politidirektoratet.
Salter, M. B., & Mutlu, C. E. (Eds.). (2013). *Research methods in critical security studies*. Abingdon: Routledge.
Sassen, S. (2007). *A sociology of globalization*. New York: W.W. Norton & Co.
Smith, P.S. P. (2012). A critical look at Scandinavian exceptionalism: Welfare state theories, penal populism and prison conditions in Denmark and Scandinavia. In T. Ugelvik & J. Dullum (Eds.), *Penal exceptionalism? Nordic prison policy and practice* (pp. 38–57). London: Routledge.
Stumpf, J. P. (2006). *The crimmigration crisis: Immigrants, crime, & sovereign power*. Bepress Legal Series, Working Paper 1635. Online. Retrieved October 28, 2017, from http://law.bepress.com/expresso/eps/1635
Ugelvik, T. (2014). *Power and resistance in prison: Doing time, doing freedom*. Basingstoke: Palgrave Macmillan.
Ugelvik, T. (2016). Low-trust policing in a high-trust society. *Nordisk Politiforskning, 3*(2), 181–198.
Ugelvik, T., & Dullum, J. (Eds.). (2012). *Penal exceptionalism? Nordic prison policy and practice*. London: Routledge.
University of Oslo (2018). Crime Control in the Borderland of Europe. Oslo: Unversity of Oslo. Retrieved February 25, 2018, from www.jus.uio.no/ikrs/english/research/projects/crimmigration/
van Maanen, J. (Ed.). (1979). *Qualitative methodology*. London: SAGE Publications.
Weber, L. (2013). *Policing non-citizens*. London: Routledge.
Weber, L., & Bowling, B. (2008). Valiant beggars and global vagabonds: Select, eject, immobilize. *Theoretical Criminology, 12*(3), 355–375.
Zehfuss, M. (2012). Culturally sensitive war? The human terrain system and the seduction of ethics. *Security Dialogue, 43*(2), 175–190.

Chapter 13

Race at the border

Alpa Parmar

Introduction

The growth in scholarship on borders and the criminology of mobility has prompted new questions about the process and consequences of conducting such research including how it is situated within existing academic frameworks of migration (Aas & Bosworth, 2013; O'Leary, Deeds, & Whiteford, 2013). In this chapter, I focus on race and ask why explicit discussions about race have not been at the forefront of scholarship on borders and the criminology of mobility. The omission of race within studies on borders represents a paradox, as whilst racialized hierarchies continue to structure the flow of humans across the globe and govern access to citizenship, academic analyses of these processes have largely subdued the salience of race (Garner, 2015; Bosworth, Parmar, & Vazquez, 2018; Parmar, 2017). Citizenship, religion, class and ethnicity are discussed as though they are hermetically sealed from racializing processes and independent from biased attitudes towards cultural 'others'. The absence of race within the criminology of mobility is a missed opportunity because politically, conceptually, theoretically, and empirically, race continues to matter, and new strategies to respond to racism and racialization are urgently required.

Beginning with a conceptual discussion of race and migration, the chapter also draws on my own research on policing migration in the United Kingdom. I discuss how I think about reflexivity in my own research, including how it intersects with my own positionality and how these factors have inflected, informed and at times challenged my analysis. I urge researchers to bring their personal challenges and opportunities to the fore in their own research and argue for the merits of embedding discussions of reflexivity (that go beyond reflections on positionality) into their frames of analysis (Phillips & Earle, 2010). Frameworks that are explicit about race can provide texture, nuance and a necessary 'lived reality' to borders scholarship as well as a channel through which to expose the social effects exercised by the research relationship (Bourdieu, 1999). This is most important at a time when there is a need to revisit race and develop anti-racist perspectives that can challenge its corrosive effects (Earle, 2017; Bhattacharya & Murji, 2013). In going some way towards this aim, I suggest that race is moved from the borders of border scholarship and instead be positioned as central to it. Clearly too, analyses of migration can only be meaningfully understood by making explicit the connections between race and imperialism and by tracing the endurance of colonialism in present times (Stoler, 2016; Gilroy, 2004).

Reviving race?

Early accounts of migration often explored patterns of racialization, racist hostility and xenophobia (Rex, 1970). Over time, however, discussions of race and racism have diverged from migration and borders research (Solomos, 2014; Erel, Murji, & Nahaboo, 2016). More specifically, the inherently 'race-making' processes of migration control are overlooked, and race tends to be mentioned by reference to the demographic breakdown of the population such as the numbers of particular ethnic groups that are mobile and the countries from which they hail. Empirical data often do not aim to capture race from the research design stage, and instead ethnicity and race become issues that researchers try to retrospectively retrace and speculate about.

The separation of race and migration as a political device was recently animated in debates about the European referendum in the UK in 2016, during which anti-immigrant narratives were presented as non-racist. As part of the referendum campaign, however, racist sentiment was utilized through both spoken and written words and visual images. For example, Nigel Farage, then leader of the United Kingdom Independence Party, straightforwardly linked migrants with disease and crime, claiming 'tuberculosis is costing the National Health Service a great deal of money and much of that is coming from Southern and Eastern Europe' (Wintour, 2014). In his campaign poster titled 'breaking point', a long line of ethnic minority people were presented as if lining up to enter Europe, alongside the subtitle 'we must break free of the EU and take back control of our borders' (Stewart & Mason, 2016). Though the poster was reported for inciting racist hatred, its message was resounding. In the United States, Donald Trump invokes animalistic imagery, straightforwardly anthroporacializing and linking migrants with dirt, danger and disease (Neate & Tuckman, 2015). The 'migrant as threat' narrative and the representation of migrants as a health or criminal threat to the social body re-actualizes a racist discourse, making the 'migrant narrative' racism's most modern form (Ibrahim, 2005).

The many facets of the migrant as (criminal) threat narrative make it a nebulous, complex issue to research empirically. Terrorism, sexual assault, violence and all manner of crimes and cultural deviance are straightforwardly attributed to migrants through the media and in public discourse, fusing diverse threats together in one stereotyped folk devil. A culture of migrant blaming provides a ready-made scapegoat around which all fears and causes of social ills coalesce despite the illogicality of attributing criminality and terrorism wholesale to entire communities. For example, terrorist attacks invoke claims by the right wing that lax immigration is to blame. Terrorists are said to cross borders alongside migrants (Slack, 2016). Indeed, in his immediate response to the London March 2017 attack on Westminster, Farage claimed that multiculturalism and uncontrolled immigration from Middle Eastern countries were to blame (Oppenheim, 2017). Such narratives overlook that the assailants in this and other attacks were British born, thereby invoking historical migration as the cause of current ills. The conflation of migration and terrorism at the national political level is said to enable Western nation-states to express their own internal crises, so that every migrant has now become a potential terrorist and vice versa (Nail, 2016). It is undoubtedly conceptually and empirically challenging to research these issues and their merger alongside their specificity and to understand the blurring of different stereotypes and unpick how they animate race, culture, nationality and religion. Some scholars have tried to understand how stereotyped identities converge through racialization (Volpp, 2002). However, the conjoining of multiple and seemingly untenable factors may partly explain why race in scholarship becomes muted and alluded to in coded ways without being explicitly mentioned (Goldberg, 2014).

At other times, visual representations (photographs and films) act as a proxy for explicit discussions of race, demonstrating that most migrants in camps, lining up and waiting at borders, being refused physical and/or documentary entry are black or ethnic others, vividly signalling the colour-coded nature of migration. Although visual images can do the work of showing powerfully who it is that researchers are talking about, not engaging with the images and only subliminally highlighting the issue of who is at the receiving end of migration enforcement through photographs only is equally problematic, as the racialized nature of migration is raised yet unexplored, rendering the underlying message implicit. Such tacit meanings, personal reflections and reflexive discussions about the process of conducting migration and borders scholarship can therefore be important for explicitly revealing these meanings and dynamics. In the section that follows, I discuss the value of reflexive accounts with regard to race despite the ambivalence towards reflexive modes of writing.

Reflexing on race

One of the reasons reflexive discussions of race might have been relegated to the peripheries of main texts or volumes is because being reflexive is at times conflated with self-effacing disclosure, the ritualistic quality of which often serves more to establish legitimacy than genuinely to advance social science (Emirbayer & Desmond, 2012). Reflexivity has been criticized for its authorial exhibitionism and solipsism (Skeggs, 2002), and being reflexive is thought to advance the conception of the self at work. This is because reflexive accounts have a tendency to suggest that problems of power, privilege and perspective can be dissolved by inserting one's self into the account and proclaiming that reflexivity has occurred in practice (Probyn, 1993).

Notwithstanding these criticisms, the merits of reflexivity, particularly in criminological discussions about race, are clear (Phillips & Earle, 2010; Lumsden & Winter, 2014). Fewer accounts have examined reflexivity in borders scholarship, as the inspiration for this volume underscores, and extant scholarship has focussed on emotions and ethics. Such accounts have shown how complex it is to forge trust in sites of border control as well as the hollow reality of ethical safeguards in the face of capturing the severe conditions that participants live with (Bosworth & Kellezi, 2017; Turnbull, this volume). Suffering and the emotional responses of researchers are often key for clarifying the purpose of research and inspiring its continuation (Gerlach, this volume). Obstacles to access are also informative in making researchers understand the function of criminal justice institutions and the various strategies agents of control use towards the subjects in their custody as well as towards researchers trying to gain entry (Bosworth and Kellezi, 2017). Researchers inflect their research in a variety of ways. As Jewkes eloquently states: 'our own personalities, histories and emotions penetrate our research in ways that can ultimately enrich our analysis and give life, vividness and luminosity to our writing' (Jewkes, 2014, p. 387; Earle & Phillips, 2015).

Reflexive accounts have revealed the implicit, yet constitutive aspects of race in the research process and the importance of researchers' own identities and biographical histories (Earle & Phillips, 2015; Duneier, 2004). The racial identities of researchers can impact access, rapport, the stories that are told by participants and how comfortable they feel in engaging with the project. The idea that race or racism may be better understood by a black or minority-ethnic-group researcher, known as the 'insider-outsider' debate, has been widely explored (Phillips & Bowling, 2003) and shown to be more complex than what a binary reading of a given situation suggests. Black and brown researchers are at times misperceived by participants (also by ethnic minority participants) as inferior, while intra-ethnic dynamics and racialized histories can come to the fore in subtle and nuanced ways (Earle & Phillips, 2015).

In my doctoral research with a Pakistani Muslim community in the UK, I was working with a male Urdu-speaking Pakistani mature student who had agreed to assist me with some of the interviews with parents. Each time we met parents for the first time, we introduced ourselves as doctoral researcher (myself) and translator. However, our respective roles did not register with participants, and they would often reverse our roles, assuming I was the less experienced assistant to the male university professor. It was hard to disentangle whether this was because of my gender or race or their cultural expectations – or all three. In the same research, the in/visibility of intra-ethnic boundaries were also salient. My identity as a British Asian woman of Hindu background (clear from my Sanskrit name) meant that at times I felt as though I was treated with suspicion and uncertainty by my Pakistani Muslim participants. This made me aware, more than ever of how names are racially coded and the implicit meaning they communicate through the seemingly benign act of introducing oneself (Daniel &

Daniel, 1998; Marable, 1997). From the outside, however (by white academic colleagues and statutory agency representatives), the shared 'Asianness' between myself and my participants was perceived as uncomplicated and rather assumed to transcend research barriers.

Participants and research access gatekeepers wanting to 'place' researchers in terms of nationality, class, ethnicity and gender can be read as part of the natural interactions that occur over the research process. Such instances raise questions about if and how we can interview across divides. Researchers often describe the way in which they have tried to blur apparent boundaries or how they have resisted opening up about their own identities in order to encourage open discussion from those they are interviewing. Differences between participants and researchers have also proven instructive – for example, low contact between whites and blacks led Lamont's (2004) participants to guess that she knew little about racism and what black people are like, therefore prompting them to explain their experiences to her in careful detail. For some, though, the opportunity to use their identities strategically is precluded because of their physical appearance (Gambetta, 2005). In the section that follows, I reflect on the inescapability of my own ethnic identity and how race and positionality have mattered in the production of my research.

Policing migration

I have been working on an empirical project to understand the policing of migration in England since 2015. Research knowledge about the daily reality of how migration is policed is limited, and thus my research aims to understand how migration management is invoked in everyday police practices. In 2015, for approximately six months, I observed the booking in process at police custody suites in England and saw how nationality, race and religion intersected in practice and how foreign national offending (and fears about it) governed the way in which people suspected of a crime were treated by the police (Parmar, 2018).

Because of my ethnic background, I was apprehensive about going into police custody spaces to research migration and to understand the impact of the collaborative scheme (Operation Nexus) under which immigration officers were embedded in police custody suites. I was concerned because I come from a colonial history of migration, and as a visible ethnic minority, it was likely that I would be regarded as a non-neutral observer from the outset. The police have an acrimonious history with minority ethnic groups in the UK (Bowling, Parmar, & Phillips, 2008), and so I thought about how my presence within the police space would be perceived and what my interest in migration and race would suggest to those officers I interviewed and observed. Would they tell me the truth? Would I influence how they spoke to me, what they said and how they behaved? All of these questions crossed my mind time and time again. Such feelings were undoubtedly instructive for the research, in which themes of misrecognition, nationality as a proxy for race and distinctions between 'good' and 'bad' migrants (Andrews, 2017) were raised.

However, the constant questioning I subjected myself to about how I would be perceived was perhaps not so productive. It left me at times feeling unconfident and apologetic for my background. I felt awkward about broaching the issue of race with individual police officers because of the negative portrayal of the police in the Macpherson Report (1999)[1] and the label of institutional racism that felt omnipresent yet remained unspoken in our discussions. Would officers watch what they said when I was around, or was I overthinking everything?

What I found through doing the research is that discussions about race are coded and expressed as nationality rather than race. For example, officers talked with me openly about certain nationalities that were 'likely to have been trafficked' (police custody detention officer) or described as bounded groups with homogeneous motives such as 'they're usually here just to work' in reference to a group of Vietnamese women (police custody sergeant). The racial and ethnic backgrounds of suspects, victims and those coming into police contact were not discussed directly. As one officer put it, "After Lawrence [Macpherson Report], you'll find that we [the police] don't wanna even whisper race, except in our strategies and plans. That's the effect it has had'. Was he saying this to me in order to avoid an uncomfortable discussion about racism? Was it really the case that the language of race had disappeared out of resentment because of the Macpherson Report? Or was he worried about what I would write? I was reminded that I would have to pay close attention to what was not said as much as what was, and I would have to interpret these spaces as best I could.

Placement and misrecognition

When conducting the observations, I often felt out of place and guilty for witnessing people in distress, treated as a 'suspect' and booked into police custody. Though my stance was to try and fade into the background and not directly influence any interactions, in practice, this was difficult. I felt visible because of my ethnicity and gender, as police custody felt like a hyper-masculine space. Many of the custody officers were young men, and most were physically tall and strong, as 'you have to be able to fight back if you have to', one of the detention officers told me. I often saw why this was the case in practice, as detainees were at times violent and difficult to pacify. Frustrations were frequently directed towards the officers, whom I saw being attacked on occasion. The feeling of imminent volatility or edginess was also something I associated with predominantly male spaces, and so I often felt out of place. The mix of formality (regular citing of legislation and procedural safeguards) alongside informality (waiting and long periods of time where nothing really happened) also made it feel like an unpredictable place to hang out. Added to this was the ambiguity of my role and reason for being there. 'Why you'd sign up to be here, I dunno ... but that's research for you, I suppose', one officer said to me.

I often felt as though I was constantly being 'placed'. With the transient staff and detainee population, I was often mistaken as the solicitor, by police officers and detectives, which is unsurprising, as law is a profession that attracts a significant number of Asian women (Bowcott, 2016). On rare occasions, I was presumed to be a police officer.

I witnessed a number of Asian people who had migrated from Pakistan via Turkey and Greece and were brought into the police station as suspected illegal immigrants. Some of them looked to me to interpret their words to the police officer or spoke with me in Urdu or Hindi to establish who I was and whether they would be all right. I responded if I could and told them I was not a police officer and that they would get the help they needed. In such instances, I ironically felt similarly positioned (because of my generational distance from them and my migratory background) with a number of custody detention officers who were also visible ethnic minorities and British. Several were British Asian Sikh, and they explained some of the conflicted emotions they encountered:

> Its hardest when an older person comes in ... we are told in our culture to always be respectful to elders and it feels like what we have to do isn't how we would treat an uncle or grandparent. It's difficult but at the end of the day it's my job and I've got to try and do it. I try and separate who I am at work from who I am when I go home.
> (Discussion with custody detention officer)

I expressed empathy towards the officers, as I understood exactly what they meant by the cultural deference towards elders that is so heavily prescribed in Asian culture. Would I have felt the same about white custody detention officers telling me the same, I wondered, or did my shared cultural background mean that I could more easily reconcile why and how they did what they did?

Seeing race

Given my interest in race and migration, I asked police officers about whether they saw migrants from particular racial backgrounds more often within police custody suites. Interestingly, most of the officers commented that they did not see more people from one racial background than another, remarking instead that they saw 'all sorts coming in now' or that 'we don't really think about their background or colour, areas like here everyone is multi-cultural' (Interview with custody detention officer). However, my observations were very often imbued with race and racialized dynamics. Was this because I was looking for race? Was it that I had a particular lens through which I always prioritized a racial interpretation? Was I hyper-sensitive to the issue of race because of my own minority ethnic background? Would other researchers have interpreted events in the same way? These are questions that I continue to ask myself whilst doing the research and analysing the findings.

The finding that positive inter-ethnic relations are expressed as part of a 'harmony discourse' (Back, 1996; Phillips & Earle, 2010) was not specific to my study but reminded me of the ways that race can be seen and unseen depending on your vantage point and the narrative one chooses to convey. The conviviality (Gilroy, 2004) expressed by the officers was a reminder of the language of fantasy through which race is discussed today – as irrelevant, no longer an issue worth thinking about, adding to the illusion that society is post-racial (Goldberg, 2014). As discussed, visual ethnic markers and language proficiency mattered very much in the initial stages of the custody process, and following that, nationality was often used to infer someone's racial background (Parmar, 2018). The verbal assurances that race didn't matter jarred with what I actually saw and heard. For example, I saw no white Americans brought in for illegally overstaying and no white Germans who were working without a permit. I did, however, see many Black British and Asian British people asked to confirm their nationality, underscoring the perceived incongruity between Britishness and being black or brown.

'Going further'

In their call for reflexive accounts of race to 'go further', Emirbayer and Desmond (2012) underline that turning our analytic gaze back upon ourselves involves much more than observing how one's social position affects one's analyses. The narrow idea that 'if I explain my own subject position, then I am being reflexive' is scrutinized and rather, Emirbayer and Desmond point out that 'reflexivity requires not only understanding one's social location as an academic, but also attentiveness to one's field, one's discipline and the entire apparatus of scholastic production that sets standards for peer review, constructive dialogue' (Venkatesh, 2012, p. 634). Importantly, they suggest that it is not enough to enquire reflexively 'who one is' or where one is positioned in the social space as a whole to understand one's position takings. One 'must also inquire into the objective position occupied by subjects of objectification within an academic discipline – and the location in turn of that discipline within the larger universe of the social sciences' (Emirbayer & Desmond, 2012, p. 39). In other words, we also need to think about the topics and areas that we choose to investigate, how minority ethnic scholars are represented in the field of academic study and how particular subjects are regarded within the social sciences more broadly. Also, we need to think about how research can become complicit in framing how we think about certain issues – why is it that we are more likely to research Filipina nurses than North American bankers? And how does research contribute to fixing particular notions of migrants with racialized groups (Anderson, 2015)?

So how can we map migration scholarship in light of Emirbayer and Desmond's (2012) frame to 'go further'? Critical reflection about the makeup of academics who research borders and migration is relatively underexplored, though the under-representation of Black and minority ethnic faculty across academia generally has been highlighted (Bhopal, 2016; Mirza, 2006, 2009; Equality Challenge Unit, 2009; Pilkington, 2011). More specifically, race and representation of scholars, the social structural and institutional barriers that reproduce an almost exclusively white, middle-class academic community across different subjects (Earle & Phillips, 2015) has influenced the field of migration too, although the representation of women is more balanced when taking a cursory glance at scholars working in the field. The distance in experience, however, between migration scholars and their participants is often palpable when reading accounts of lived experiences. However, the ways that distances have been negotiated, overlooked or even are instructive tends to remain implicit in borders analyses. Further still, the ways power imbalances between researchers and their participants are amplified when researching migration, and the Global North–South polarities that are inherent to migration research are also striking. Uncomfortable ethical questions arise when we think about the fact that research findings are then part of a profit-based process, rendering stories of migration commodities of the broader migration industry (Anderson, 2014).

Some scholars have reflected on these very issues and highlighted the complexities of being a white researcher asking migrants about their experiences of incarceration, racialization and being categorized as a 'foreigner', thereby forcing confrontation with researchers' own sense of positionality and privilege (Bosworth et al., 2005). Making a conscious effort to foreground subjects' own voices in all their complexity is one way in which Kaufman (2012) approaches her research with foreign nationals in prison. She draws on Spivak's (1988) essay 'Can the Subaltern Speak', which critiques post-colonial scholarly approaches for ironically re-inscribing neo-colonial imperatives of political and economic domination and for being complicit in the process of cultural erasure. Aside from a handful of accounts which critically engage with the colonial repercussions and possible meanings of borders scholarship and its expansion as a scholarly enterprise, detailed discussions about race and colonialism have been few, thus creating a metaphorical elephant in the room. Possibly the residue of the anthropological origins of inquiries into migration, or because discussions of race are not regarded as 'novel', the result is that the often nuanced and textured nature and sometimes racialized frame of research exchanges is left unspoken and unwritten.

Such silences are paradoxical because revealing racialized dynamics are important for demonstrating the contradictory and often myopic lens through which migration control is rationalized. For example, research has revealed the subtle expression of intra-ethnic/racial hierarchies and cultural essentialism when participants who are immigration or police officers also belong to racialized groups themselves (see, for example, Bosworth, 2018). In my own research on policing migration, in one instance, a younger police custody detention officer of British Asian background referred to migrants who had recently arrived in the UK derogatorily as 'freshies', presumably to indicate his perceived social distance from them. 'Freshie' is a pejorative, racist term often used intra-ethnically by settled ethnic minorities to stereotype and distinguish themselves from recent migrants (Phoenix, 2011; Shankar, 2008; Charsley & Bolognani, 2016). The detention officer went on to tell me that although he understood Punjabi and felt guilty about it, he would not reveal his ability to understand Punjabi to recent migrants in an effort to efface his shared ethnic, racial and cultural membership with the group. Instances such as these reminded me of the work of Back, Sinha, and Bryan (2012) on the need for us to understand how new hierarchies of belonging operate and order humanity in the neoliberal globalized world. People are marked by their immigration status, and this affects the politics of racism in Britain in ways which have shifted yet still carry the lasting legacy of Empire. New foreigners who physically resemble old foreigners are ranked on a lower hierarchy of belonging. The old foreigners are, however, intricately tied and complicit with the system because of the economic gains that come with jobs.

To summarize, viewing migration research through a critical race lens is perturbing and forces researchers to confront how research is part of the 'race-making' process. Does research on borders and migration enlist itself as part of the racialization and ossification of categories about who is defined as a migrant? How are colonial relationships of power re-inscribed by researchers who extract and profit from stories about suffering from racialized groups of vulnerable and people experiencing perpetual precarity? Although these research dilemmas are disconcerting and somewhat irresolvable, awareness and acknowledgement of these researcher–participant dynamics are important to air, if only to demonstrate that our interactions with and representations of the subaltern (racialized groups) are inevitably loaded (Spivak, 1988). It is also important to calibrate such complexities along with the possibility for change and the human connection that borders scholarship enables, as I discuss in the next section.

Affinities

One of the great advantages of the ethnographic approach (often applied in borders scholarship) is that it 'involves listening to people, seeing what they do, attempting to feel what they feel and hear what they say', which means that it creates an implicit politics of affinity (Earle & Phillips, 2015, p. 247). Although a politics of affinity may not be the same as experiencing how migrants experience racialization, an understanding of race and ethnic boundaries and their everyday negotiated realities (even in the research process) may be more likely to relate or promote reflection about experiences of migration.

As someone belonging to a minority ethnic group and with a family history of migration to the UK, while researching borders and race, I have at times been able to feel solidarity with my participants because of their links to my own background, shared experiences of racism and through my feelings towards my own British Asian identity. At times, it has allowed for research interactions to truly be a form of reciprocal exchange, in which I have discussed my own or my family's experiences in reference to or as a starting point for the accounts that participants have shared with me. I have also felt able to reflect on participants' feelings of marginalization in relation to my experiences of feeling 'out of place' in the academy (Puwar, 2004). The embodiment of race and gender that I represent as an Asian woman is at times instructive for my research but also inimical to being taken seriously, as I have on occasion found. Cast as inherently standpointist[2] and therefore incapable of seeing other perspectives or through an imagined objectivity, there is often scrutiny about the underlying motives for my research – scrutiny which is seldom applied to white academics researching topics that appear to be unconnected to their own ethnic, gender and class backgrounds. For example, at a recent conference, when I presented a paper on the silence of race within criminology, I was asked whether my focus on the issue of race in reference to the Macpherson Report (1999) was biased and whether I was speaking from a specific, politicized perspective. This was disappointing but also telling; as Ahmed (2017) reminds us, naming racism or exposing the problem of race or sexism runs the risk of being cast as *the* problem and is often heard as sensationalist (see also Eddo-Lodge, 2017). So although my affinity to the subject I was researching was instructive for adding meaning and verve to my work, an assumption about my personal motives for presenting the argument that I did also served to delegitimize my voice in the eyes of a white male middle-class academic.

Conclusion

How might race be better incorporated into borders scholarship? As discussed, being explicit about *how* our research focus exposes or verifies forms of racialization is important. Being open about the ways that researcher and participant positionality enters the research encounter can also be instructive in the ways that the discussion in this chapter has illuminated. Paying critical attention to the concepts and categories of ethnicity and race that are used in migration scholarship is crucial. Rather than race being pushed to the border of migration scholarship or relegated to the appendix, this chapter's premise has been to suggest that race should be made central to many of the questions that research on borders and the criminology of mobility aims to excavate. Given that migration research offers a lens through which to study societies (Anderson, 2015), the question of race seems ineluctable. In addition, modern-day discussions of race are usually expressed as though race is separate from histories of colonialism or 'remain safely sequestered on the distant fringes of national narratives', a framing which has been criticised for being myopic (Stoler, 2016, p. 122; Hesse, 2004). As Moffette and Vadasaria (2016) explain, modern colonialism required political technologies, such as racism, to expand colonial projects of empire. Borders scholarship could arguably be more emphatic about the role of colonial histories, their lasting presence and their continuing consequences.

Finally, the style of this chapter, which is punctuated with questions that I ask myself when designing, conducting and writing up my research, is written in this way in order to encourage researchers to acknowledge, raise and speak about such questions (with regard to race) in their own projects. I have also described the role of emotions – both positive and negative – in relation to race and racialized experiences in the discussion. Arguably, borders scholarship is in a prime position to reveal, document and explain how race is felt and to 'take emotions seriously and try and clarify the nexus between material and emotional racialized processes' (Bonilla-Silva, 2017).

Notes

1 The Macpherson Report was published following the inquiry into the racist murder of Stephen Lawrence, a black teenager from South London. The Macpherson Report stated that the Metropolitan Police were institutionally racist and made a number of recommendations to try and excise racism from the police force.
2 Standpointism began with feminist standpointism (Harding, 1987), which refers to a commitment to try and understand the world from the perspective of the socially subjugated. Feminist standpointism has encouraged theoretical and personal reflexivity in relation to knowledge and the process of knowledge production through research (Heidensohn & Gelsthorpe, 2007).

References

Aas, K., & Bosworth, M. (Eds.). (2013). *The borders of punishment: migration, citizenship and social exclusion*. Oxford: Oxford University Press.

Ahmed, S. (2017). *Living a feminist life*. Durham, NC: Duke University Press.

Anderson, B. (2015). 'Heads I win: Tails you lose': Migration and the worker citizen. *Current Legal Problems, 68*, 179–196.

Anderson, R. (2014). *Illegality Inc. clandestine migration and the business of bordering Europe*. Oakland, CA: University of California Press.

Andrews, A. (2017). Moralizing regulation: The implications of policing 'good' versus 'bad' immigrants. *Ethnic and Racial Studies*, Taylor & Francis Online, *40*(14). doi:10.1080/0141 9870.2017.1375133

Back, L. (1996). *New ethnicities and urban culture: Racisms and multiculture in young lives*. London: Routledge.

Back, L., Sinha, S., & Bryan, C. (2012). New hierarchies of belonging. *European Journal of Cultural Studies, 15*(2), 139–154.

Bhattacharya, G., & Murji, K. (2013). Introduction: Race critical public scholarship. *Ethnic and Racial Studies, 36*(9), 1359–1373.

Bhopal, K. (2016). *The experiences of Black and minority ethnic academics: A comparative study of the unequal academy*. London: Routledge.

Bonilla, Silva, E. (2017). 2018 theme 'feeling race: An invitation to explore racialized emotions. *American Sociological Association*. Online. Retrieved August 31, 2017, from www. asanet.org/ annual-meeting-2018/2018-theme

Bosworth, M., Campbell, D., Demby, B., Ferranti, S., & Santos, M. (2005). Doing prison research: Views from inside. *Qualitative Inquiry*, *11*(2), 249–264.

Bosworth, M. (forthcoming). This place makes you racism. In M. Bosworth, A. Parmar, & Y. Vazquez (Eds.), *Race, criminal justice and migration control: Enforcing the boundaries of belonging*. Oxford: Oxford University Press.

Bosworth, M., & Kellezi, B. (2017). Doing research in immigration detention removal centres. *Criminology and Criminal Justice*, *17*(2), 121–137.

Bosworth, M., Parmar, A., & Vazquez, Y. (2018). *Race, criminal justice and migration control: Enforcing the boundaries of belonging*. Oxford: Oxford University Press.

Bourdieu, P. (1999). *The weight of the world-social suffering in contemporary society*. Cambridge: Polity.

Bowcott, O. (2016). Almost half of all solicitors in England and Wales are women. *The Guardian*. Online. Retrieved May 1, 2017, from www.theguardian.com/law/2016/may/17/almost-half-solicitors-england-wales-women-bame-lawyers-black-background

Bowling, B., Parmar, A., & Phillips, C. (2008). Policing minority ethnic communities. In T. Newburn (Ed.), *Handbook of policing*. Devon: Willan.

Charsley, K., & Bolognani, M. (2016). Being a freshie is (not) cool: Stigma, capital and disgust in British Pakistani stereotypes of new subcontinental migrants. *Ethnic and Racial Studies*, *40*(1).

Daniel, J., & Daniel, J. (1998). Preschool children's selection of race-related personal names. *Journal of Black Studies*, *28*, 471–490.

Duneier, M. (2004). Three rules I go by in my ethnographic research on race and racism. In M. Bulmer & J. Solomos (Eds.), *Researching race and racism*. London: Routledge.

Earle, R. (2017). Anti-racist criminology? In T. Amatrudo (Ed.), *Social censure and critical criminology: After Sumner*. London: Palgrave.

Earle, R., & Phillips, R. (2015). Prison ethnography at the threshold of race, reflexivity and difference. In D. Drake, R. Earle, & J. Sloan (Eds.), *The Palgrave handbook of prison ethnography*. London: Palgrave.

Eddo-Lodge, R. (2017). *Why I'm no longer talking to White people about race*. London: Bloomsbury.

Emirbayer, M., & Desmond, M. (2012). Race and reflexivity. *Ethnic and Racial Studies*, *35*(4), 574–599.

Equality Challenge Unit. (2009). *The experience of Black and minority ethnic staff in higher education*. London: Equality Challenge Unit.

Erel, U., Murji, K., & Nahaboo, Z. (2016). Understanding the contemporary race – migration nexus. *Ethnic and Racial Studies*, *39*(8), 1339–1360.

Gambetta, D. (2005). Deceptive mimicry in humans. In S. Hurley & N. Chater (Eds.), *Perspective on imitation: From cognitive neuroscience to social science* (pp. 221–241). Cambridge, MA: MIT Press.

Garner, E. (2015). Crimmigration: When criminology (nearly) met the sociology of race and ethnicity. *Sociology of Race and Ethnicity*, *1*(1), 198–203.

Gilroy, P. (2004). *After empire: Melancholia or convivial culture?* London: Routledge.

Goldberg, D. (2014). *Are we all postracial yet?* Cambridge: Polity.

Harding, S. (1987). Introduction: Is there a feminist method? In S. Harding (Ed.), *Feminism and methodology: Social science issues* (pp. 1–14). Bloomington, IN: Indiana University Press.

Heidensohn, F., & Gelsthorpe, L. (2007). Gender and crime. In M. Maguire, R. Morgan, & R. Reiner (Eds.), *The Oxford handbook of criminology* (pp. 381–420). Oxford: Oxford University Press.

Hesse, B. (2004). Im/plausible deniability: Racism's conceptual double bind. *Social Identities*, *10*(1), 9–29.

Ibrahim, M. (2005). The securitization of migration: A racial discourse. *International Migration, 43*, 163–187.
Jewkes, Y. (2014). An introduction to 'doing prison research differently'. *Qualitative Inquiry, 20*, 387–391.
Kaufman, E. (2012). Finding foreigners: Race and the politics of memory in British prisons. *Population, Space and Place, 18*, 701–714.
Lamont, M. (2004). A life of sad, but justified, choices: Interviewing across (too) many divides. In M. Bulmer & J. Solomos (Eds.), *Researching race and racism*. London: Routledge.
Lumsden, K., & Winter, A. (Eds.). (2014). *Reflexivity in criminological research: Experiences with the powerful and powerless*. London: Palgrave Macmillan.
Macpherson, L. (1999). *The Stephen Lawrence inquiry*. Cm 4262-I. London: The Stationery Office.
Marable, M. (1997). The last word: What's in a name? *Black Issues in Higher Education, 14*, 112.
Mirza, H. S. (2006). Transcendence over diversity: Black women in the academy. *Policy Futures in Education, 4*(2), 101–113.
Mirza, H. S. (2009). *Race, gender and educational desire: Why black women succeed and fail*. London: Routledge.
Moffette, D., & Vadasaria, S. (2016). Uninhibited violence: Race and the securitization of immigration. *Critical Studies on Security, 4*(3), 291–305.
Nail, T. (2016). A tale of two crises: Migration and terrorism after the Paris attacks. *Studies in Ethnicity and Nationalism, 16*, 158–167.
Neate, R., & Tuckman, J. (2016). Donald Trump: Mexican migrants bring tremendous infectious disease to the US. *The Guardian*. Online. Retrieved May 12, 2017, from www.theguardian.com/us-news/2015/jul/06/donald-trump-mexican-immigrants-tremendous-infectious-disease
O'Leary, O. A., Deeds, C., & Whiteford, S. (2013). *Uncharted terrains: New directions in border research methodology, ethics, and practice*. Tucson, AZ: University of Arizona Press.
Oppenheim, M. (2017). Nigel Farage blames multiculturalism for London terror attack. *The Independent Online*. Retrieved April 2017 from http://www.independent.co.uk/news/uk/home-news/nigel-farage-london-terror-attack-multiculturalism-blame-immigration-lbc-radio-ukip-mep-leader-a7645586.html
Parmar, A. (2017). Intersectionality, British criminology and race: Are we there yet? *Theoretical Criminology, 2*(1), 35–45.
Parmar, A. (2018). Policing belonging: Race and nation in the UK. In M. Bosworth, A. Parmar, & Y. Vazquez (Eds.), *Race, criminal justice and migration control: Enforcing the boundaries of belonging*. Oxford: Oxford University Press.
Phillips, C., & Bowling, B. (2003). Racism, ethnicity and criminology: Developing minority perspectives. *British Journal of Criminology, 43*(2), 269–290.
Phillips, C., & Earle, R. (2010). Reading difference differently? Identity, epistemology and prison ethnography. *British Journal of Criminology, 50*, 360–378.
Phoenix, A. (2011). Somali young women and hierarchies of belonging. *YOUNG, 19*(3), 313–331.
Pilkington, A. (2011). *Institutional racism in the academy: A UK case study*. Stoke-on-Trent: Trentham Books.
Probyn, E. (1993). *Sexing the self: Gendered positions in cultural studies*. London: Routledge.
Puwar, N. (2004). *Space invaders: Race, gender and bodies out of place*. London: Berg.
Rex, J. (1970). *Race relations in sociological theory*. London: Weidenfeld & Nicholson.
Shankar, S. (2008). *Desi land*. Durham, NC: Duke University Press.

Skeggs, B. (2002). Techniques for the reflexive self. In T. May (Ed.), *Qualitative research in action*. London: SAGE Publications.

Slack, J. (2016). 'Staggering' number of European jihadis: EU's own border agency admits terrorists are exploiting refugee crisis and lax controls but has no idea how many illegal immigrants there are. *The Daily Mail*. Online. Retrieved May 14, 2017, from www.daily mail.co.uk/news/article-3525279/Mass-migration-allowingterrorists-pour-Europe-EU-s-border-agency-admits-s-revealed-false-documents-not-facing-thorough-checks.html

Solomos, J. (2014). Racism and migration. In B. Anderson & M. Keith (Eds.), *Migration: A COMPAS anthology*. Oxford: COMPAS, University of Oxford.

Spivak, G. C. (1988). Can the subaltern speak? In C. Nelson & L. Grossberg (Eds.), *Marxism and the interpretation of culture* (pp. 271–313). Urbana, IL: University of Illinois.

Stewart, H., & Mason, R. (2016). Nigel Farage's anti-migrant poster reported to the police. *The Guardian*. Retrieved July 15, 2017, from https://www.theguardian.com/politics/2016/jun/16/ nigel-farage-defends-ukip-breaking-point-poster-queue-of-migrants

Stoler, A. L. (2016). *Duress: Imperial durabilities in our times*. Durham, NC: Duke University Press.

Venkatesh, S. (2012). A race to reflexivity. *Ethnic and Racial Studies, 35*(4).

Volpp, L. (2002). The citizen and the terrorist. *UCLA Law Review, 49*, June 2002.

Wintour, P. (2014). Nigel Farage defends plan to bar immigrants with HIV from NHS care. *The Guardian*. Retrieved August 15, 2017, from www.theguardian.com/politics/2014/oct/10/nigel-farage-defends-plan-immigrants-hiv-nhs

Chapter 14

One of us or one of them?

Researcher positionality, language, and belonging in an all-foreign prison

Dorina Damsa and Thomas Ugelvik

Introduction

Over recent years, Norway has seen an increase in control and punitive measures against migrants. This phenomenon is not unique to Norway but is rather a trend that has emerged in other countries (see Weber, 2013; Aas, 2013; Bowling & Sheptycki, 2015; Bosworth & Turnbull, 2015). Among the prominent examples of this development is the increased use of longer prison sentences for immigration offences (Plassen, 2016), a sharp increase in deportations (Politiets utlendingsenhet, 2016), and the emergence of what has been called a general 'more exclusionary penal culture directed at non-citizens' (Aas, 2014: 520). In this context, the profile of the Norwegian prison population has changed. According to official statistics, 34 per cent of the prisoners in the Norwegian system are currently foreign citizens, a considerable increase from 13 per cent in 2000 (Kriminalomsorgen, 2016).

Norwegian prisons have always held a handful of foreign national prisoners. The increase in their numbers has recently rendered their presence in prison from a fact of prison life – something that is just there and that does not really warrant much thought – into a major social problem that has been given substantial attention in the public and political spheres (Ugelvik, 2013). As of November 2016, 102 nationalities could be found in the Norwegian prison population: 652 individuals from Central and Eastern Europe, 225 from African states, 220 from Asia, 196 from Western Europe, and 34 from other states (Kriminalomsorgen, 2016). To respond to the growing numbers, the Norwegian Correctional Services have resorted to a number of solutions, from leasing prison spaces in the Netherlands (Pakes & Holt, 2017) to opening the country's first and so far only all-foreign prison at Kongsvinger in 2012.

By Norwegian standards, Kongsvinger prison is a medium-sized men's prison. Located about 90 minutes northeast of Oslo, it has the capacity to hold 117 prisoners in total. Nearly two-thirds of these men (69) are placed in the high-security unit behind a concrete wall, while 48 are housed in the lower-security part of the prison between the wall and a much more climbable fence. Few of the men on either side speak Norwegian. Instead, English operates as a common-ground language that makes communication between prisoners and officers at least haltingly possible.

Based on our experiences of conducting research in Kongsvinger prison, we will discuss the challenges connected to the lack of a shared language between researchers and participants and the barriers this may create. However, as we will argue here, language-related challenges should not necessarily be a problematic feature of the research process, but, with reflexive examination, they can also become important sources of data collection and analysis in their own right. One author, Thomas, was only able to converse with prisoners using prison English, a sort of pidgin language that has evolved through the everyday interaction between officers and prisoners. A number of Norwegian words such as 'luft' (literally meaning 'air' in Norwegian, but used to communicate 'yard time'), 'besøk' (visit, or the visits unit) and 'kjøkken' (kitchen) are mixed with basic English into a language that is tailored to and heavily influenced by the practical life-world of the prison. In contrast to his work with the prisoners, Thomas communicated with prison officers in his native Norwegian. The other author, Dorina, is of Romanian origin and thus was able to interview Romanian citizens imprisoned at Kongsvinger in their native language. At the time she was not yet fluent in Norwegian and had to talk with prison officers in English.

A shared language will open doors, but in a fieldwork site such as a prison, the opening of one door often means that others close. As a result of our distinct linguistic abilities and deficits, we each experienced different challenges and opportunities. In the following, we will reflect on the impact that our different language skills had on our research field experiences and how our language skills gave us membership in some groups while at the same time they were closing us off from others. In so doing, we describe how we, as two different researchers, who were working on two different research projects in the same field site, were positioned in the field, how we constructed and were constructed by the research field based on our different language skills, and how these processes were connected to questions concerning belonging and difference in the foreign-national prison research setting.

Background and methods

Thomas did four months of sustained fieldwork in Kongsvinger prison in the fall of 2013, collecting participant observation data. Dorina, in contrast, visited the prison on numerous short-term research trips over the course of 2015 and 2016, collecting interview data while also doing participant observation. Thomas conducted fieldwork as part of a multi-sited ethnographic study of what he calls 'crimmigration prisons' (Ugelvik, 2014a, 2014b, 2014c, 2017). Dorina's project was more specific. She studied the release process of Romanian nationals and their transition from Norwegian prisons to freedom. While the projects somewhat differed, both authors sought to understand the life of foreign nationals imprisoned at Kongsvinger prison through fieldwork.

During his fieldwork, Thomas had a more permanent and stable presence in the prison than Dorina. He carried keys and an assault alarm on his belt, which meant he could move around in the various spaces of the institution as he pleased. As a native Norwegian speaker, he quickly and effortlessly established positive relationships with prison officers. His research project was perceived as ultimately beneficial to the prison, so officers, in a sense, felt that they had a stake in it. However, in many cases, he found building rapport with prisoners more difficult than he was used to from other prison field sites because of the inherent language barrier between himself and the foreign-national prison population. This meant that, at times, conversations with inmates were laborious, halting, and frustrating for everybody involved.

Unlike Thomas, Dorina made more irregular visits to the prison in order to interview specific prisoners. She was, therefore, not given keys and was instructed to always stay 'within sight' of an officer to have her 'safety ensured'. This limited her independent movement to the small area around the officers' office. She had to be escorted by an officer when moving between different spaces, much like the prisoners themselves. Not fluent in Norwegian, she struggled to communicate with officers and often felt she had to work to establish a connection with them. She often felt like a burden to their already-full schedule. Her language skills and clear distinction from the officers, however, allowed her to bond very quickly with prisoners. In conversations with them, Dorina used Romanian and some Italian and French to collect data.

A prison can be described as a system of positions and rules that exist in more or less rigidly defined relationships and hierarchies (Sykes, 1958), the most important being the prisoner/officer divide (Lindberg, 2005; Sparks, Bottoms, & Hay, 1996). This system exists before the researcher enters the institution, and it will continue to exist after she or he has left; but while there, the researcher cannot avoid being part of it. As a result, the researcher entering into this rigidly defined pre-existing system is in most cases seen as something of an oddity (Ugelvik, 2014c), neither a prisoner nor an officer. As such, the researcher is a liminal figure. In important ways she or he falls between established positions in the prison's system of categories and hierarchies. Researchers must carve spaces for themselves in their field through continuous negotiation. Careful self-positioning, impression management, and relationship work all play a role in negotiating a meaningful position in what has been described as an inherently politicized space (Sparks, Bottoms, & Hay, 1996; Rowe, 2014; Ugelvik, 2014c). Such matters apply to all research projects that involve a sustained researcher presence on the wings. In all-foreign wings or prisons, however, this process is profoundly impacted by the presence or absence of a shared language.

Several studies suggest that foreign-national prisoners experience the pains of imprisonment as more or less direct results of their non-citizen status (*inter alia* Kaufman, 2015; Ugelvik, 2014a, 2014b, 2017; Warr, 2016). Warr (2016) argues, for example, that foreign nationals in prison experience uncertainty and hopelessness about their immigration situation that, together, undermine the legitimacy of their imprisonment. Issues related to their residence status and possible post-release deportation especially frustrate many foreign nationals in prison.

Other studies suggest that the most common and significant problem reported by foreign-national prisoners is narrower: a lack of knowledge of the national language (Kalmthout, Hofstee-van der Meulen, & Dünkel, 2007; Kaufman, 2012; Singh Bhui, 2008). Communication problems, these authors assert, are at the root of a range of everyday frustrations. In many cases, both verbal and written communication is severely hampered. This may lead to feelings of social isolation, uncertainty, and helplessness. Prisoners are frustrated at not being understood by staff, having little to read in their own language and no television channels available, and at missing out on basic provisions because they had not understood instructions. Moreover, foreign inmates are entitled to as many visits as nationals, but in practice they generally receive far fewer for practical and economic reasons. Many foreigners are isolated, both literally and symbolically and culturally. In extreme cases, language problems may lead to what one might call cultural deprivation. The language barrier will colour every part of the everyday prison experience for prisoners but also for officers. Correctional officers on their part have often told us that they are frustrated at the lack of language skills (and time to develop such skills) and available resources to work constructively with foreign nationals.

The lack of a shared language also shapes the experience of prison researchers. In the field, language competency or the lack thereof raises particular difficulties for researchers interacting with participants or writing a text in a foreign language. Some degree of language equivalence between the researcher and the participants is necessary to understand and interpret what is being said (Aneas & Sandin, 2009). Differences in verbal style may affect communication and interpretation adversely. The use of slang may also represent a barrier; even when researcher and informant share the same first language, communication can be hampered by the use of different 'tribal dialects'. On the other hand, field research can be described as a process in which a researcher enters into the world in order to learn things that she or he does not know to begin with, and learning how to efficiently communicate with the people one encounters in the field is a vital and potentially constructive and rewarding part of the process. The various ways the data collection process is impacted by the flow (or in some cases, rather, the trickling) of communication can be said to be particularly easy to spot in research projects in which the importance of 'foreignness' and the everyday communication problems (or, frequently, breakdowns) are part of the study object. In short, the fact that in ethnographic fieldwork, language is both tool and end product is made very clear indeed in projects such as ours.

Language, culture, and belonging in prison

Our different language skills did affect our researcher positions at Kongsvinger prison. Our linguistic abilities intersected with other matters, like differences in age and gender, as well as our different capacities to move freely around the prison. As a result, we were co-opted differently by the prisoner and officer 'tribes', while we established rapport with specific participants in the field. In the following and for the purpose of our analysis in this chapter, we will discuss how this may have impacted our data. We will specifically look at our own 'foreignness' in an all-foreign prison (mediated by our citizenship and overall cultural positioning in addition to language), which was the aspect of our identity and field persona we perceived as most salient during the data collection.

Kongsvinger prison houses people from a range of countries who are united in one institution by the fact that they, through their immigration status, share a status of non-belonging from the point of view of the Norwegian state. There is a great variety when it comes to the language skills and background of prisoners in Kongsvinger prison. Some prisoners are part of large language groups in which it is easy to find someone to talk to in one's native tongue. Others speaking minority languages may experience feelings of isolation, without anyone to communicate meaningfully with, apart from sign language or very broken English. According to Honigsberg (2013), linguistic isolation can be seen as a distinct form of isolation in prisons with effects that are comparable to those of physical isolation. A shared language, on the other hand, can create an important sense of group belonging and common ground. Language skills can temporarily tie strangers together. Along with the understanding of language may come an understanding of cultural codes that may be used as a resource while people interact, begin to know each other, and bond.

For Dorina, being Romanian and speaking Romanian was probably the most important factor in successfully establishing relationships with prisoners. Language worked as a universal passkey; most Romanian prisoners automatically assumed her to be on their side, to understand what it is like to be Romanian and to be a Romanian in Norway more specifically. Thus, she effortlessly became an associated member of one of the largest language groups in the prison. As a fellow national, she was expected to understand and empathize with the participants' lifestyle, as she was supposed to understand the state of poverty of so many Romanians and their lack of options to make ends meet: 'you know how it's like in Romania'; 'you know the hardship', 'you have no choice' but to leave the country and ultimately participate in criminal activities.

With an understanding of French and Italian, Dorina was able to communicate with other prisoners too. She soon became an informal messenger or translator in the communication between foreign-national prisoners and Norwegian prison officers. Shared citizenship and language presumed same knowledge, similar views of sameness or otherness, and created a shared space, as one participant commented, a respite from the 'day in, day out' of prison life. In short, shared foreign languages allowed Dorina to be seen as an honorary member of the prisoner tribe almost instantly:

> The four of us [Dorina and three prisoners] decide to sit and talk in the cafeteria, as it was snowing heavily outside. We got some coffee, and then looked for a table. I placed my things on the officers' dining table, since

it was the first table as you walked in. One prisoner commented that we should sit at another table, in the corner, as 'not to get infected', presumably from sitting at the officers' table.... As the prisoners went in and out of the cafeteria for smokes, they always returned with a grin, reporting the officers' curiosity regarding our conversation. 'To them, you are the enemy within. The one they cannot get rid of', says one prisoner. They seemed satisfied by this. They were satisfied too that officers could not understand us when we spoke. They told the officers that we were talking about post-release, about their plans, and such. They didn't want the officers to know that they were 'dishing it out, all the shit that happens' there.

(Dorina, fieldnotes, 2015)

Thomas, on the other hand, had to resort to English (and in a few cases Norwegian) in his communication with prisoners. As a result, he experienced a greater distance that needed to be overcome initially. In most cases, being positioned as Norwegian and speaking English therefore marked him from the outset as an outsider to the prisoner community, and, perhaps to some, as someone who might be aligned with the prison or the Norwegian government in some way. Even when he could communicate reasonably well with prisoners in English, he sometimes got the impression that the conversation was based on a lack of fundamental trust. Sometimes, the circumstances simply chose a side for him, and there was not much he could do about it, even if he wanted:

In the low-security part of the prison, the office area is right next to the prisoners' canteen. Officers working the evening shift often eat dinner with prisoners. They use their own plates and cutlery, which are washed separately in the officers' dishwasher, however. The blue pattern makes the plates clearly separable from the prisoners' white china. The plates are bigger and looked nicer. When an officer asked me early on in the fieldwork if I would like some dinner, I say yes, looking forward to having dinner with the prisoners. She brings me an officer's plate and officer's cutlery however, symbolically positioning me as part of one group and not the other. The one guy I know well and sit down with to eat leaves soon after because he has finished his dinner early and wants to make a phone call. I end up sitting at a table all by myself, eating dinner off my blue patterned prison officers' plate.

(Thomas, fieldnotes, 2013)

We were positioned very differently in the same fieldwork site – actually in the very same room, if not at the same table – on these two occasions. Thomas was clearly not a prison officer, but he was somehow associated with them, and his position vis-à-vis the prisoners was ambiguous at best. Dorina was clearly not a prisoner, but she was included in the Romanian language community and was made part of the group.

As time passed, Thomas did manage to create a few extended relationships with individual key informants among the prisoners, of the kind that he had depended on in previous research projects in prisons, but he had to work a lot harder over a longer period of time to get there than Dorina did. Predictably enough, he ended up spending most of his time talking with prisoners who knew at least a fair bit of English. Similarly, the prisoners who had spent a lot of time in Norway were easy to get to know and get along with for Thomas. A few times he experienced a bit of the frustration reported by prisoners himself when he was approached by men who had heard about his project and felt that they had something important to tell him, but where the lack of a common language made data collection almost impossible. At other times, he was seen as a Norwegian exception, someone who could become a valuable ally or even advocate, someone who could finally relay the truth about the Norwegian system to the Norwegian public. It is reasonably common for prison researchers to be positioned as potential advocates, but it is even more problematic than usual when the language barriers make it even more difficult to adjust the position initially ascribed to the researcher.

Both Dorina and Thomas frequently interacted with prisoners who felt that the prison was essentially a racist institution created to provide foreign-national prisoners with a second-class prison experience. In both studies, prisoners often took the sort of hyper-critical censorious stance towards the prison, the Norwegian criminal justice system, and the Norwegian government in general as described by Mathiesen (1965, p. 23) as a 'criticism of those in power for not following, in their behaviour, principles that are established as correct within the social system in question'. However, unlike Mathiesen's study, we found that this stance was coupled with a strong sense of in-group solidarity and common destiny; prisoners often reported feeling like members of a group of outcasts that the Norwegian government was basically trying to spend as little money on as possible and then have them transferred or deported as quickly as possible. Unsurprisingly, they did not hold the Norwegian prison system in high regard. Prisoners routinely presented Dorina with a more or less accurate criticism of a racist Norwegian system enforced by racist prison officers:

PRISONER: Everything has changed in Norway. So, you, as a Romanian, or any other nationality, you will never benefit from those jails you see on TV. Those are made for Norwegians. These are made for Romanians. Specially made jails for Romanians, for immigrants. There is not one Norwegian in this prison and there are 200 persons, 200 inmates. And there are a few others. And in Oslo, the majority are immigrants. A thousand inmates fit in there.[1] You've been there. You've seen how ugly it gets. (Dorina, interview, Kongsvinger, 2015)

PRISONER: High security is better, because there are Norwegians there.[2] (Dorina, fieldnotes, in conversation with a new prisoner at Kongsvinger, 2015)

We both found that prisoners at Kongsvinger often understand any negative decision or any kind of bad experience as connected to their status as foreigners and the fact that they were being held in an all-foreign prison. Discrimination and outright racism were frequently used and widely shared catch-all explanatory frames. In cases in which prisoners only had limited or wrong information, decisions were often seen in the context of their general view of Kongsvinger as a racist institution. Even in the cases when we felt that Kongsvinger prison was compared favourably to other Norwegian prisons, prisoners at Kongsvinger often chose to reconstruct their experiences as examples of discrimination and racism.

Within this frame of understanding and in connection thereto, prisoners positioned both of us as advocates who would bring forth the alleged human rights abuse taking place in Kongsvinger. Some prisoners took Thomas to be, in a sense, a representative of the Norwegian state that had decided to deport them. He experienced a few – but not many – awkward finger-pointing conversations with prisoners who wanted him to explain why 'your people have decided to throw me out of the country'. Dorina, seen by prisoners as equally foreign, did not experience this at all.

In Dorina's and Thomas's cases, the differences between their research personas resulted in distinct positions in the field and consequent opportunities and challenges. Dorina's shared foreignness, citizenship, language, and connected feelings of community with the participants allowed her to construct a more textured account of their experiences yet prevented her from accessing certain spaces within their environment and subsequent insights into their experiences. Not yet fluent in Norwegian, she chose to speak to officers in English, which substantially limited communication. Officers are used to speaking English with the inmates at Kongsvinger and do it quite well. At the same time, using the language that officers use to communicate with most prisoners marked Dorina as 'outsider'. Simply put, officers at Kongsvinger prison use English as a working language, but they relax in Norwegian. Her project was understood to have some relation to the Romanian prisoners and Romania and was thus seen as somewhat disconnected from the prison staff.

Thomas, for his part, got to see firsthand the limits of this communication and experience it for himself, with its inherent frustrations. He therefore got a lot of data on the practical communication difficulties experienced by prisoners and officers alike. On the down side, some willing prisoners could not participate in the research because of the language issues. He may therefore have contributed to the language-based pains of imprisonment experienced by some foreign national prisoners. Some prisoners may also have chosen not to talk with him because they did not understand the purpose of his visit.

Conclusion

Ever since the 'linguistic turn', language is seen as performative (Austin, 1962; Searle, 1969; Madison, 2012) and fundamental to the performance of the self and social relations (Madison, 2012; Myhre, 2012). According to Austin (1962), language does not just describe, it also creates. Through 'speech-acts', material and situational change is produced. Building on speech-act theory, Searle (1969) argues that *all* language is performative. The position was further developed by Derrida (1973, 1978, 1982), who argued that speech is citational, constantly reproducing the reality it refers to within a specific context, through a certain identity, and contingent on culture and history. What we know and say, we have inherited. According to Madison (2012, p. 179),

> words are indeed performative and *do* have material effects ... they *do something* to the world; and that something is to reiterate (in terms of Derrida) speech, meaning, intent and customs that have been repeated through time and that are communicative and comprehensible because they are recognizable in their repetition.

Language is also essential to the performance of collective identities and belonging. It works as a mark that differentiates groups and is often sufficient to identify one's membership in a specific group (Edwards, 1985; Kamwangamalu, 2007). From this perspective, language is a conditional marker of identity, solidarity, and groupness (May, 2000; Tannenbaum, 2009) and the 'most salient way we have of establishing and advertising our social identities' (Lippi-Green, 1997, p. 5). Speaking a language, then, is a performance of the self and of one's position in the social world.

The linguistic turn in ethnography has led to the proliferation of critical discussions of ethnography as practice and of the status of the resulting ethnographic text. Ethnographies are no longer seen as (more or less) faithful representations of an unproblematic external reality; they are the result of a series of productive meetings between researchers and researched in which some parts of the real are put into focus while other parts are ignored. Seen as a discursive practice, ethnography is the result of a communicative relationship between researcher and participant. Ethnographic data are for a large part talked into being through a shared process that is at its very core structured and shaped by language. Researcher and researched are both seen as speaking subjects, within specific settings, at given times. The ethnographer no longer just represents her or his experience, nor does she or he automatically hold the authority to speak on behalf of others. Ethnography is thus revealed as a 'function of specific positions within wider power relations' (Myhre, 2012, p. 186). Language is a core part of how these power relations are experienced.

Language also plays an important role in the social construction of a collective identity and feelings of belonging. Ever since Anderson's (1983) 'imagined community', language has been seen as an important element in the construction and mobilization of group solidarity. Furthermore, when participants do not speak the dominant language in a certain context, they may become dependent on the researcher to speak for them (Temple & Young, 2004, p. 164). Translation and writing from/into a foreign language bring further issues to the ethnographic endeavour. Because languages are associated with group membership and identities, researchers will be positioned by the language they use, even when they are trying hard to avoid it.

As researchers, our language capabilities did significantly impact the data collection process: how we were positioned in the field, who we talked to and who talked to us, and the perspectives we were exposed to. Language was essential to the field site construction of our identities and the relationships we were able to strike up and maintain within the Kongsvinger prison context. In short, for Dorina, being a foreigner, like the prisoners, and for Thomas, being a Norwegian, like the officers, had both advantages and disadvantages.

Our two different field positions came with specific opportunities and also had different limitations. These were connected to and an intrinsic part of the field of linguistic power relations that was at Kongsvinger prison. Again, in ethnographic fieldwork, language is both tool and end product. A common language can open some doors, but it will also, at the same time, close others. In contexts like Kongsvinger prison, in which a certain language represents power, the researcher may even have the responsibility of naming and speaking for the 'other' thrust on her or him, even when she or he is trying to avoid it. According to Temple and Young (2004, p. 162), these are issues 'that just will not go away' – hierarchies of language power, epistemologies of researchers, and issues around naming and speaking for people seen as 'other' will continue to present themselves to new generations of researchers that have to take them seriously. Issues related to researcher positionality, language, and belonging are not simply problems to be avoided though; they are inherent to the research process and potentially very productive sources of ethnographic data in their own right.

Acknowledgements

The writing of this chapter has been funded by a European Research Council starting grant (Thomas) and a Norway-Romania EEA grant (Thomas and Dorina). We would like to thank the editors, as well as the participants of the University of Oslo Department of Criminology and Sociology of Law writing workshop and in particular Sveinung Sandberg for important comments on an earlier draft.

Notes

1 Oslo prisons have a capacity of a little more than 400 prisoners, of which approximately 50 per cent were foreigners as of June 2016.
2 There are no Norwegian prisoners at Kongsvinger.

References

Aas, K. F. (2013). The ordered and the bordered society: Migration control, citizenship, and the Northern penal state. In K. F. Aas & M. Bosworth (Eds.), *The borders of punishment: Migration, citizenship, and social exclusion*. Oxford: Oxford University Press.

Aas, K. F. (2014). Bordered penality: Precarious membership and abnormal justice. *Punishment & Society, 16*(5), 520–541.
Anderson, B. (1983). *Imagined communities: Reflections on the origin and spread of nationalism.* Verso. Ann Arbor, MI: University of Michigan.
Aneas, M. A., & Sandin, M. P. (2009). Intercultural and cross-cultural communication research: Some reflections about culture and qualitative methods. *Qualitative Social Research, 10*(1). Retrieved from www.qualitative-research.net/index.php/fqs/article/view/1251/2738Intercultural
Austin, J. L. (1962). *How to do things with words.* London: Oxford University Press.
Bhui, H. S. (2008). *Race and criminal justice.* London: SAGE Publications.
Bosworth, M., & Turnbull, S. (2015). Immigration detention, punishment and the criminalization of migration. In S. Pickering & J. Ham (Eds.), *The Routledge handbook on crime and international migration.* Abingdon: Routledge.
Bowling, B., & Sheptycki, J. (2015). Global policing, mobility and social control. In S. Pickering & J. Ham (Eds.), *The Routledge handbook on crime and international migration.* Abingdon: Routledge.
Derrida, J. (1973). *'Speech and phenomena' and other essays on Husserl's theory of signs.* Evanston: Northwestern University Press.
Derrida, J. (1978). *Writing and difference.* Chicago: University of Chicago Press.
Derrida, J. (1982). *Margins of philosophy.* Chicago: Chicago University Press.
Edwards, J. (1985). *Language, society and identity.* Oxford: Basil Blackwell.
Honigsberg, P. J. (2013). Linguistic isolation: A new human rights violation constituting torture, and cruel, inhuman and degrading treatment. *Northwestern University Journal of International Human Rights, 12*(1), 22–45.
Kalmthout, A. M. v., Hofstee-van der Meulen, F. B. A. M., & Dünkel, F. (2007). *Foreigners in European prisons.* Nijmegen: Wolf Legal Publishers.
Kamwangamalu, N. W. (2007). One language, multi-layered identities. *World Englishes, 26*(3), 263–275.
Kaufman, E. (2012). Finding foreigners: Race and the politics of memory in British prisons. *Population, Space and Place, 18*(6), 701–714.
Kaufman, E. (2015). *Punish and expel: Border control, Nationalism, and the new purpose of the prison.* Oxford: Oxford University Press.
Kriminalomsorgen. (2016). *Årsstatistikker, NOU, stortingsmeldinger og rapporter.* Retrieved from www.kriminalomsorgen.no/publikasjoner.242465.no.html
Lindberg, O. (2005). Prison cultures and social representations: The case of Hinseberg, a women's prison in Sweden. *International Journal of Prisoner Health, 1*(2–4), 143–161.
Lippi-Green, R. (1997). *English with an accent: Language, ideology and discrimination in the United States.* London: Routledge.
Madison, D. S. (2012). *Critical ethnography: Method, ethics, and performance.* Los Angeles, CA: SAGE Publications.
Mathiesen, T. (1965). *The defences of the weak: A sociological study of a Norwegian correctional institution.* London: Tavistock.
May, S. (2000). Uncommon languages: The challenges and possibilities of minority language rights. *Journal of Multilingual and Multicultural Development, 21*(5), 366–385.
Myhre, K. C. (2012). The pitch of ethnography: Language, relations, and the significance of listening. *Anthropological Theory, 12*(2), 185–208.
Pakes, F., & Holt, K. (2017). The transnational prisoner: Exploring themes and trends involving a prison deal with the Netherlands and Norway. *British Journal of Criminology, 57*(1), 79–93.

Plassen, A. (2016). Skjerpet strafferamme for brudd på innreiseforbudet: Et nødvendig og forholdsmessig tiltak for å ivareta innvandringskontroll? *Kritisk Juss*, 47(3), 181–216.
Politiets utlendingsenhet. (2016). *PU uttransporterte 7.825 personer i 2015.* Retrieved from www.politi.no/politiets_utlendingsenhet/nyhet_15691.xml
Rowe, A. (2014). Situating the self in prison research. *Qualitative Inquiry*, 20(4), 404–416.
Searle, J. (1969). *Speech acts*. Cambridge: Cambridge University Press.
Sparks, R. F., Bottoms, A., & Hay, W. (1996). *Prisons and the problem of order.* Oxford: Clarendon Press.
SSB. (2016). *Nøkkeltall for innvandring og innvandrere.* Retrieved from www.ssb.no/innvandring-og-innvandrere/nokkeltall/innvandring-og-innvandrere
Sykes, G. M. (1958). *The society of captives: A study of a maximum security prison.* Princeton, NJ: Princeton University Press.
Tannenbaum, M. (2009). What's in a language? Language as a core value of minorities in Israel. *Journal of Ethnic and Migration Studies*, 35(6), 977–995.
Temple, B., & Young, A. (2004). Qualitative research and translation dilemmas. *Qualitative Research*, 4(2), 161–178.
Ugelvik, T. (2013). Seeing like a welfare state. In K. F. Aas & M. Bosworth (Eds.), *The borders of punishment: Migration, citizenship, and social exclusion.* Oxford: Oxford University Press.
Ugelvik, T. (2014a). Paternal pains of imprisonment: Incarcerated fathers, ethnic minority masculinity and resistance narratives. *Punishment and Society*, 16(2), 152–168.
Ugelvik, T. (2014b). The incarceration of foreigners in European prisons. In S. Pickering & J. Haam (Eds.), *The Routledge handbook on crime and international migration.* London: Routledge.
Ugelvik, T. (2014c). Prison ethnography as lived experience: Notes from the diaries of a beginner let loose in Oslo prison. *Qualitative Inquiry*, 20(4), 471–480.
Ugelvik, T. (2017). The limits of the welfare state? Foreign national prisoners in the Norwegian crimmigration prison. In P. S. Smith & T. Ugelvik (Eds.), *Scandinavian penal history, culture and prison practice: Embraced by the welfare state?* London: Palgrave Macmillan.
Warr, J. (2016). The deprivation of certitude, legitimacy and hope: Foreign national prisoners and the pains of imprisonment. *Criminology & Criminal Justice*, 16(3), 301–318.
Weber, L. (2013). *Policing non-citizens.* Abingdon: Routledge.

Chapter 15

Voices in immigration detention centres in Greece

Different actors and possibilities for change

Andriani Fili

Introduction

Detention centres are filled with voices. Sometimes they are loud and their echo is strong; other times they are muted. But who is their audience? Does listening enable representation? Can we ever speak for others? Drawing on work I have conducted across a number of Greek detention centres in a variety of roles, I explore whether it is possible to represent the voices of immigrant detainees in a way that may have a positive impact on their situation.

Voice has frequently been privileged by qualitative (Mazzei & Jackson, 2009) and feminist (Hartsock, 1983; Harding, 1993) researchers who seek to represent the truth of experience. As Britzman (1989) argues, 'a commitment to voice attests to the right of speaking and being represented.' The drive to make voices heard and understood has inspired critical research with marginalised populations and their interactions with oppressive systems. Criminological accounts of confinement, for example, have been dedicated to ventriloquising or speaking for silenced and subjugated voices in prison (see, for example, Carlen, 1981; Sparks, Bottoms, & Hay, 1996; Bosworth, 1999; Liebling, 2004; Crewe, 2009; Phillips & Earle, 2010) and immigration detention (Bosworth, 2014; Bosworth & Kellezi, 2014; Bosworth & Slade, 2014; Hall, 2010). In this work, voices from those subject to immigration detention may not only illuminate these hidden institutions but also make them come alive.

Lived experience in hidden and secretive institutions has, for much academic work, become a criterion for understanding and one that could potentially bear transformative power. Researchers, thus, develop theories that express and encompass the voices and needs of others in a bid to challenge power relations and improve material conditions for the lives of individuals or groups. Practitioners, too, seek to speak out for immigration detainees, not just to tell their stories but to demand change in light of their accounts.

While there is much to be admired in this body of qualitative work, questions remain. Whereas the flow from practice to impact seems straightforward, the potential or even desire of research to shape progressive change is less smooth. Do academics and practitioners wield legitimate authority in representing the voices of others? What are the epistemological limits of voice? Can any of this work actually challenge the many drivers of detention policies and practices?

This chapter attempts to answer these questions by reflecting on my experiences as a researcher and NGO practitioner in the field of immigration detention in Greece. It is a tale of naivety, hope, disappointment and the desire to find hope again in the grimmest environment. I pay particular attention to the challenges of the ethical implications and personal ambiguities of speaking for others. I have no doubt that some of the issues highlighted in this chapter reflect the naivety that may come with the territory of being a novice researcher, a young practitioner and a white female, so they are specific to my positionality(ies) and should not be regarded as generalised observations. Nevertheless, I hope that my experiences will be useful for other researchers grappling with similar questions.

The chapter will unfold as follows: The following section will provide an outline of the Greek detention system, which forms the context against which both my research experience and work in the non-profit sector occurred. I will then move on to describe my journey as a researcher and a practitioner and the challenges of representing detainees. Drawing on this discussion, I refer to the different ways that detainees' voices and stories are collected and used by different actors. In doing so, I will explore the limits and possibilities of the impact that research and practice can generate and its benefits for the individuals in detention. I argue that for representation to have the potential to open detention sites to a global gaze, it must grapple with a series of issues, which can be summarised as a *who, how, who to and why* of representation (Pickering & Kara, 2017).

The maze of immigration detention in Greece: challenges of listening to immigration detainees

Immigration detention has, for many years, been Greece's key policy in managing irregular arrivals. It offered a means of satisfying European Union (EU) demands by increasing the rate of 'safe' and legal returns, appeasing Greek citizens by discouraging the visibility of undocumented people and attempting to deter prospective arrivals by wilfully making detention facilities unlivable (Fili forthcoming). The situation in detention, particularly at border locations, was described as a 'humanitarian crisis' by UNHCR (2010) long before the so-called European refugee crisis in 2015 due to its arbitrariness, overcrowding and poor conditions.

After many years of expansion and a short halt in 2015 following the inauguration of the first left-wing government,[1] the Greek state has resumed confinement and detention tactics to manage the rising number of refugees and migrants. At the moment, there are around 30 refugee camps[2] and 5 hotspots on the Aegean islands, partly operating as detention centres, as well as a number of informal sites, spread all over Greece. The current government is not only trying to build more detention centres but is also hoping to convert small reception centres, especially those hosting unaccompanied minors, into large military camps. In addition to these new facilities, Greece continues to use a number of pre-removal detention centres, older dedicated detention facilities and numerous border guard and police stations.

Despite the scale of this practice, surprisingly little is known about them, other than what we can glean from reports by human rights organisations (Amnesty International, 2010; Amnesty International, 2012; Human Rights Watch, 2008; MSF, 2014; Pro Asyl, 2012). Yet detainees throughout Greece have been very vocal about their experiences. They often engage in hunger strikes, and isolated incidents have at times triggered larger protests. They issue statements about conditions in detention, demanding change. However, has anyone ever listened to them? More importantly, have their actions had an impact on life in detention? Such aspects of detention rarely attract the public eye or government attention, and when they do, all too often they are dismissed as manipulative behaviour.

As governments have restricted access to detention centres, detention practices have become resistant to change. Political parties and media on the left express their concern about what is going on behind iron doors; however, they cannot effect change beyond their own circles. The growing activist movement against detention, racism and fascism and NGOs that work in detention, though strong, have limited political capital or influence vis-à-vis the state.[3] While the latter have, to a certain extent, conformed to the Greek state's interests and agendas, activists have been demonised by the government and by mainstream media.

Academia is strangely silent on all counts (although see Bosworth, Fili, & Pickering, 2016, forthcoming). That is to say, despite sustained media and political interest in Greece as a key site of European border security and several disturbing accounts about life in the country's detention, reception and refugee facilities, there is little academic scholarship about daily life in Greek detention centres.[4] For the most part scholarship on detention is purely theoretical and relies merely on secondary data (Cheliotis, 2013; Angeli & Triandafyllidou, 2014; Triandafyllidou, Angeli, & Dimitriadi, 2014; Mantanika, 2014). As has been argued in the UK context, immigration detention is the topic of independent academic scrutiny (Bosworth & Kellezi, 2016a).

Three factors are relevant in explaining the continued marginalisation of immigration detention in academic debate in Greece. First, detainees make up a statistical minority of the foreign population in the country. Hence, the issues that they face in detention pale into insignificance when compared to the general fear of crime and social insecurity the undocumented population on the streets of Athens represents. If anything, in an era of rising xenophobia and anti-immigrant rhetoric (Voutira, 2013), the public is happy that immigrants are kept out of sight, regardless of the conditions in which they are placed.

Second, researchers face insurmountable obstacles in their attempts to conduct research in closed institutions (Koulouris, 2009). Indeed, a report by the Greek Ombudsman (2006) exposes the entrenched and long-standing bureaucratic practices and ideas about research in administrative fields like prisons that 'favour corruption' (Koulouris, 2009, p. 313). In this context, researchers are perhaps discouraged from venturing into a bureaucratic struggle. Third, social science research in general is severely underfunded in Greece, with no systematic effort to form or assess strategies for the future of the humanities and social sciences, apart from a few instances.[5] Hence, social research in Greece, including that on border control and immigration detention, is not as well developed as in other countries in Europe.

Against this context, it seems that few actors can and will represent immigrant detainees in Greece, while the voices of those in detention have been continuously silenced. The following sections will examine two instances of commitment to the voices of detainees, my role in them and my hopes for change.

Getting to know the field of immigration detention in Greece: becoming a researcher

Contemporary qualitative research on closed institutions, such as immigration detention centres, often focuses on making marginalised voices heard. Similarly, social scientists whose research focuses on migration and refugee issues argue that speaking for those who are vulnerable also has to make an impact. Researchers tend to think, albeit often not explicitly, that they should not only contribute to a theoretical understanding of the world but also help the people caught up in humanitarian emergencies (Jacobsen & Landau, 2003). However, this approach to knowledge assumes that research subjects want to speak and be represented. But 'if suffering is the unspeakable, as opposed to what can be spoken; if it is what remains concealed, impossible to reveal' (Frank, 2001, p. 355), can we ever be sure about what we know? Put another way, can we ever claim we speak for the other (Alcoff, 1995)?

As I attempt to answer these questions, I relate the discussion to research I conducted in a Greek immigration detention centre. To the best of my knowledge, this was the first such academic study in Greece with free access to staff and detainees. In that project, I sought to examine women's decision making in relation to border policing, based on their testimonies, and aimed to develop a more comprehensive understanding of unauthorised border crossing and its policing.[6] The empirical part of this project, which included formal and informal interviews with migrant women and police officers, was conducted over a month in 2011 at Petrou Ralli, a detention facility for migrants in Athens, followed by two months of participant observation. The Hellenic Police were the approving body for undertaking this research and the directing authorities of the centre. In negotiation with them, I was given full access to interview staff and migrants as well as free movement throughout the centre but not the cells. Respondents were recruited through the social service on site and in consultation with detention officers. Together I formally interviewed 40 migrant women, police officers and administrative staff.

Schooled in social research methods yet a novice in undertaking empirical research, I initially felt very grateful for the opportunity to conduct this piece of research. Upon entering the field, though, and given the lack of information about it, I was rapidly overwhelmed. In common with young female researchers in environments that encompass dominant forms of masculinities (Gurney, 2002; Bosworth & Slade, 2014), I decided early on to lend authority to myself by emphasising my academic background. Hence, I soon became the '*girl from the [foreign] university*', detached from the Greek context. While being an outsider 'expert' positioned me in the field as a 'phenomenological stranger' with license to ask 'dumb questions' (Sparkes, 1994), it also raised uncomfortable expectations that I would provide answers. On many occasions, detention officers would ask my opinion about the financial crisis and the migration situation in the country. In other instances, participants appeared to want answers about whether I thought their overtly racist ideas were 'right.' Afraid that an honest response would taint their trust and hamper my access to detainees, I remained most of the times silent, nodding along, as I listened to officers' comments about inadequate women for their contravention of gender-based expectations and failing cultures (Bosworth et al. forthcoming in 2018).

Over time, my silence became a great source of anxiety. I soon realised that my reactions in the field would be the lens through which the data would be generated (Woodthorpe, 2009) and through which my supervisors' interpretation of immigration detention in the country would come. This insight led me to wonder what implications instances like this would have in terms of me becoming a 'good' ethnographic researcher. Would I live up to my supervisors' expectations? Was I being careful enough in the interview process? More importantly, if I did not speak up to defend detained women, why was I there? In raising these questions, I confronted my limitations as a researcher and saw my own powerlessness to speak for them.

As soon as I could leave the field, I rushed with feelings of relief and excitement to the analytical phase of the project. Somewhat optimistically, I assumed that committing women's words on paper would matter (i.e. make an impact) and make up for my silences while in the field. Yet as I sat in front of my computer screen re-reading my interview transcripts and fieldnotes about life inside a Greek detention centre, I had the nagging suspicion that the research and articles which would be produced drawing on it would be irrelevant to the women I interviewed. They would never read them, nor would the questions we asked and sought to answer be likely to affect their living conditions drastically. In an era of mass mobility that entails so much human suffering, academic work often seems self-indulgent and somewhat removed from the immediate problems facing participants (Bosworth & Kellezi, 2016a). As others have reported elsewhere (Bosworth & Kellezi, 2016b), I found it hard to reconcile myself to the aspirations of research participants for the research to make things better for them.

As I was striving to make my work intellectually sophisticated in order to justify my place in academia, I feared that I was no longer speaking for the women I interviewed but rather only addressing other academics. Therefore, I grew more and more convinced that if I were to continue being in the field, my work would have to make a difference to detained women and men. I did not feel academia could achieve change. So I left the field as a researcher and began working for an NGO.

Getting too close to the field of immigration detention: becoming an NGO practitioner

The welfare framework for refugees and migrants in Greece, like the welfare regime as a whole (Lyberaki & Tinios, 2014), is rudimentary at best. In response to years of austerity politics, social actors and NGOs have taken on many social welfare services for vulnerable populations, effectively forming a hybrid shadow state (Skleparis, 2015, p. 150) in which the Greek government is little more than a 'coordinator' of refugee and migrant welfare provision services (Sitaropoulos, 2002). NGO interventions in immigration detention facilities have been triggered by unmet humanitarian needs and by the obstacles detainees face in accessing basic provisions, such as legal aid, health and social support. However, acknowledging the challenges of independence and autonomy in detention settings (Kotsioni, 2016) and due to problems of access, as well as funding constraints, few organisations actually provided services inside detention, rendering many detainees, especially those in remote detention locations, at the mercy of piecemeal interventions.

The organisation where I worked was the only one that, at the time, offered psycho-social and medical support to economic migrants and asylum seekers detained in six migrant detention centres in Athens with permanent locally established teams.[7] I was situated in the Athens airport detention centre as a social worker, together with a psychologist and a doctor. During my time there I conducted more than 900 interviews with detainees and held informal conversations with several detention officers.

The centre was in dire need of humanitarian intervention (Fili, 2013). At the time we started working there, 120 men were detained in nine single-occupancy cells with very little natural light and two toilets to share. The men were not able to lie down or sleep at the same time. Their only physical movement was limited to going to the toilet for a few minutes in the morning and the evening. At all other times they were locked inside their cells. In fact, our daily operations, which mainly involved meeting with detainees, were fully dependent on the consent of police officers on duty despite framework arrangements being signed between the NGO and the authorities. Other rules restrained them: they were not allowed to smoke more than three cigarettes a day, they were not given cutlery for 'security' reasons and conditions of hygiene were never properly observed.

As a young practitioner, I began with humanitarian, albeit contested (Perkowski, 2016), ideals of 'saving' people in detention. As has been shown elsewhere (Slim, 2005: p. 2), 'ideals and idealism are frequently associated with excessive optimism, even naivety', to the point where they become unrealistic. Not long after my first days at work, a 'sense of realism' crept in born not only of self-knowledge but also of empirical observation of the world around me which gave few grounds for optimism that my work in detention would make a difference.

Acknowledging that effective provision of aid can only be delivered in a safe and secure environment, which a detention setting cannot ensure, I had to come to terms with significant compromises in my work and concede my humanitarian principles, which led me to get involved in the first place.[8] My colleagues, who had been in the field for much longer, tried to reassure me:

> You know the beginning is always difficult. Don't worry about it, you'll get used to it. We've been here for a very long time and we don't respond like this anymore, our sentiments have frozen, which is good about us but not good for the job because we get very suspicious. We've seen a lot and we have to screen everyone. We have to realise who needs help and who's lying. Sometimes we make mistakes but that's the way it is. We are humans and we have to deal with it. It's a strategic response to the difficulties of the work I think. You have to be neutral and not let anything affect you so much.
> (Personal conversation with colleagues, March 2011)

Remaining neutral is extremely challenging under conditions that so provocatively contravene basic standards of decency and humanity (CPT, 2012) and was not my intention in any case. I was there to speak for the detainees at the top of my voice. So I implored the NGO director to act on the information about abuse and ill treatment we reported almost every day. Yet each time we were discouraged from pursuing further action, because this would, allegedly, disrupt our relations with the police and would affect our daily routine. Not surprisingly, depending on state authorities for economic survival was effectively eroding the NGO's capacity for advocacy. However, she was right. The dissemination, to relevant ministries and the media, of the letter to the minister we ended up writing created outrage. Officials at the centre threatened to file lawsuits for slander. Detention officers compromised our access to detainees. Yet in the long run, the managing authorities grew more receptive to our recommendations, or at least appeared to do so by allowing for more 'freedoms' (e.g. cutlery, more cigarettes, more visits to the toilet). Our success was celebrated but soon forgotten as the situation gradually went back to 'normal'. For speaking to authorities that do not want to hear for people that do not officially 'matter' cannot have meaningful impact on the detainees' situations.

Being exposed to the daily realities of a detention facility, which had the unenviable – albeit deserved – reputation as the worst in Athens, and not being able to help them was paralysing. I became more cynical, which, over time, affected my efficiency and productivity. Indeed, no stories of harrowing border crossings, death and loss would shock me anymore. Moreover, I often questioned whether all this suffering was real. Did it honestly affect the person that was in front of me, or had it become the same standardised testimony I heard about every day? How can I tell if what I am listening to is true, I wondered? Feelings of burnout, disillusionment and compassion fatigue are common among aid workers, who face increasing demands they cannot resolve and work in distressing contexts (Cardozo et al., 2012); qualitative researchers encounter similar issues in the field (Dickson-Swift et al., 2007). After a few months I sought to spend as little time in the centre as possible and went home every day feeling exhausted; I found it unbearable to be confronted with my own powerlessness in the face of so much hardship.

Elsewhere, I have described detention centres in Greece as mazes which trap those within (Fili, 2013). To return to this metaphor, I think it is important to ask whether researchers or practitioners can help detainees find their way out. Do some locations offer people a vantage point with more freedom to speak up and represent others? The previous sections highlight that speaking for others in immigration detention is severely constrained by the everyday realities of the institutions and people who work inside them. Still, as I conclude, the different ways we collect people's voices and use them and to whom they are disseminated matter for the impact on these voices being heard.

Voices from immigration detention: concluding thoughts

This has been a rather bleak representation of my experiences as a researcher and a practitioner in immigration detention in Greece. While I understand that this account might leave my or others' work open to challenge, I prefer to see it as a way of accounting for 'emotional baggage' (Knowles, 2006). To imply that challenging encounters such as the ones recounted in this chapter do not happen is to ensure that novice researchers and practitioners are not prepared or equipped to face them. It hides emotionally and intellectually demanding components of our work in immigration detention.

I have, thus, taken to writing about my experiences in order to help make sense of them and what they might suggest for the role of academic scholarship and the third sector in places of confinement. But this has not been so much about what they can do but more about what they cannot achieve; for only when we are reflexive about the limitations of our practices can we understand the way forward. My intention, therefore, has not been to show that speaking for immigrant detainees is futile. I have sought rather to point out that speaking in ways that may have impact on people's lives is riddled with challenges.

The tendency of civil society and academia to avoid conversing with each other, with each side claiming a kind of moral high ground (hearing, understanding and representing the voices of others), assumes a compulsive quest that 'truth' about life in detention can be attained from one perspective or another. However, can we ever be sure about what we know? Can we ever achieve reliable representation of the other? While researchers and practitioners ebb and flow in and out of detention centres, dependent on their funding and access arrangements, detainees either float in the murky waters or sink hard and fast in the detention maze. Since I first encountered the immigration detention system in Greece in 2011, little has changed. The institutions remain resistant to academic scrutiny and practitioners' recommendations, and people inside them continue to suffer. Without ethical accounts of representations that seek to address the *who, how, who to and why* of representation (Pickering & Kara, 2017), we end up with a scattering of painful stories that fail to achieve change in research participants'/beneficiaries' situations.

Detainees do have a voice; sometimes they let it be heard, other times they prefer to be silent. Detainees speak to the authorities and to each other. They speak above and beyond fences. Researchers and practitioners listen and, by virtue of their positions, report. Before they do, though, they have to make decisions about how to take the words out of their participants' mouths and represent them in other outlets. Those acts of representation take myriad forms: from writing an article to presenting conference papers to liaising with the authorities. But who listens? As these representations hit the brick walls of self-indulgent academic communities and indifferent governments, it becomes all the more evident that audiences matter. The impact of words can depend significantly on who else is engaging with those representations (Pickering & Kara, 2017). For representation should be defined not only by what is said but also by the audience and/or others' recognition of and reaction to what is actually said (Fili, 2013). Understanding the interaction between speakers, audiences and other parties is thus at the heart of understanding representation, which seeks to effect change.

According to Flynn (2017), to effectively challenge the many drivers of detention policies and practices requires flexibility of thought, analysis, strategies and tactics. While there is no prescriptive recipe for ethical involvement with detained people, serious consideration of the ethics of representation may provide a start to a reflexive, collaborative journey towards a shared ethics of engagement in social scientific research and practice. This would take into account a variety of voices, the urgency of particular situations, the lessons learned from the history of failed attempts to 'save' detainees and the objectives and needs of different governments, social groups and – most importantly – detainees (Flynn, 2017). In this way, representing immigrant detainees in a way that may achieve political change must have many sides to be effective. It is this journey I would like to begin to actively engage with a large audience for all the wrongs I was a silent witness to while researching and working in immigration detention centres in Greece. I hope that my commitment to reflection – indeed public reflection – on my choices about the *who, how, who to and why* of representation will invite more companions on the collaborative path to opening detention centres in Greece to a global gaze.

Notes

1 Following its election pledge to break with anti-immigrant practices of the past, the government started evacuating detention centres (Chrysopoulos, 2015). However, as people on the move found fences and walls on their way to Europe, they became stranded in Greece, forcing the government to turn again to detention.
2 There is administrative confusion around the number of refugee camps in Greece (www.newsdeeply.com/refugees/articles/2017/03/06/the-refugee-archipelago-the-inside-story-of-what-went-wrong-in-greece).
3 For a discussion on this issue please see Clarke, J., Houliaras, A. and Sotiropoulos, D. (Eds.), 2015.
4 It must be noted that bordering control and border crossing practices (Green, 2010; Bacas, 2010; Topak, 2014; Pallister-Wilkins, 2015; Trubeta, 2015), the asylum procedure (Cabot, 2012; McDonough & Tsourdi, 2012) as well as immigration policies and management (Voutira, 2013; Karamanidou, 2014) have been extensively explored. Scholarship has focused on the economic, political and sociocultural changes connected to migration processes and the development of migration policy (see, inter alia, Triantafyllidou, 2009; Skordas, 2002; Fakiolas, 2003).
5 National Centre for Social Research (EKKE), www.ekke.gr/index.php?lng=en.
6 The fieldwork was supported by the Oxford University Research Support Fund at the Faculty of Law as well as by the Australian Research Council Future Fellowship of Sharon Pickering for the project 'Border policing: Gender, human rights and security'.
7 Other organisations offered services, mainly legal aid and representation, but only on a temporary basis, when funding allowed it.
8 This is what Frances Webber describes as 'the vexed question of when, if and how we should engage with statutory bodies and whether it is possible to do so without jeopardising the principles which led us to get involved in this work in the first place' (in Tyler et al., 2014).

References

Alcoff, L. (1995). The problem of speaking for others. In L. Bell & D. Blumenfeld (Eds.), *Overcoming racism and sexism*. Lanham, MA: Rowman & Littlefield.
Amnesty International. (2010). *Greece: Irregular migrants and asylum-seekers routinely detained in substandard conditions*. London: Amnesty International.
Amnesty International. (2012). *Greece: The end of the road for refugees, asylum-seekers and migrants*. London: Amnesty International.
Angeli, D., & Triandafyllidou, A. (2014). *Is the indiscriminate detention of irregular migrants a cost-effective policy tool? A case-study of the Amygdaleza Pre-Removal Center*. Midas Policy Brief, ELIAMEP, Athens.
Bacas, J. L. (2010). No safe haven: The reception of irregular boat migrants in Greece. *Environment and Planning D: Society and Space, 32*, 815–833. doi:10.1068/d13031p

Bosworth, M. (1999). *Engendering resistance: Agency, power and women's prison*. Aldershot: Ashgate.
Bosworth, M. (2014). *Inside immigration detention*. Oxford: Oxford University Press.
Bosworth, M., Fili, A., & Pickering, S. (2016). Women's immigration detention in Greece: Gender, control, and capacity. In M. J Guia, V. Mitsilegas, & R. Khoulish (Eds.), *Immigration detention, risk and human rights*. New York: Springer.
Bosworth, M., Fili, A., & Pickering, S. (forthcoming in 2018). Women and border policing at the edges of Europe. *Journal of Ethnic and Migration Studies*.
Bosworth, M., & Kellezi, B. (2014). Citizenship and belonging in a women's immigration detention centre. In C. Phillips & C. Webster (Eds.), *New directions in race, ethnicity and crime* (pp. 80–96). Abingdon: Routledge.
Bosworth, M., & Kellezi, B. (2016a). Getting in, getting out and getting back: Access, ethics and emotions in immigration detention research. In S. Armstrong, J. Blaustein, & A. Henry (Eds.), *Reflexivity and criminal justice: Intersections of policy*. Practice and Research. London: Palgrave Macmillan.
Bosworth, M., & Kellezi, B. (2016b). Doing research in immigration removal centres: Ethics, emotions and impact. *Criminology & Criminal Justice, 17*(2), 121–137.
Bosworth, M., & Slade, G. (2014). In search of recognition: Gender and staff-detainee relations in a British immigration detention centre. *Punishment & Society, 16*(2), 169–186.
Britzman, D. (1989). Who has the floor? Curriculum, teaching and the English student teacher's struggle for voice. *Curriculum Inquiry, 19*(2), 143–162.
Cabot, H. (2012). The governance of things: Documenting Limbo in the Greek asylum procedure. *Political and Legal Anthropology Review, 35*(1), 11–29.
Cardozo, B. L., Gotway Crawford, C., Eriksson, C., Zhu, J., Sabin, M., Ager, A., . . . Simon, W. (2012). Psychological distress, depression, anxiety, and burnout among international humanitarian aid workers: A longitudinal study. *PLoS One, 7*(9).
Carlen, P. (1981). *Women's imprisonment*. London: Routledge and Kegan Paul.
Cheliotis, L. (2013). Behind the veil of philoxenia: The politics of immigration detention in Greece. *European Journal of Criminology, 2013*(10), 725.
Chrysopoulos, P. (2015, May 2). Migrants from Amygdaleza detention center released in Athens. *Greek Reporter*. Retrieved from http://greece.greekreporter.com/2015/03/02/migrants-from-amygdaleza-detention-center-released-in-center-of-athens/
Clarke, J., Houliaras, A., & Sotiropoulos, D. (Eds.). (2015). *Austerity and the third-sector in Greece: Civil society at the European frontline*. Abingdon: Routledge.
CPT. (2012). *Report to the government of Greece on the visit to Greece carried out by the European Committee for the prevention of torture and inhuman or degrading treatment of punishment (CPT) from January 19–27, 2011*. Strasbourg: Council of Europe.
Crewe, B. (2009). *The prisoner society: Power, adaptation and social life in an English prison*. Oxford: Oxford University Press.
Dickson-Swift, V., James, E., Kippen, S., & Liamputtong, P. (2007). Doing sensitive research: What challenges do qualitative researchers face?. *Qualitative Research, 7*(3), 327–353.
Fakiolas, R. (2003). Regularising undocumented immigrants in Greece: Procedures and effects. *Journal of Ethnic & Migration Studies, 29*(3), 535–562.
Fili, A. (2013). The maze of immigration detention in Greece: A case study of the airport detention facility in Athens. *Prison Service Journal* (205).
Fili, A. (forthcoming in 2018). Containment practices of immobility in Greece. In M. Karakoulaki, L. Southgate, & J. Steiner (Eds.), *Crossing lines and climbing walls: Critical perspective on migration in the 21st century*. Bristol: E-International Relations Publishing.

Flynn, M. (2017). *Putting immigration detention in interdisciplinary perspective* (Part I). Retrieved September 20, 2017, from www.law.ox.ac.uk/research-subject-groups/centre-criminology/centreborder-criminologies/blog/2017/05/putting

Frank, A. W. (2001, May). Can we research suffering? *Qualitative Health Research, 11*(3), 353–362.

Greek Ombudsman. (2006). *2005 annual report.* Report, Greek Ombudsman, Athens.

Green, S. (2010). Performing border in the Aegean. *Journal of Cultural Economy, 3*(2), 261–278; *Ethnologia Balkanica, 14.*

Gurney, J. N. (1991). Female researchers in male-dominated settings. In *Qualitative approaches to criminal justice: Perspectives from the field* (pp. 169–189). California: SAGE Publications

Hall, A. (2010). These people could be anyone: Fear, contempt (and empathy) in a British immigration removal centre. *Journal of Ethnic and Migration Studies, 36*(6), 881–898.

Harding, S. (1993). Rethinking standpoint epistemology: What is 'strong objectivity'? In L. Alcoff & E. Potter (Eds.), *Feminist epistemologies* (pp. 49–81). New York: Routledge.

Hartsock, N. C. M. (1983). The feminist standpoint: Developing the ground for a specifically feminist historical materialism. In S. Harding & M. B. Hintikka (Eds.), *Discovering reality: Feminist perspectives on epistemology, metaphysics, methodology, and philosophy of science* (pp. 283–310). Dordrecht, The Netherlands: Reidel.

Human Rights Watch. (2008). *Stuck in a revolving door: Iraqis and other asylum seekers and migrants at the Greece/Turkey entrance to the European Union.* New York: Human Rights Watch.

Jacobsen, K., & Landau, I. (2003). Researching refugees: Some methodological and ethical considerations in social science and forced migration. *Evaluation and Policy Analysis Unit United Nations High Commissioner for Refugees,* CP 2500, Geneva, Switzerland.

Karamanidou, L. (2014). Political parties and immigration in Greece: Between consensus and competition. *Acta Politica, 50*(4), 442–460.

Knowles, C. (2006). Handling your baggage in the field reflections on research relationships. *International Journal of Social Research Methodology, 9*(5), 393–404.

Kotsioni, I. (2016). Detention of migrants and asylum-seekers: The challenge for humanitarian actors. *Refugee Survey Quarterly, 35,* 41–55.

Koulouris, N. (2009). *Surveillance and penal justice: Alternative sanctions and the dispersal of prison.* Athens: Nomiki Vivliothiki.

Liebling, A. (2004). *Prisons and their moral performance: A study of values quality and prison life.* Oxford: Oxford University Press.

Lyberaki, A., & Tinios, P. (2014). The informal Welfare state and the family: Invisible actors in the Greek drama. *Political Studies Review, 12,* 193–208.

Mantanika, R. (2014). Confinement practices of undocumented migrants at the borders of Europe: The case of Greece. In C. Michella & L. Nicola (Eds.), *The EU, immigration and the politics of immigration detention* (pp. 109–127). Abingdon and New York: Routledge.

Mazzei, L. A., & Jackson, A. Y. (2009). *Voice in qualitative inquiry: Challenging conventional, interpretive, and critical conceptions in qualitative research.* London: Routledge.

McDonough, P., & Tsourdi, E. (2012). The 'Other' Greek crisis: Asylum and eu solidarity. *Refugee Survey Quarterly, 31*(4), 67–100.

Medicins Sans Frontieres. (2014). *Invisible suffering: Prolonged and systematic detention of migrants and asylum seekers in substandard conditions in Greece.* Athens: MSF.

Pallister-Wilkins, P. (2015). The humanitarian politics of European border policing: Frontex and border police in Evros. *International Political Sociology, 9,* 53–69.

Perkowski, N. (2016). Deaths, interventions, humanitarianism and human rights in the Mediterranean 'migration crisis'. *Mediterranean Politics, 21*(2), 331–335.

Phillips, C., & Earle, R. (2010). Reading difference differently?: Identity, epistemology and prison ethnography. *British Journal of Criminology, 50*(2), 360–378.

Pickering, L., & Kara, H. (2017). Presenting and representing others: Towards an ethics of engagement. *International Journal of Social Research Methodology, 20*(3), 299–309.

.Pro Asyl. (2012). *Walls of shame: Accounts from the inside: The detention centres of Evros*. Frankfurt/Main: Pro Asyl.

Sitaropoulos, N. (2002). Refugee welfare in Greece: Towards a remodelling of the responsibility-shifting paradigm? *Critical Social Policy, 22*(3), 436–455.

Skleparis, D. (2015). Towards a hybrid 'shadow state'? The case of migrant-/refugee-serving NGOs in Greece. In J. Clarke, A. Huliaras, & D. A. Sotiropoulos (Eds.), *Austerity and the third sector in Greece: Civil society at the European frontline* (pp. 147–166). Series: Southeast European Studies. Ashgate: Farnham, Surrey. ISBN: 9781472452689.

Skordas, A. (2002). The new immigration law in Greece: Modernization on the wrong track. *European Journal of Migration and Law* (4), 23–48.

Slim, H. (2005, October 5). *Idealism and realism in humanitarian action*. Two Talks Given at the ACFID Humanitarian Forum Canberra.

Sparkes, A. (1994). Life histories and the issue of voice: Reflections on an emerging relationship. *Qualitative Studies in Education, 7*(2), 165–183.

Sparks, E., Bottoms, A. E., & Hay, W. (1996). *Prisons and the problem of order*. Oxford: Oxford University Press.

Topak, Ö. E. (2014). *The biopolitical border in practice: Surveillance and death at the Greece–Turkey borderzones. Environment and Planning D: Society and Space, 32*(5), 815–833.

Triandafyllidou, A. (2009). Greek immigration policy at the turn of the 21st century: Lack of political will or purposeful mismanagement? *European Journal of Immigration and Law, 11*, 159–177.

Triandafyllidou, A., Angeli, D., & Dimitriadi, A. (2014). *Detention as punishment: Can indefinite detention be Greece's main policy tool to manage its irregular migrant population?* Midas Policy Brief, ELIAMEP, Athens.

Trubeta, S. (2015). 'Rights' in the grey area: Undocumented border crossers on Lesvos. *Race & Class*, Institute of Race Relations, *56*(4), 56–72.

Tyler, I., Gill, N., Conlon, D., & Oeppen, C. (2014). The business of child detention: Charitable co-option, migrant advocacy and activist outrage. *Race and Class, 56*(1), 3–21.

UNHCR (2010). Submission by the United Nations High Commissioner for Refugees for the Office of the High Commissioner for Human Rights' Compilation Report. *Universal Periodic Review*, Greece.

Voutira, E. (2013). Realising 'fortress Europe': 'Managing' migrants and refugees at the borders of Greece. *Social Sciences Review, 140–141*, 57–69.

Woodthorpe, K. (2009). Reflecting on death: The emotionality of the research encounter. *Morality, 14*(1), 70–86.

Criminal justice research in an era of mass mobility
Concluding remarks

Synnøve Jahnsen, Rebecca Powell and Andriani Fili

> "Do not deplore, do not laugh, do not hate – understand!"
> —(Spinoza quoted in Bourdieu, 1993, p. 1)

Introduction

At a time when nationalism and conservative 'law and order' discourses seem to merge with calls for repressive migration policies, Spinoza's precept cited here serves as a helpful reminder that humanity has struggled to find meaning through centuries. At the same time, his words also suggest that our ability to 'understand' our situation is connected with our ability to control our emotions. Yet we ask, what does it mean to 'understand' crime control and migration regimes at a time when Europe is closing its borders, political figures such as Donald Trump vow to incarcerate an estimated 2 to 3 million non-citizens, and former Australian state officials respond by taking pride that "the world is catching up to Australia" on border control (Scott Morrison, former immigration minister quoted in Murphy, 2017). Is it enough to simply adopt Weber's notion of 'verstehen' as "a process of subjective interpretation on the part of the social researcher, a degree of sympathetic understanding between social researcher and subjects of study" (Ferrell, 1997, p. 27)? Or are we better off conceptualising our 'understanding' as inspired by Hannah Arendt, which always leaves us like Sisyphus doomed to carry out an unachievable task, recognising that 'understanding' is a state one seeks rather than arrives at?

More acutely, for some, perhaps, should we leave our emotions at the door as we enter the field to conduct interviews and engage in ethnographic studies or wrestle with statistical datasets as we try to build models while pouring over endless streams of news reports and policy documents in a constantly changing field? Are we not allowed to laugh or cry as we try to make sense of the world we live in? Is it even possible? Is it not wiser to accept our emotional repertoire as part of our cultural prescripts, as central parts of our collective and individual capacity to understand not only ourselves, our sympathies and our frustrations but each other as human beings, equally vulnerable and dependent on each other? In more provocative terms, are we living in times that allow us to lean back and rely on the advice of old and long-dead men like Spinoza?

Coming together

This chapter is written from a sense of doubt, not only about what lessons we should take from past thinkers but also about how we should write a concluding chapter that does justice to a collection of unique accounts of research practices at the same time as we stay sensitive to the personal and often emotional experiences that lie behind them. Despite our uncertainties, as the editors of this book we share a strong belief that by being open about where we write from, it will be easier for other scholars to engage constructively with some of the challenges and dilemmas that might await.

This edited collection seeks to answer the call for a 'reflexive turn' within the social sciences. At large, these debates share a position that there is no value-free, neutral or objective viewpoint from which to see the social and, as such, serves to open up for debates about lived experiences, our modes of understanding and the quality of our methodological resources. It seems however, that while there is an increased recognition that 'reflexivity' is important when thinking about one's research projects and that the individuals involved are 'subjects', not 'objects', fewer researchers offer reflexive accounts or discuss how reflexivity should be understood and operationalised. Rather, 'the reflexive turn' in social sciences and 'reflective research methods' can mean a variety of things, both depending on the disciplinary perspective and, to some extent, one's methodological preferences and ideological influences (Nelken, 1994; Lumsden & Winter, 2014; Bourdieu & Wacquant, 1992; Wacquant, 2011). While some researchers will seek to draw attention to the power structures involved in the ways in which knowledge is produced and applied, others will turn their attention towards the researcher, one's positionality and/or personal 'quality' (Lumsden & Winter, 2014). It also seems, as pointed out by Jahnsen and Slettvåg (this volume), that the few publications available for criminologists interested in the relationship between migration and crime are skewed against qualitative research projects focusing on migrants as subjects of research or are limited to more narrow discussions of flawed datasets. The literature, in other words, does not cover the whole spectre of research on the intersections between crime and migration. As a result, researchers coming into the field are offered little guidance on how to identify, articulate and take account of the range of influences that might be shaping their research project at various stages, from data collection and analysis to writing it up.

By coming together as editors, we have moved beyond initial inhibitions to discover common ground across various migration regimes and institutional and national contexts. We have also gained insights into the uniqueness of individual research experiences and the various ways researchers negotiate their relationship with the field, the stories they hear and the stories they are willing to share. In sum, this collection weaves together a larger discussion of research processes and the setbacks and challenges that occur. Together, the chapters offer a better understanding of the often-messy process of criminal justice research and honest reflections about 'good' and 'bad' research practices. In doing so, this book offers examples of the multiple ways in which knowledge is produced in collaboration with and respect of the researched and how researchers negotiate their relationship with the field. More importantly, it explores how a researcher's background and location, as well as conceptualisations of the field, can affect the access, interpretation and presentation of prescient criminological questions and answers.

It is within a context of increased social and political unrest that the contributors of this collection have been asked to reflect on their experiences of 'doing' research and share what they see as methodological possibilities and limitations in the field. Most authors, at various stages of their careers, have done ethnographic studies on and at the border, whether in the past or more recently. In these studies they have entered physical, social and political spaces at the fringes or edges of nation-states, spaces which are marked by being both a beginning and an end but also the front of our research field. In their projects, researchers are often dealing with the management of wanted migration and the management of unwanted migration. The fallout of welfare state services combined with increasingly restrictive border control laws and policies has real, difficult and sometimes devastating impacts on the life quality of those who seek protection within asylum arrangements or who seek to cross borders by irregular means. At the same time, for those of us working in this relatively new field, it often feels as though there are few available academic resources or colleagues. Some of these challenges feel personal: How far should we be willing to go for scientific progress, to obtain access to closed institutions and hard-to-reach populations? To what extent should we put ourselves in situations which at best are uncomfortable and at worst are physically and emotionally dangerous? How do we know we are in danger, and how do we deal with the inequalities we experience and that are part of the field, where some levels of risk will be unacceptable for the institutions we work for yet tolerated and/or created by the institutions we research or are doing research for?

While mainly framed within the discipline of criminology, this edited collection has evolved from an interdisciplinary research group conducting research that involves both qualitative and quantitative research data. Authors have not only provided accounts of the relations between their conceptualisations of the field and methodologies (see for example Gundhus; Johansen; Skilbrei; Weber, this volume), mainstream methodological considerations, such as the benefits and pitfalls of qualitative and quantitative data (see for example Jahnsen and Slettvåg; Cochrane; Aitken, this volume), the use of new technology and media platforms (Turnbull, this volume) or the importance of a multicultural and multilingual background (see for example Damsa and Ugelvik, this volume) as well as the challenges that can arise from being researchers with such a background (see for example Parmar; Aliverti, this volume); we have also asked our authors to transform what for some might feel as private and personal vulnerabilities into public discourse (see for example Turnbull; Gerlach; Fili; Powell and Segrave, this volume).

In her chapter, Sarah Turnbull shares her reflections about the dangers of burnout after doing community-based and remote follow-up research with women and men that she first met at immigration removal centres in the UK, and later when they were living their 'post-detention lives'. She describes her experience of participants who looked to her for help out of their predicaments. As she makes clear, while ethical considerations were helpful, they did not prevent her from feeling powerless and distressed at various stages of her project, nor did they change the lives of her participants. In this context, Gerlach's observation (this volume) about the scarcity of institutional support available for academics and students experiencing secondary trauma is alarming. As Gerlach points out, the risks of secondary and vicarious trauma are often overlooked in qualitative research literature yet constitute a real danger for border control ethnographers. For her, intrusive thoughts would creep up in otherwise normal situations, reminding her about bestialities and traumatic experiences in her interview data. The blurred lines between fieldwork site and 'home' not only can make it difficult to complete a project but affect physical health and emotional well-being of the researcher.

Conclusions

Honest accounts from researchers who at one stage of their project have felt vulnerable or have had to deal with a sense of discomfort or failure are not only useful moments of self-reflection but also benefit researchers collectively. While such accounts might feel risky, uncomfortable and even painful to write, doing so can also be empowering, as they reveal the power dynamics and positionalities of those engaged in various research processes. Above all, writing about the research process offers crucial transparency that holds us accountable, collectively and individually, towards each other and to our respective fields and disciplines.

One conclusion that can be drawn from this edited collection is that our conceptions of possibilities and limitations are connected to how we conceptualise and think about our criteria for failure and success and that this, in turn, seems directly linked to our ability to overcome challenges and create or gain access to (knowledge about) data, systems and procedures. As such, our collection contains accounts from researchers who have overcome practical and ethical dilemmas, at the same time as they manoeuvre what Skilbrei (this volume) refers to as political and ethical 'tricky waters'.

We might also conclude that the challenges and opportunities researchers might run up against are not equally distributed. For example, while members of our research network have been able to visit and do research at detention centres in Norway and the UK, the Australian authorities have been far less forthcoming in providing researchers with access. Not only is access to Australian offshore immigration detention centres currently blocked, but, due to the sheer size of the country, onshore systems facilitating incarceration and deportation of non-citizens are dispersed, making it difficult for researchers to get access (albeit not impossible; see for example Powel and Segrave, this volume) and challenging to gain an overview of how the regime works across Australian states (see Jahnsen, 2018). Similarly, the chapters reveal variation in opportunities for funding. Opportunities and incentives not only vary across institutional and national context but also depend on our positions within the university system and our abilities to create networks and allies within and across the systems we are researching. In this respect, the Leverthulme Network on External Border Control, which drew together the three research groups represented in this book, is a testimony to the benefits that come from joint efforts to enhance research on border control regimes, as it has created a unique opportunity for early-career researchers to meet and share their insights and experiences.

The final part of our conclusion serves as a reminder that research will be judged not only in terms of its results, analysis and dissemination but to which extent a researcher achieved his or her success within traditional standards of ethical and legal regulations for conduct. Yet according to Düvell et al. (2010) researchers on migration, with a few exceptions (see for example Van Liemp & Bilger, 2012; Hugman et al., 2011; Tyldum, 2012; Surtees & Brunovskis, 2016), often miss out on ethical discussions. For us, it seems that the combination of an increasing number of asylum seekers and refugees, their precarious life situations and the heightened political tension surrounding the issue of crime and migration have increased the complexity of ethical and practical dilemmas. Thus, one way to read the book is also to consider it as a contribution to moral issues in migration research. While the struggles faced by individual researchers may appear uniquely situated in time and space, the chapters speak of a shared experience across borders, disciplines and institutional affiliation, namely a commitment to develop best practices for research and live up to universal standards for ethical principles.

By editing this collection we have learned that the 'choices' we make (or consciously and unconsciously do not make) with regard to ontological and epistemological positioning, methodological and theoretical perspective and the adoption of particular research methods are bound up not only with our personal or academic biographies, nor are they motivated exclusively by intellectual concerns. The interpersonal, political and institutional contexts in which researchers are embedded also play a key role in shaping these 'decisions'. Many of our contributors expressed discomfort when considering their research practices reflexively, some seemingly afraid of criticism, others seemingly uncomfortable with the 'emotional', 'wishy-washy' or 'navel-gazing' direction a more reflexive account of our research practices might produce. Others have turned their discomfort into the object of analysis, laying bare their preconceptions and sympathies for scrutiny. In this respect Powell and Segrave's contribution to our book seems particularly significant in its effort to open up a discussion about how researchers' conceptions of sympathy can be seen as a valued emotional resource that links to power structures inherent in the ways we as a collective steer our research interests. Sympathy, as well as the absence of sympathy, not only speaks of the relationship that exists between the researcher and the researched and how it is embedded in moral hierarchies but also how our research is valued as useful or devalued as not, by whom and why.

Seen this way, the absence of sympathy not only renders visible the micro politics involved when researchers engage with non-citizens who have committed serious and violent crimes. It also renders visible the politics of 'desirable' and 'undesirable' research topics and methods and how it corresponds with social and political discourses about 'deserving' and 'undeserving' migrants, as well as discourses about 'innocence' and 'guilt', where the migrant is the 'perpetrator' and the 'victim' is the state. This way there is a lesson, not explicitly told, by Powell and Segrave, but one which we can draw out of their chapter about the dangers of letting our research be guided by populist public debates about migration, where women and children are more frequently and successfully presented as victims of restrictive state policies, while convicted male non-citizens are presented as the threat so 'foreign' and 'intolerable' that it legitimises increased restrictions. As such, we might conclude that while pointing one finger to a problem in the field, the chapter points four back at the research community. We are all accountable for thinking more critically about the ways in which we disseminate research as a resource and how our emotional attachments become relevant when considering to whom we give voice, why, how and when, but also when considering to whom we might not (see Fili, this volume).

Final remarks

We started this chapter provocatively asking whether emotions have a place in social sciences, challenging common perceptions about what it means to seek knowledge and understanding. We also reminded our readers about Sisyphus, who in Greek mythology was punished for his curiosity and for revealing the secrets of the gods. In the myth Sisyphus is not only doomed to the eternal task of rolling a huge stone up a hill, he also has to endure the futility of it, as once he reaches the top, he knows that it will roll right back and hit him on its way. In Western culture, the tragedy of Sisyphus speaks not only about tasks seen as both laborious and futile, it also speaks of those who feel compelled to engage in routines in order to build and maintain professional integrity and identity. Seen this way, the knowledge that the stone will fall back on Sisyphus reminds us that for researchers, their labour does not stop once they find the answers to the questions that originally guide them. Rather, once we reach that hill, the landscape will hopefully open up, allowing us to see other hills. Once we find an answer it usually leads to another question, and so we carry on, both as individuals and as a collective. The stones we leave unturned are the stones that might hit us, or the stones we carry could be the image of the weight of the emotional burden that comes with the work we do, each of us carrying it differently.

As with any good story, this collection will not reveal the secrets of the gods. And just as a good story is partial and leaves its readers curious, our collection by no means provides a set of guidelines or easy-fix solutions nor addresses the full gamut of methodological challenges one might face when conducting research on and at the border. Yet the key policy implications of criminal justice research on immigration control regimes suggest that it is timely to explore the purpose of academic research in this area and the different ways it is carried out. We therefore expect this collection to be drawn upon by our contemporaries and by future generations. As such, our labour has not been carried out in a Sisyphean fashion but rather with the hope that we, stone by stone, have created a foundation from which other researchers can overcome their challenges by adding their experiences to future discussions.

The struggle itself towards the heights is enough to fill a man's heart. One must imagine Sisyphus happy. (Albert Camus)

References

Aitken, D. (forthcoming). Life and death in immigration detention. In A. Fili, S. Jahnsen, & R. Powell (Eds.), *Criminal justice research in an era of mass mobility*. Abingdon: Routledge Press.

Aliverti, A. (forthcoming). Spotting foreigners inside the courtroom: Race, crime and the construction of foreignness. In A. Fili, S. Jahnsen, & R. Powell (Eds.), *Criminal justice research in an era of mass mobility*. Abingdon: Routledge Press.

Bourdieu, P. (1993, 1999). To the reader. In P. Bourdieu & P. P. Ferguson (Eds.), *The weight of the world: Social suffering in contemporary society*. Cambridge: Polity Press.

Bourdieu, P., & Wacquant, L. J. D. (1992). *An invitation to reflexive sociology*. Chicago: The University of Chicago Press.

Camus, A. (1942). *The myth of Sisyphus*. London: Penguin Books.

Cochrane, B. (forthcoming). Expectations and realities of fieldwork by a nascent qualitative researcher. In A. Fili, S. Jahnsen, & R. Powell (Eds.), *Criminal justice research in an era of mass mobility*. Abingdon: Routledge Press.

Damsa, D., & Ugelvik, T. (forthcoming). One of us or one of them? Researcher positionality, language, and belonging in an all-foreign prison. In A. Fili, S. Jahnsen, & R. Powell (Eds.), *Criminal justice research in an era of mass mobility*. Abingdon: Routledge Press.

Düvell, F., Triandafyllidou, A., & Vollmer, B. (2010). Ethical issues in irregular migration research in Europe. *Population, Space and Place, 16*(3), 227–239.

Ferrell, J. (1997). Criminological verstehen: Inside the immediacy of crime. *Justice Quarterly, 14*(1), 3–23.

Fili, A. (forthcoming). Voices in immigration detention centres in Greece: Different actors and possibilities for change. In A. Fili, S. Jahnsen, & R. Powell (Eds.), *Criminal justice research in an era of mass mobility*. Abingdon: Routledge Press.

Gerlach, A. (forthcoming). Researching vulnerable women: Sharing distress and the risk of secondary and vicarious trauma. In A. Fili, S. Jahnsen, & R. Powell (Eds.), *Criminal justice research in an era of mass mobility*. Abingdon: Routledge Press.

Gundhus, H. O. I. (forthcoming). Turning researcher position into theorizing: Conceptualizing the police role in migration control. In A. Fili, S. Jahnsen, & R. Powell (Eds.), *Criminal justice research in an era of mass mobility*. Abingdon: Routledge Press.

Hedwards, B., & Suwinthawong, S. (forthcoming). Migrant voices in the Global South: Challenges of recruitment, participation and interpretation. In A. Fili, S. Jahnsen, & R. Powell (Eds.), *Criminal justice research in an era of mass mobility*. Abingdon: Routledge Press.

Hugman, R., Pittaway, E., & Bartolomei, L. (2011). When 'do no harm' is not enough: The ethics of research with refugees and other vulnerable groups. *British Journal of Social Work*, 41(7), 1271–1287.

Jahnsen, S. (2018). Banishing and banning outlaw motorcycle clubs. In K. Rønn, H. Gundhus, & N. Fyfe (Eds.), *Moral issues in intelligence led policing*. Milton Park, UK: Routledge.

Jahnsen, S., & Slettvåg, K. (forthcoming). 'Crimmigration' statistics: Numbers as evidence and discourse. In A. Fili, S. Jahnsen, & R. Powell (Eds.), *Criminal justice research in an era of mass mobility*. Abingdon: Routledge Press.

Johansen, N. B. (forthcoming). Funnel politics: Framing an 'irreal' space. In A. Fili, S. Jahnsen, & R. Powell (Eds.), *Criminal justice research in an era of mass mobility*. Abingdon: Routledge Press.

Lumsden, K., & Winter, A. (2014). *Reflexivity in criminological research: Experiences with the powerful and the powerless*. Basingstoke: Palgrave Macmillan.

Murphy, K. (2017, January 30). Scott Morrison says Trump travel ban shows 'world is catching up' to Australia. *The Guardian*. Retrieved November 8, 2017, from www.theguardian.com/australia-news/2017/jan/30/scott-morrison-trump-travel-ban-world-is-catching-up-to-australia-border-protection

Nelken, D. (Ed.). (1994). *The futures of criminology*. London: SAGE Publications.

Parmar, A. (forthcoming). Race at the border. In A. Fili, S. Johansen, & R. Powell (Eds.), *Criminal justice research in an era of mass mobility*. Abingdon: Routledge Press.

Powell, R., & Segrave, M. (forthcoming). In the absence of sympathy: Serious criminal offenders and the impact of border control measures. In A. Fili, S. Johansen, & R. Powell (Eds.), *Criminal justice research in an era of mass mobility*. Abingdon: Routledge Press.

Skilbrei, M. L. (forthcoming). Manoeuvring in tricky waters: Challenges in being a useful and critical migration scholar. In A. Fili, S. Johansen, & R. Powell (Eds.), *Criminal justice research in an era of mass mobility*. Abingdon: Routledge Press.

Surtees, R., & Brunovskis, A. (2016). Doing no harm – ethical challenges in research with trafficked persons. In D. Siegel & R. de Wildt (Eds.), *Ethical concerns in research on human trafficking*. Cham: Springer International Publishing.

Turnbull, S. (forthcoming). The challenges and opportunities of researching life after immigration detention. In A. Fili, S. Johansen, & R. Powell (Eds.), *Criminal justice research in an era of mass mobility*. Abingdon: Routledge Press.

Tyldum, G. (2012). Ethics or access? Balancing informed consent against the application of institutional, economic or emotional pressures in recruiting respondents for research. *International Journal of Social Research Methodology*, 15(3), 199–210.

Van Liemp, I., & Bilger, V. (2012). Ethical challenges in research on vulnerable groups. In C. Vargas-Silva (Ed.), *Handbook of research methods in migration*. Cheltenham: Edward Elgar Publishing.

Wacquant, L. (2011). From 'public criminology' to the reflexive sociology of criminological production and consumption. *The British Journal of Criminology*, *51*(2), 438–448.

Weber, L. (forthcoming). Taking the border for a walk: A reflection on the agonies and ecstasies of exploratory research. In A. Fili, S. Johansen, & R. Powell (Eds.), *Criminal justice research in an era of mass mobility*. Abingdon: Routledge Press.

Index

Aboriginal: justice 16; people 18, 21
Administrative Appeal Tribunal (AAT) 167, 168
Afghan mothers: interview format for 75–77; interviews of 80–81; migration to Australia 70; *see also* vulnerable women
Ahmed, Sara 88
Anderson, Bridget 10n3
Arendt, Hannah 226
Asian identity, British 189–190, 192, 196
assisted return 32–34
Australia 4, 7; agenda for criminal deportations 168–169; border control in 226; criminal deportation in 161; internal borders methodology 19–22; positionality in researching with unsympathetic 162–163; refugee and asylum-seeking populations 72; refugees from Iran and Afghanistan 70; research design 163–164; research methodology 161–162; *see also* border control
Australian Border Deaths Database 10, 10n5
Australian Research Council (ARC) Future Fellowship 16
Awkward Yeti, The (cartoon) 147, 157

Back, Les 30
Barnett, Robert 105
Birmingham courts 85–86; citizenship 88–89, 90; diversity 88; doing research in 86–90; dominant ideology of democratic rights 92–93; foreigners in courtroom 90–93; foreign national clientele 87–88; language proficiency and nationality 92; migrant population of 87; race and crime in multicultural city 93–95; racism and nationalism 95–96; Romanians in 93–95

border as method, exploratory research 15, 18–19, 25–26
border control: adopting a sympathetic position 160, 161–162; agenda for Australian criminal deportations 168–169; brief history of criminological studies 2–5; experiences from field 164–168; interviewing a sex offender 165–167; interviewing stakeholders 167–168; research design in Australia 163–164; secondary and vicarious trauma in 149–152, 157
Border Criminologies website 2, 10n1
Border Crossing Observation website 73, 82n1
border research: finding structures of internal 19–22; methodology 6; taking border for a walk 15–19
Boswell, Christina 32
Bosworth, Mary 91, 114, 127n1, 150, 151
Bowling, Ben 17
Breivik, Anders Behring 182, 184n9
Burawoy, Michael 29

Camus, Albert 232
Canfield, Julie 152
China, power of authorities in India 105–106, 111
Christie, Nils 29
citizenship: as control policy 64; criminal courts 85–86, 88–89; crimmigration research 89–90; foreigners in courtroom 90–93; hierarchies within internal borders 17–18, 20–21; language of 96
communication: of immigration detainees 119; in Kongsvinger prison 202, 204–206, 208; in policing migration 174; relationship of researcher and

participants 136–138; in research projects 34–35; social media for researchers and participants 137, 139–140; verbal, in recruitment 71
Council of Europe Convention on Action Against Trafficking in Human Beings 36
courts *see* Birmingham courts; criminal courts
Crime Control at the Borderlands of Europe 174, 183
criminal courts: in Birmingham 86, 87, 89; citizenship and migration status 85–86; foreigners in courtroom 90–93; foreign national offenders 96; race and crime in multicultural city 93–95; racism and nationalism 95–96; *see also* Birmingham courts
criminal foreigner 45, 93
criminal justice and migration 41–42, 52; accounting for 'crimmigration' 44; allowing scrutiny of researchers 50–52; challenges and opportunities for researchers 229–231; counting groups or categories 45–46; 'crimmigration' statistics 42–43; determining counting strategies 46–48; Norway 41–42, 47–51; problem of bureaucratic data and feedback 44–45; problem of nationally bound data 49–50; researching a 'moving target' 48–49; research practices coming together 227–229
criminological studies: brief history of border control 2–5; race and migration 186–187
crimmigration: citizenship in research 89–90; as political issue 44; processes within Norwegian police 178, 178–179; term 183n5; *see also* criminal justice and migration
crimmigration law 2, 62; term 43
CUREC (University of Oxford's Central University Research Ethics Committee) 155

deaths: Australian Border Deaths Database 10, 10n5; border-related 2, 220; of children 76, 77; in detention centres 7, 114–115, 120–126; *see also* immigration removal centres (IRCs)
detention *see* immigration detention; immigration detention centres; immigration removal centres (IRCs)

diversity: in Birmingham court 86–88; in immigration removal centres 115–117; in policing migration 174, 178

enforced return, term 34
epistemology 26n2; border research 15–19
Ethiopians in Norway 63
European Union (EU) 214: migration management 28–29; research funding 31
exploratory research: border as method 15, 18–19, 25–26; internal borders methodology 19–22; taking border for a walk 15–19; theory pyramid 21–22; translating into practice 22–25

Farage, Nigel 187, 188
foreigners: in courtrooms 90–93; race and crime in multicultural city 93–95; research in Birmingham courts 86–90; *see also* Birmingham courts
framing 16, 18, 23, 180, 193, 196; concept of 55; crime and crime control 181; deportation in combatting crime 178; as method 55–56; of migration 29; problem of 33–34; problem of language 57
Franko, Katja 174, 183n4
freshie 195
funnel, term 57
funnel politics 55–56; framing as method 56–57; as imagery 63–65; IOOI (insiders outside/outsiders inside) tale 57–60; IOOI differences and similarities 60–61; IOOI framing politics 64; maintenance of control mechanism 62–63; reality of in IOOI 61–62; waiting camps for irregular migrants 58, 59
Future Fellowship, Australian Research Council (ARC) 16

Gilroy, Paul 95–96
globalization 174, 181
Global North 69–70, 75, 194
Global South: gatekeepers in recruitment process 105–107; Global North–South polarities 194; immigration status of participants 102–105; interpreting interviews of irregular migrants 108–110; migration from 69–70; participation and engagement in interview 107–108; recruiting participants at research site 101–107; research stories of migrants 100–101, 110–112

governing spaces 58–59
Greece 4, 8; immigration detention in 214–216, 220–222; *see also* immigration detention centres
Greek mythology, Sisyphus in 226, 231–232

humanitarian crisis 214
Human Research Ethics Committee 24

Immigration Act, Norwegian Parliament (2008) 62
Immigration Appeals Board 35
immigration control, impact on service provisions 24
immigration detention: boundaries of researcher-participant relationship 136–138; challenges of follow-up research 133–138; communication logistics in 135–136; ethical dilemmas and challenges 133–135; field of research 130–132; method and data for life after 132–133; United Kingdom (UK) 130–132
immigration detention centres: becoming a researcher in 216–218; becoming NGO practitioner in 218–220; challenges of listening to detainees in Greece 214–216; Petrou Ralli 216; voices from 213, 220–221
immigration removal centres (IRCs) 7, 114; aftermath of deaths in 124–126; detainee custody officers (DCOs) 116–117; detention research 114–115; diversity in 115–117; Heathrow IRC 116, 127n2; pain and suffering in 119; researching deaths in custody 120–126; segregation unit 118; social environments of 119; sources and subjects 122–124; staying put in 117–120
Independent Advisory Panel on Deaths in Custody 122
India: asylum seeking from Tibet to 100; gatekeepers for research recruitment 105–106, 111; immigration status of Tibetan refugees 103–104; India-Nepal border 4, 7; interpreting interviews of Tibetans in 109, 110; interviews of Tibetans in 107–108; power of Chinese authorities in 105–106, 111; recruitment process in 102; Tibetan refugees in 101
insider-outsider debate, race 189; *see also* IOOI (insiders outside/outsiders inside)

internal bordering practices: hierarchies of citizenship 17–18, 20–21; methodology for structures of 19–22; policing public space 17, 20; structurally embedded border 17, 20; themes of 17–18, 20–21; *see also* exploratory research
interpreters: deciphering messages 79–81; expectations of 78–79; translating in interviews 78–81
IOOI (insiders outside/outsiders inside): differences and similarities 60–61; framing politics 64; project 57–60, 65; reality of funnel politics 61–62; waiting camps for irregular immigrants 58, 59; *see also* funnel politics
Iranian mothers: interviews of 80, 81; migration to Australia 70; *see also* vulnerable women

Jacobsen Christine 31
Jamaica 4, 86–87, 148–149, 152, 156

Kaufman, Emma 91
Kellezi, Blerina 151
Klee, Paul 15
Kongsvinger prison: background and research methods at 202–204; language, culture and belonging in 204–208; language as performative 208–209; language in constructing identity and belonging 209–210; narratives of researchers of 202, 205–208; in Norway 201–202
Kovalevskaya, Sophia 26
KRIPOS (Norwegian National Criminal Investigation Service) 174

labour migration, Laos to Thailand 100, 101, 109
language 8, 18, 110; body 108; of border control 24; of citizenship 96; of compassion 179; in constructing identity and belonging 209–210; in courts 88–89; culture and belonging in prison 203–208; in detention centres 119; English language 23, 73; framing in problem of 57; interpreters of 78, 79; Lao 106; national belonging 85–86, 92, 191, 193; of race 93, 95, 191, 193
Laos: border with Thailand 4, 6, 101; labour migration to Thailand 100, 101, 109; *see also* Thailand

Index

Lawrence, Stephen 191, 197n1
Leverhulme Network on External Border Control 1, 2, 183n7, 230
Linking Act 64

McBarnet Doreen 92
McCann, Lisa 149
Macpherson Report 191, 196, 197n1
maintenance: as control mechanism 62–63; notion of order 64
marginalized populations: interpreters for 78–81; navigating narratives of 74–78; recruitment and access to 71–74; *see also* qualitative researcher
Maribyrnong Immigration Detention Centre (MIDC) 163, 165
Mezzadra, Sandro 18–19
migration: policing 190–193; race and 186–187; *see also* criminal justice and migration; policing migration; race
Migration Act (1958) 170n8
Migration Act (2014) 169n3
migration crisis 8–10, 28
migration management 28–29, 37–38; enlisting research in 31–33; mobility and 38; problem of embeddedness 34–36; problem of expected loyalty 36–37; problem of framing 33–34; problem of oversocialisation of researchers 29–31, 37–38; research integrity 38
Ministerial Council on Deaths in Custody 122, 125
mobility, migration and 38, 186–187
motivational interviewing (MI) 61
Munro, Alice 26

National Health Service 187
National Police Immigration Service (NPIS) 175, 183n7
Neilson, Brett 18–19
non-citizens, categorizations of 45
nongovernmental organisations (NGOs) 2, 31, 60: Australian research 164; health services 59; immigration detention in Greece 214–215, 218–220; Thailand research 102
Norway 4, 6, 8; criminal justice and migration 41–42; human trafficking research 47; Kongsvinger prison 201–202; maintenance as control mechanism 62–63; migration crisis 9–10; migration management 28–29; policing migration 173–174; problem of embeddedness 34–36; problem

of expected loyalty 36–37; problem of framing 33–34; problem of oversocialisation of researchers 29–31; researching a 'moving target' 48–49; researching policing migration in 174; sociology in migration research 29–31; tax license for holding job 63; terrorist attack 22 July, 2011 182, 184n9; *see also* Kongsvinger prison; policing migration
Norwegian Aliens Act 48–49
Norwegian Correctional Services 201
Norwegian Directorate of Immigration (UDI) 30, 34–36
Norwegian Police Directorate (POD) 42, 49–50, 174, 175, 177, 179
Norwegian Police University College 173, 174, 181, 183n2
Norwegian Social Science Data Services (NSD) 177

Operation Nexus 91, 190
Organised Crime Unit, Oslo police district 174

Pearlman, Laurie 149
Pew Research Center 43
Police Immigration Service, Norway 175
policing: of public space 17, 20, 22–23; shaping globalization 181
policing migration: dealing with discomfort and complicity 179–182; emerging and contested field 175–176; in England 190–193; negotiation in field 177–179; in Norway 173–174; placement and misrecognition 191–192; positionality as analytical concept 176–177; recognizing police agency 182–183; research of in Norway 174; seeing race in 192–193
post-traumatic stress disorder (PTSD) 147, 148, 154
Powell, Enoch 85, 87, 91
prison: description of 203; *see also* Kongsvinger prison
Prisons and Probation Ombudsman (PPO) 122

qualitative methodologies 69
qualitative research, motherhood influence during interviews 77–78
qualitative researcher: interpreters for translating 78–81; interviewing participants 74–78; for marginalized populations 69–70, 81–82; recruitment and access to participants 71–74; snowball sampling 71

race: freshies 195; insider-outsider debate 189; migration scholarship 193–195; Pakistani Muslim community in UK 189–190; policing migration 190–193; politics of affinities 195–196; reflexive discussions of 188–190; reviving 187–188; seeing, in migration 192–193
refugee crisis 28, 175, 214
research: migration management 31–33; snowball sampling in recruitment 71; trauma in border control 149–152
Research Council of Norway (RCN) 30, 33
Research Excellence Framework 30
research integrity 38
Rose, Nikolas 32

secondary trauma: awareness of 152; description of 148–149; ethical boundaries 155–156; vicarious and 147–148; *see also* trauma
secrecy 62, 114
segregation, in immigration removal centres 118
Sisyphus, Greek mythology 226, 231
Smith, Tuhiwai 90
snowball sampling, for recruitment 71, 102
social media, researcher-participants relationships 135–136, 137, 139–140
social scientists: crossing ethical boundaries 155–156; self-care for 156; supervision and support for 154–155; time for supporting victims 156; *see also* trauma
Spinoza, Baruch 226, 227
standpointism/standpointist 196, 197n2
sympathy: definition of 169n1; in research methodology 161–162; role in research and policy 160; *see also* border control

terrorism: London March 2017 attack 188; Norway attack 22 July, 2011 182, 184n9; in United kingdom 187–188
Thailand: gatekeepers for research recruitment 105–106; immigration status of migrants to 103; interpreting interviews of irregular migrants 108–110; labour migration from Laos to 100, 101, 111; recruitment process for research 102; *see also* Laos

There Ain't No Black in the Union Jack (Gilroy) 95
Tibet: asylum seeking to India via Nepal 100; social and religious oppression in 101; *see also* India
trauma: awareness of 152; constrictive reactions 153; effective supervision and support of researchers 154–155; impact on research 152–154; intrusive reactions 153–154; post-traumatic stress disorder (PTSD) 147, 148; prevalence in border control research 149–152; secondary 148–149; supporting social scientists 154–156; vicarious 149, 152, 153–154
Trump, Donald 187, 226

United Kingdom (UK) 4, 6–7; immigration detention and deportation in 130–132; Independence Party 187; Pakistani Muslim community in 189–190; *see also* Birmingham courts; immigration detention
United Nations Convention, human trafficking 42
UN Trafficking Protocol 36

vicarious trauma: awareness of 152; constrictive reactions to 153; description of 149; intrusive reactions to 153–154; secondary and 147–148; *see also* trauma
Villawood Immigration Detention Centre 163
voluntary return 34
vulnerable women: crossing ethical boundaries 155–156; research details 149–152; secondary trauma 147, 148–149; social scientists studying 154–156; trauma in border control research 149–152; vicarious trauma 147, 149; *see also* trauma

Wacquant, Loic 162
waiting camp, irregular migrants 58, 59
Weierstrass, Karl 26
Welfare, Working Life and Migration (VAM) 30
women *see* vulnerable women

xenophobia 9, 187, 215

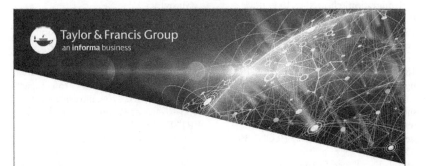